FAITHS IN THEIR PRONOUNS

FAITHS IN THEIR PRONOUNS

WEBSITES OF IDENTITY

Kenneth Cragg

sussex
ACADEMIC
PRESS

BRIGHTON • PORTLAND

2 4 6 8 10 9 7 5 3 1

First published 2002
in Great Britain by
SUSSEX ACADEMIC PRESS
PO Box 2950
Brighton BN2 5SP

and in the United States of America by
SUSSEX ACADEMIC PRESS
5824 N.E. Hassalo St.
Portland, Oregon 97213-3644

British Library Cataloguing in Publication Data
A CIP catalogue record for this book is available from the British Library.

Library of Congress Cataloging-in-Publication Data
Cragg, Kenneth.
Faiths in their pronouns : websites of identity / Kenneth Cragg.
p. cm.
Includes bibliographical references and index.
ISBN 1–903900–15–8 (alk. paper) — ISBN 1–903900–16–6 (alk. paper)
1. Religions. 2. Language and languages—Religious aspects. 3. Grammar, Comparative and general—Pronoun. I. Title.
BL85 .C775 2002
210′.1′4—dc21   2002021715

The cover illustration depicts part of the "Studies of the Heads and Hands of the Apostles" by Raphael, and is reproduced by the kind permission of The Ashmolean Museum, The University of Oxford.

Typeset and designed by G&G Editorial, Brighton
Printed by Bookcraft, Midsomer Norton, Bath
This book is printed on acid-free paper.

Contents

I beseech you, enter your life.
I beseech you learn to say "I" when I question you.
For you are no part but a whole.

Ezra Pound

Since I came into this vale of tears
I cannot tell you who I am.

ʿUmar Khayyam

Between eternity and time –
Your consciousness and me.

Emily Dickinson

Fixed in this parenthesis, I cannot contain my life.

Sylvia Plath

I was aware of me myself in the exact middle of a living story and
my body was my adventure and my name.

Dylan Thomas

Then it was that my whole ME stood up, in native, God-created
majesty and with emphasis recorded its protest.

Thomas Carlyle

But one man loved the pilgrim soul in you
And loved the sorrows of your changing face.

Buland al-Haydari

By so many more there are that say "ours"
So much the more of good doth each possess.

Dante Alighieri

Introduction

The pronoun, grammarians say, is "a part of speech". Grammar aside, we would have to say that it is the very mother tongue of thought. Verbs are conjugated for persons and nouns are promptly possessed, some so completely that no pronoun is necessary, being hidden or attached and so inherently there in either case. "I" and "you", "us" and "ours", "we" and "they" are endlessly traded in the barter of life. Pronouns – personal, relative, possessive, demonstrative – are the very websites of identity and, as such, obsessive whether in the very being of selfhood or in the collective pride of tribes and structures in the human scene. "What does it take to be me?" we have severally to ask. "What's ours is not yours" tends to be the instinctive assumption of possession. Being in identities is the perennial puzzle of philosophy, the burden of social ethics.

The puzzle and burden cling even to the forms of grammar. Languages like English name their pronouns as if serving notice of an imperial habit – "I" being dubbed the first person, "thou" the second and the absent party merely third. Semitic tongues are more ethical and refer more deferentially to "the speaking one", "the addressed one" and "the absent one", making no claim to priority. Culpable as the other self-centredness may be, heirs of Greek and Latin are innocent of the subtle discriminations mandatory in languages in Asia, where the speaker has to be keenly alert for social distinctions of class, wealth and status and be in careful use of forms and pronouns due to superior, or right for inferior, ranking of the other party. Then a lofty or a humiliated awareness prevails thanks to a grammar conspiring with exclusions and despisings in society.

"Pro-nouns" are well so styled. For they always function on behalf of rights, powers, claims, dignities and demands. Acquisitive, defensive, aggressive, impulsive, assertive, discursive – they take guard on the frontiers of personality, transacting the business of existence singular and plural. The work of the world being done by words, pronouns will contrive to hitch to most of them and commandeer their purposes.

It quickly follows that pronouns personal demand those of interrogation. "Who?" and "whose?" follow hard on the heels of "me" and "mine" where identity moves in the toils of community and property is at stake in conflict. Or identity itself, the self and the other, becomes the theme of perpetual enquiry. "Who will tell me who I am?" stems from every experience of the mystery. "Who art Thou Lord?" is the ultimate question of faith. These pronouns capture the inherently possessive nature of selfhood. They are the very counters in the exchanges of relationship.

In every way, then, pronouns are the essence of religion, their use the ever present liability of religious faith. On every count they have to be the first focus of honesty in the converse of religious diversity. The handling they have is a fair index to the mind of believers, how they are construed a sure clue to the mosque or the idiom of a temple's creed or ritual. Judaism, indeed, made the "I am" of its exclusive YAHWEH and the "we" and "ours" of "His people" the heart of its mind. Even if we are compelled to hold that, in the end, "God has only chosen peoples" in the plural, a tenacious identity between the "Thou" of worship and the "us" of worshippers is the fact about every traditional shrine, every house of reverence, however disparate their cultures or their tenets. The onus of that situation prompts the impulse to ventures of religious dialogue. It is no light burden if "inter-faith" is to be truly such and more than "inter-interest".

To embark, then, on some study of "pronouns in faiths" is to take in hand a compass integrity must read in such waters. Or, to change the figure, "consult the web" makes fair imagery for what pronouns are and the business they transact in their tangling sequences – the sites to which we quickly come when we work the net. The net is, because they are: they continually intercept what gives them occasion. Let the web be society, the transactable world, then the pronouns – I, we, us, ours, they, thou, you, them – print themselves on keyboard encounters and the whole is a "catch-endless" situation.

Such was the "catch" in Robert Browning's poem, "The Pope and the Net", about a fisher's son who, through all his graduation from deacon to priest to cardinal, kept a fisher's net for his insignia, to keep always in mind his humble origins. It disappeared when he was raised to the Papacy. "Why, Father, is the net removed?" he was asked. "Son, it hath caught the fish" was the reply.[1] Motives are always shading meanings, with pronouns at the heart of them. The same poet in "Love in a Life" has a lover seeking through all the rooms in the other's soul as in a physical dwelling.

> Room after room I hunt the house through
> We inhabit together . . . I range the whole house
> From the wing to the centre.
> Still the same chance. She goes out as I enter,
> Spend the whole day in the quest . . .
> Such suites to explore, such closets to search . . .[2]

"Et tu Brute" echoes from Shakespeare's *Julius Caesar*. "Tityre, tu" is the opening of Virgil's First Eclogue, with Tityros, a name meaning a Greek shepherd's flute, the one who plays it, or a warbling bird these resemble, or again the poet's lines made to sound like a bird's twitter.

Selfhoods are by nature ambiguous, enigmas in part both to others and themselves, in the bewildering quests of love or hope or deep conjecture. "Nets" and "webs" in their recent computer coinage are apt analogy for these endless "interstices between the inter-sections" in our human-ness, if we borrow Samuel Johnson's definition of the earlier sort. In a characteristic poem Walt Whitman borrowed the web language. Writing of "A Noiseless Patient Spider" he "marked on a little promontory how it explored"

> . . . the vacant vast surrounding . . .
> . . . launched forth filament, filament, filament out of itself,
> Ever unreeling them, ever tirelessly speeding them.

Pursuing his imagery he went on:

> And you, O my soul, where you stand
> Surrounded, detached in measureless oceans of space,
> Ceaselessly musing, venturing, throwing, seeking the spheres to
>   connect . . . them,
> Till the bridge you need will be formed . . .
> Till the gossamer thread you fling catch somewhere, O my soul![3]

For this precarious, vulnerable, ever opening–closing experience in the pronounal world, faiths are given, devised, employed, sifted, to be mentors and guides, or to be crutches and comforters in the haplessness of being, womb to tomb, on a sequence ever attended by memory, the lostness of the past and the awaitedness of the future. The time factor means that pronouns act like verbs registering what has been and what might yet be. They are possessed by yearning forward and recollection backward, hallowed by heritage or haunted by resentment, restless with apprehension or fired by ambition. They are inwardly fixed points in the ever moving shape of outward circumstance where "meshes we have woven bind us to each other".[4]

Such "weaving", furthermore, "binds" often to discriminate. There is the rubric of the restrictive pronoun. "We" and "our" are globally inclusive if we are saying: "We are one humanity on our single planet earth." But such usages, though always necessarily wise for us, find scant purchase on our minds under the rule of nation, land, race and culture. The plurality of these serves to intensify the singularity of each expression, so that while we are many in our human identities, we hold them in their interior sanctions as exclusive to ourselves.

This phenomenon of self-aware identities, in the broad denominators of ethnicity and history, fragments endlessly into sub-cultures and privacies of every kind. For these, religions have been massively responsible, inevitably so, given the religious impulse to bring absolute criteria and demand singular loyalty. There are few sharper warrants for a "them and us" mentality than the privileged event of final revelation or the mystique of "chosen-ness" or the prerogative of some sublime illumination lastingly guru-ized. These, in their turn, being so possessively professed and guarding so vital a secrecy, give rise to internally competing versions of their decisive authority. These in turn are vexed again by the stresses of envy and the vagaries of strife round orthodoxy.

Pronouns, thus personal, relative, hidden, attached, restrictive, interrogative, are the readiest clue to the discourse of religions, the first preoccupation of faiths in converse Who we are, explores who are you? Things held are always people holding them. Identities, perceiving and being perceived, are the stock in trade of faiths and their faithfuls.

The aim in "Websites of Identity" is to review and search the liability for their pronouns as religions use them, and think into the task they have with doctrines and the institutions that enshrine "we" and "us" and "ours" in the "why" and "how" that tell themselves. Grammar has often supplied an analogy for faith.[5] Pronouns are the first candidates inside it.

Pronouns immediately require that the point of departure in the venture must be the experience of personhood itself, the mysterious unison of the physical, mental and spiritual in the human individual. That is where the great faiths of Asia have opted to begin. Unlike the Semitic faiths they have not presumed to cry to identifiable deity: "Oh God, Thou art my God," or to claim: "Thus says the Lord." Rather the enigma and burden of self-hood has been their starting-point. Transcendent unity in mystical attaining may come to be their goal and destiny but from a first long brooding on "being-in-a-self" and that self frustrated by the pain of transience and caught in puzzling mortality.

To that mind and mood we come in CHAPTERS TWO and THREE but it is well to start with selfhood in the perceptions of the theism of Hebrew psalmody supremely captured in Psalm 139. It takes us to what elsewhere (Psalm 119:54) is poetically described as "the house of my pilgrimage" – the body-shrine of personal identity. "The house" is more than the locale, the terrain, even the exilic land, through which, in the perennial sojourn of his mortal flesh, he individually went. It is "the bone-bound island" in which he "learned all he knew".[6] With this – which more vulgar times might merely dub "the body shop" – as a first mentor of the worth of personhood, we are the more alert for the perplexity so ardent and so probing in Hindu and Buddhist distrust of it.

In wary suspicion of the trustworthiness of human meaning Semitic faiths have sponsored, the Asian mind can be our surest tutor in whatever argument ensues. The Bhagavad Gita is, indeed, a sort of psalmody in its soul poetry, its capacity for rapture, but with all the sacred texts of Asia around it its Arjuna is no "wresting Jacob". There is a deep contrast in the ethos. Only in knowing it can study reckon well with the shared human-ness so diversely read.

CHAPTER THREE reaches for that reckoning, taking the familiar plea: "So help me God!" with a ?, a query, in the place of "God". In the bleaker forms of Buddhism among the Theravada or Hinayana there were no "helpers", no Bodhisattvas, to succour the disciple, whose only reliance had to be on the Dharma, the Teaching itself. "Help" – in its first but now much attenuated meaning – was always a crucial theme in Biblical vocabulary, opened out into the New Testament understanding of "grace".

If only a lost quest for the non-existent, the formula: "So help me – who?" can serve to carry further the implications of two initial chapters. Where the unknown psalmist of the 139th and the Arjuna of the Gita take us in their differing worlds opens out the radical religious issues in the human condition, comprised as they are in the art, or the absurdity, of "being me". Contemporary literature has much to say on these. Its queries around them, its picturing of them, are steady running commentary on the verdicts of the faiths in history. The resulting situation has to be the prime incentive to their mutual encounter.

The objective in CHAPTERS FOUR to EIGHT is to study the role of the personal pronoun, singular and plural, in the Jewish, Islamic and Christian Scriptures and structures of faith. The centrality of a social personalism is definitive in each, though in crucially differing terms. The role of what we take on from Asian traditions has to be one of a constant scepticism about Semitic assurance around personhood, peoplehood, prophethood and the theism these sustain and invoke. Focus on the theology of human pronouns makes it that way. That only theists are in such love of them, makes them in honest need of Hindu/Buddhist suspicion round the role their selfhoods claim to play.

There is little doubt that the Judaic form of how that role is seen, possessed and practiced is unique, alike in the origins it found and the history it wrote. For, with Judaism, it is not simply that religion shapes identity but that identity is itself religion, rooted in the concept of "chosen-ness". Thus YAHWEH bestows the land on His people, that the land through the people, the people in the land, mutually fulfill themselves. He is glorified in that exclusive bond. All was sanctioned and sanctified by an ancestry pledged to it, a history shaped in it and a conquest made for it.

That conviction of a tribally divine "election" and a divinely tribal destiny held at its heart an enormous paradox. It lived with a perennial dilemma around how to comprehend the rest of humankind, the *ethnoi*, the "Gentiles", whom it necessarily excluded from its self-awareness but could never feasibly exempt from its relationships. The nobility of its finest prophets strove to envisage some inclusiveness of "benediction" to "the ends of the earth", but as long as this insistently required the unbroken tenure of the copyrighted agency that could bestow it, the vision was for ever thwarted by its own prescript. It is a paradox painfully sharpened by the degree to which contemporary Zionism has darkly politicized the Judaism that gave it birth, so that a Judaic "us" and "ours" – the who we are and where – have thereby become prone to intolerance. It would be fair to say that Jewry through all the centuries has carried all the burdens and suffered all the hurts of its uniquely pronounal religion. The very people whose ritual lawyers first contrived the idea of "the scape-goat" have tragically been made to play the role in a world unready for their exceptionality in the only terms they said it could consist. For the terms consigned the rest of humankind to a dubious differential status. These have to be the themes of CHAPTERS FOUR and FIVE, age-long and contemporary.

For reasons which become clear later, the Christian resolution of that paradox in the New Testament best follows CHAPTERS SIX and SEVEN, which are devoted to the personal pronoun, singular and plural, in the faith of the Qur'an and Islam. For while Islam carefully distinguished itself from the people-criterion of Jewry,[7] it strenuously maintained the Judaic themes of "law and prophet", perpetuating the concept of a divine relation to humankind that was directive, legal, hortatory and didactic, based on precept and "messengers", who invoked lessons from nature and examples in story enshrining "reminder" and moral education. These proceeded on the assumption that, duly chastened, taught and guided, humanity was amenable to divine discipline and submissible to divine sovereignty, the more so in that Islam would organize the structures of ritual, community and authority within which those ends could be assured, including the political state, the *Dawlah* that could corroborate the *Din*.[8]

This comprehending in Islam of the human scene is illuminated by a study of pronouns in the Qur'an, both the frequent "thou" addressing Muhammad himself and the "you" belonging to Muslims in general. There will be occasion to see how Islam is at once an intensely personal religion, with "no soul bearing the burden of any other",[9] and yet also a faith grounded more firmly than any other in solidarity and sustained habituation. Those characteristics, predictably, have been maintained when sectarianism supervened. The Islamic will to be monolithic, "God's own religion", has never been forfeit since the Prophet's Hijrah told its intention so to be.[10]

Alerted by all these implications CHAPTER EIGHT moves into the "we"

---

and "I" of the Christian's New Testament. There are two fundamental contrasts from all the foregoing that interdepend. The one is the new dimension of redemptive self-giving as definitive of "God in Christ". The other is the making of a new peoplehood-in-faith, heir to the Judaic theme of divine peoplehood but now no longer in "seed", or "land", or tribal "exodus", or Davidic "kingship", but in a personal, private faith, available to all, place and kin and tongue apart. That individual response to "the Christ of God", intelligently realized and inwardly loved, at once incorporates into "the body of Christ", so that allegiance is never solitary but always communal. The resultant peoplehood is retrieved from exceptionalizing categories of birth and sex and habitat and grounded in common grace.

On that prime condition, it becomes entirely capable of cultural diversity with "the nations bringing their glory and their honour into it", having their idiosyncrasies recruited into its fulfilling discipline. It follows that the pronounal usages of the New Testament are a ready index to this being "in Christ", as Paul loved to have it. The Book itself is a fertile study in the radical revision of divine peoplehood, the pain and stress of it. For, since it was for the most part under wholly Jewish auspices, it proved a deeply vexing transition taking nervously joyous shape in the tide of dispersion from "Jerusalem round about unto Illyricum" – a dispersion engrossed in moral education and spiritual nurture in the often hostile milieu of Graeco-Roman pagan imperialism. Theology could wish no richer veins of pronounal exegesis than those the Gospels and Letters yield in the New Testament.

After the long Semitic retrospect in hand through CHAPTERS FOUR to EIGHT, and before returning in CHAPTER TEN to the Asian quest for self-abeyance, we must engage with where pronouns are most fraught with mystery in the wonder of sexual intimacy. "Two great sexes," as John Milton had it, "animate the world." "I" and "thou" – we might say – are the generative pronouns whence all else derives. "Male and female created He them" and what ensues is the primary net-working of our human experience. Sexuality is the first testing ground of religions, the quarry of much of their imagery, the least tractable realm of their ethical tuition.

The tractability of the sexual impulse has rarely been so problematic as in our contemporary society. Ancient Rome was no doubt profligate enough and all societies have struggled to read, interpret and achieve their sexual fulfilment. But with the erosion of prestigious orders of tribal sanction or primal custom on every hand, and in the current preoccupation with grimly reductionist patterns of sexual exchange expressed in the vulgarity of merely "having sex" in the ambiguously sophisticated West, religious readings are hard pressed either to inform the mind or retrieve the soul by their comprehending of the body.

7

Numerous factors demand a studious attention – things social in the relevance of the family, nuclear or extended; things economic in the continuity of lineage and property; things political in the care of education, health, welfare and the sanity of culture. Supremely, through all these is the liability on religion to interpret and guide both concept and practice. The surest clue will be the sense of sexuality as "sacrament" as the ultimate principle by which "the inter-animating of the world" via "the two great sexes" truly moves. What, then, is that supreme principle and how may it find shape in each and every religious ordering? Whether monitored by Islam, imaged in Hinduism, hallowed in Jewry, or indulged in secularity, our "male and female" mutuality tells and transacts its truest intimacy in being known and fulfilled in sacramental trust.

Two final chapters are evidently necessary. CHAPTER TEN is concerned with how our "dividual" existence[11] has long excited in many quarters an urge somehow to escape from itself or lose itself in a final obsolescence of all pronounal awareness by attainment of utter "non-duality". We have to ask whether, inhabiting as we do an inalienable personhood, there is any mystical "unitive" condition which does not violate the personhood that seeks it.

Ascetics pursuing one may well be "detached" from all willed acquisitiveness. Will they be thereby detached from the self that sought to be?[12] "Entering" non-identity leaves the open question what it was that did so. The problem has been perennial for mysticisms everywhere. Maybe it has to be contained in paradox.

Faiths that aim to forego personal identity may be deeply healing, earnestly venturing, ideologies about unselfishness and deeply enriching in their social benison. Can they overcome the liability to be which is the gist of human experience? Striving to "non-entify" the self seems only to signal again the fact of it. The selflessness that is fully moral must be other than unselfing an ego it will always need.[13]

That there are deep issues here is evident enough. They go to the very core of religions and their capacity for honest realism. What, then, of faiths' pronoun-users now? Their "I"s, "thou"s, "we"s and "ours" – ever in the foreground – speak from the hinterlands of rites and creeds and codes, the shadowlands of their prejudice and pride. "We" in church or mosque, in gurdwara or synagogue, in temple or shrine, are in perpetual liability for ourselves. The world stays uneasily sceptical of how well any can discipline, the better to commend, themselves. It remains apprehensive lest they only perpetuate their enmities and forfeit their assumed vocation. How restrictive are their pronouns? how inwardly interrogative? how patiently expressive? "Find us on our website" they say: but what for the finding?

CHAPTER ONE

The House of My Pilgrimage

I

"Here in the body pent," sang the eighteenth-century hymn-writer, James Montgomery, musing on his mortal journey. He wanted "pent" to suit his coming rhyme with "tent", the moving thing he "nightly pitched nearer home" in eternity. His instincts were very Biblical. For the early Hebrews were a nomadic people and "the tent" or "tabernacle" was loved imagery for divine companionship in safeguard of their destinies. "Penthouse" aside, the "pent" word is somewhat archaic as meaning "confined within narrow limits" or "having something overfull within" as emotions can be.[1]

"Here in the body spent" we might guess the athlete thinking, wearied at the end of a marathon, or the unsaid admission of the dying, reaching for a sip of water.[2] For it is precisely the energies of the living physique that underline the pain and fate in their demise. The marvel of the chemistry of the body rides with the final wistfulness of its exhaustion.

The Biblical writers were apt in borrowing from their nomadism the frame of their piety, making "tentedness" the pattern of the divine presence and the transient tenure of their home in the body. The psalmist (119:54) brings the two together when he sings: "Thy statutes have been my songs in the house of my pilgrimage." His habitat in place and time is only a tenancy by dint of a physique of limb and sinew, bone and flesh, nerve and flow of blood in veins. Only these sustain the consciousness wherewith he registers "statutes" to obey and "songs" to voice the joy of them.

There are translations which prefer "the house" to mean either "the land of exile" or "the reach of my wanderings", but in either event there was no pilgrimage without a pilgrim. The personal equation is always in the circumstantial, and prior to the geographical. The body is always the quintessential "tent" of transit, and "tent-language" central to Judaic story.[3]

When Paul, in writing to Corinthian Christians (2 Cor. 5:1), returns to it, he reads the dissolution of the body at death as a "taking-down" of "the earthly tabernacle" of human habitation, to be replaced by "a building from God eternal in the heavens".[4] As "not made with hands", it is in studied contrast to "your (God's) hands have made and fashioned me" of our psalmist's world (119:77) – a theme to be told still more vividly by Psalm 139. That the body is the human tent and a mere tent the body are evident enough, and a rich mine for the reverent imagination. If transience, impermanence (*anicca*) was the defining perception of the Buddhist mind concerning humankind, the Biblical muse, in its differing idiom, had it no less crucially in view.

II

Rarely, in poetry of the soul, has this sense of the journeying self in the life and limb of the body been more intimately told as an experience of the divine presence than in the *Domine Probasti* of the Biblical Psalter – Psalm 139. "Lord, thou hast searched me out, explored me, and known me."[5] The whole might be called "the song of the discovered God, the hymn of the awakened and alerted self" and each in the reality of the other.

The commentators write freely of abstractions like "omnipresence, omniscience and omnipotence" but here is no abstract philosophy of these. All is vivid inter-awareness. The pronouns "Thou" and "I", "Thine" and "mine" take over the syntax and occur in every verse. It is not simply that the singer is personally conscious of YAHWEH but that YAHWEH is ever watchful over his being. There is an all-embracing theme of mutuality – of the divine unceasing presentness, to the human an inescapable reality. No "they", no "them" enter into the equation until, for reasons we must examine later, v. 20, where the psalmist relates painfully outside the "Thou"– "I" bond with which he is awesomely pre-occupied, "pre-empted" we might almost say. Elsewhere his whole being is consciously anticipated by divine solicitude, steadily pursued by divine mindfulness.

This intense personalism is in sharp contrast to the Atharvaveda verses of the Hindu Scripture with which, for striking reasons of phrase and detail, it has sometimes been compared. There the third person is steadily used and the theme is told in academic abstraction. The sky-god Varuna's intervention is being sought against the designs of a cunning enemy and, in that interest, praise of His omnipresent, omnicompetent majesty is the reassuring ground of hope.

> The great lord of the world sees as if he were near at hand. If any one thinks that he walks unseen, the gods know it all. Whether one walk, or stand, or hide oneself, lying down or standing up . . . the counsel which two take sitting together – King Varuna knows it: he is between them as a third. If

10

anyone flew far off to the other side of heaven, even there he would not escape Varuna our King . . . With a thousand eyes his scouts search the world. As a gamester casts the dice, so he orders all things.[6]

The incidentals are uncannily close. They are those of the body's habits available for all such discourse. For the rest, the contrast is total. Psalm 139 is oblivious of "divine scouts". The soul is realizing, not discoursing.

Though, as the Psalm's conclusion sharply indicates, the poet is fully in the world of his time, his song, nevertheless, is remarkably free of the prejudices of "covenant" and "tribe". His ultimate antipathies are ethical, not ethnic. Like the parables of Jesus, his lines belong with what is human per se and prescribe no national or racial criteria to limit their range and truth. His humanness is free of jealous considerations of locale, being completely alive to the intimations of a physicality common to all. There is no mention of some "promised land", nor of – as in so many other psalms – the unique "people of God", the only ones to "know the joyful sound".

For something inherently inclusive possesses him. If, as we may assume from the Aramaic and other factors, he is writing in exilic time and place, he is still mentally where "taking the wings of the morning" would convey him to "the uttermost parts of the sea". So morning would be moving, for one dwelling still in mind and heart on the coast of Philistia. From Babylon west-bound morning moves over the dry plains of desert earth.

The strophes of the psalm tell soul-emotions but transcend contentious particularity, absorbed as the singer is with the divine exploration of his physically conscious being. For the penetrating awareness of the divine presence informs his whole physique.

> Thou knowest my down-sitting and my uprising: Thou understandest my thoughts long before. Thou art about my path and about my bed and spiest out all my ways. For lo! there is not a word in my tongue, but Thou, O Lord, knowest it altogether.

He is "toward God" and God is "toward him" in all the mundane ways of the working day, resting and rising, walking and talking. YAHWEH is his intimate, anticipating his thoughts and "scanning", "discerning", even "winnowing", his working mind, divinely "known through and through". "Fashioned behind and before", he is aware in his very frame of being "besieged" like a city encompassed all around. The Biblical imagery of the Lord as "a hand", holding, containing, shaping his being, spells "a knowledge too wonderful", a mystery for which he has no explaining clue, ever alert as he remains to the embracing reality.

Here is no localized divinity of territorial limits and preserves, such as belong with the old plural tradition content to credit "gods many and lords many" whose precincts one might expect to escape.

> Whither shall I go then from Thy spirit, or whither shall I flee from Thy presence. If I climb up into heaven, Thou art there: if I go down to hell Thou art there also. If I take the wings of the morning and remain in the uttermost parts of the sea, even there also shall Thy hand lead me and Thy right hand shall hold me.

Instinctively his poetry finds the chords of Hebrew parallelism. "Even there" tells the exceptionless "seizing" of the divine "grasp" of him, where-ever his imagined routes of escape devise to take him. "Winging swiftly into the morning" or "nestling in the nether world" will not avail him to elude – not so much a "hound of heaven" as an unslumbering vigilantes who is already there and everywhere.

It will be futile to invoke darkness and light. For

> If I say: Peradventure the darkness shall cover me, then shall my night be turned to day. Yea, the darkness is no darkness with Thee, but the night is as clear as the day: darkness and light to Thee are both alike.

The fundamental divide of the created world, being inside one handiwork, allows no "cover" from the creating cognizance where the creature could securely lurk. The "even there" of far dawn and deep Hades holds also of "creeping murmur and the pouring dark". All lies under the living ken of the eternal grasp where "no secrets are hid".

Yet, somehow, this perennial divine reality spells no creaturely intimidation tending towards counsels of despair. It bodes no constraint towards suicidal verdicts on the self, no trend towards mystical will to self-annihilation. On the contrary, it impels the psalmist to a keener alertness around the possession of the body and the strange dowry in his birth. Here, in being born and being alive in his generation, he reaches for the ever renewed wonder of pronounal religion.

> For my reins are Thine. Thou hast covered me in my mother's womb. I will give thanks unto Thee, for I am fearfully and wonderfully made: marvellous are Thy works, and that my soul knoweth right well. My bones were not hid from Thee: though I be made secretly and fashioned beneath in the earth. Thine eyes did see my substance, yet being imperfect and in Thy book were all my members written, which day by day were fashioned when as yet there was none of them.

William Tyndale's text has the eloquence the theme deserves, albeit that his renderings need the closer attention of the exegetes. "Reins", to be sure are obsolete, but not "the awful wonder of our birth", its "meant-to-be-ness" under God. "Embryo" is the word we need now, for the initiation in the womb and the sequence of "weaving" and "knitting" by which limbs and sinews, bones and nerves, veins and lungs, are moulded into babe for "house" and "pilgrimage", for life and destiny.

Birth holds the mystery of life as something in the contriving all
unpremeditated by its inner hero, unconsulted on the hazards of the dual
parenthood, but – in the awed reverence of the psalm – bound over into
glad acceptance of its embarkation into selfhood. The poet here is not
complaining about "the night my father got me his mind was not on me"
– if such had been his case. He is reading, in every event concerning intercourse, the sacramental sequences of his wombing as an architecture of
God.[7]

Nativity, ever unsolicited by the embryo, the self to be, has ever been a
focal theme of the religious mind. It inaugurates the pronounality of our
personal existence. The psalmist teaches us the terms in which a sacred
sanity should "take it in" and "take it on" in the daily business of being
the self it set on the way. Once born, there is no non-accepting the onus
of it. Thus it constitutes the deepest of religious issues, the crucial setting
of decisions of faith made inescapable by its being, in its incidence, beyond
our option yet, in its eventfulness, the supreme point of our volition in its
reading and reception. Our babyhood begins and continues in expectation – the expectation of a significance awaiting a societal responsiveness,
entailing a reciprocal responsiveness of ours progressively with the
maturing of our powers. It tells of a monumental indebtedness inside a
mutual creaturehood and, thereby, a perennial mindfulness of the loom
of the Lord in the womb of the mother.

So the poet-psalmist, his hymn renewed or contrasted in ever fertile
birth-poetry celebrating or lamenting the incidence of our nativities.
Among such was the Swedish polymath, Linnaeus, echoing this very
psalm.

> Thou sawest my happiness when I was still lying
> In the darkness. Thou settest my clock,
> Thou cuttest my bread. Say why, Almighty Hero,
> Should'st Thou forget me now?
> My house I have built by the grace of God.
> Therefore I sleep unafraid.[8]

In contrasted moods about nativity were G. K. Chesterton and Louis
MacNeice. The former – in "The Babe Unborn":

> In dark I lie, dreaming that there
> Are great eyes cold or kind
> And twisted streets and silent doors
> And living men behind.

Waiting eagerly to enter the living scene he cries:

> They shall not hear a word from me
> Of selfishness or scorn

13

If only I could find the door,
If only I were born.[9]

The latter – suspecting Buddhist-style the malign world:

I am not yet born, console me.
I fear that the human race with tall walls will wall me,
With strong drugs dope me, with wise lies lure me . . .

He fears he will commit treasons of word and deed that are "engendered by traitors beyond" him, and wants to be "rehearsed" in the clues he must catch, the parts he must play, the hectors he will suffer. Will he be like water, held – and spilled – in the hand?[10]

"Fearfully made" is what the psalmist realized, a "substance being imperfect" as an embryo could well presage a substance in the person only precariously attained. Most poetically confident and wonder-full a celebrant of his own nativity was Thomas Traherne, whose poem "Salutation" wonders "where he was before he was", and why "they should be mine" – those "treasures lodged in this fair world, strange all and new to me", "who nothing was" from all eternity.

It was this sense of grateful selfhood that enabled him, in his now famous *Centuries* (of reflection),[11] to realize how to "enjoy the world aright", "all his care being to be sensible of God's mercies and to behave himself as the friend of God in the universe". It was not that, for him, God was held to be in some way "immanent" in every flower. Rather it was that God "resided in the esteeming of it according to its real value".[12] As an alert selfhood was drawn out by and into the day to day world in responsive awareness of its being, so appealingly *there*, the reality of the divine presence was duly perceived and received within the soul through the ever availing ministry of the body's mediating powers.

Though the psalmist in 139 is no Traherne in the Herefordshire countryside, this was the meaning of his "Thou art about my path", so that where I walk is where Thou art. In the intensity of his theology he does not need Traherne's warning, but can still cry with him:

He often visiteth our minds
But cold acceptance frequently He finds . . .

O happy ignorance of other things
Which made me present with the King of kings.[13]

Both knew well that the encompassing presence was sublimely responsive to the human responsiveness where it was ever contriving to be discovered. The mystery of the body in the homing of the soul was the instrumental register of the divine presence. Old "mother earth" was

14

indeed a fit analogy of the mortal pregnancy whence the psalmist's life had sprung. Was not "the womb of time" the surest imagery whereby to comprehend the arena of human history?

> How dear are Thy counsels unto me O God, O how great is the sum of them
> . . . when I awake I am still with Thee.

III

This "waking" out of "reverie" – if so we understand the text – seems to have been a mathematician's grappling with an unmanageable sum, the inexhaustible "thoughts of God" more multitudinous than the sands of every shore. He realizes that all his doings have been anticipated by the divine knowledge. "The book of the living" was a familiar concept elsewhere in Psalms 56:8 and 69:26. There is an uncanny aptness in "all members" – not limbs merely in a growing embryo but "actions" awaiting the full empowerment of those bodily functions, the means to ends of personhood.

But does this proleptic divine knowledge mean that YAHWEH is a "tyrant throned" and the psalmist a doomed cog in His wheels? Hardly so, else how could he be praying with such ardour to have his will to integrity tested, how end his hymn with pleading to have all his thoughts examined?

> Try me, O God, and seek the ground of my heart, prove me and examine
> my thoughts.

The hapless slave of deity seeks no scrutineer. The psalm ends in a deliberate identity with the realization it knew at its start: "Lord you have examined me and known me." "All my members written" are not in the script of fate but in the crisis of a personhood, in the utmost scruple writing them.

Personhoods may devise against themselves "all the ways a heart can kill its owner", and then learn how a "script overtook them in their ways",[14] but "member" and "counsels" have always responsibly contrived it so. Or, as Charlotte Mew had it in her lament on one such:

> Here lies a prisoner.
> Leave him, he's quiet enough: and what matter
> Out of his body or in, you can scatter
> The frozen breath of his silenced soul,
> Of his outraged soul, to the winds that rave:
> Quieter now than he used to be, but listening still
> To the magpie chatter over his grave.[15]

Psalm 139, too, comes to a bitter end but in a very different terms.

> Do not I hate them. O Lord, that hate Thee, and am I not grieved with those
> that rise up against Thee? Yea, I hate them right sore, even as though they
> were my enemies.

There is something dangerous here. A man saying "God's enemies are
mine too", can soon be thinking: "My enemies are God's also", and he is
set to be another Saul en route to his Damascus. What are we to make of
the abrupt sequence of the psalm at v. 19 where the poet banishes all
"bloodthirsty men" and bids his YAHWEH "slay the wicked"? Does he not
need an Isaiah to suggest to him that "God's thoughts are not like his
thoughts"? We need urgently to face the issue. Does the anger forfeit the
other glad dimensions of body–soul in pilgrimage.

The question presses. This ardent "Thou–I" relation of Psalm 139 is
wonderful – we have argued – in having no alien "them" in its cognizance,
not until vv. 19–22. Only then does a third party come into its ken but
when it does it is with a passionate hatred. The devotee of YAHWEH
becomes a fanatical accuser sparing no vehemence. How should we understand him? There are those who, regretting the harsh transition, view him
as "a man of him time" and, if indeed an exile, then legitimately a verbal
scourger of Babylon. Then the harshness, though regrettable and
unworthy, might be forgiveable. We can wait, Biblically, for a wiser mind
about "love your enemies".

Yet the psalter keeps its place, if only because the problem goes deeper.
Is religion, or its psalmodies of fervent piety, intrinsically divisive and, the
more intense, the more rejectionist outside itself? It is a question we must
remit to where we encounter it again in the study of religious pronouns –
Jewish, Christian and Muslim, in CHAPTERS FOUR to EIGHT. Presently the
sharp turn of temper in Psalm 139 holds in suspense a forceful clue. It is
that the "Thou–I" world of theological love can never escape the contra-
dictions of the actual world nor the co-presence of the contradictors. No
"You and I" is exempt from the fact – and the factors – of third parties.
All situations are at length three-pronounal. "Should I not hate those,
Lord, who hate thee?" is a key question of any faith equation.

Moral issues are not to be evaded if worship is to be honest. There is
the ever painful riddle of human perversity. "Men who speak deceitfully
and abuse the Name shamefully" are perennially with us if outside the
sanctuary. The ethical issue belongs with the transcendent reference.
Refusing the one is to forsake the other. The psalmist's very devotion has
to engage him with the contrary world, unless it be a fond delusion. There
is no respite from the "grief" of them except in relinquishing all things
divine. There has thus to be a political corollary to honest worship, a reach
for righteous polity in the whole practice of prayer.

There are those who see the intense personalism of Psalm 139 as belonging to "the individual as king". The hymn in some cultic sense has been read as a ritual preparation for power, a plea for vindication in the shape of protested innocence. Hence the psalm's introit: "You have examined me" reaches to its conclusion "try me and prove me . . ." and the two hold in themselves the entire theme of the whole. This is a ruler finding his ground to be such in the proven warrant of his fitness "in the knowledge of his God". He who is thus fully "in God's presence" has occasion to identify "God's own enemies", and to aver his "hatred" of them. Perhaps "the everlasting way" is the Ark in godly procession. "I shall count them mine enemies" has to do with both miscreants inside Israel and evil-wishers outside it. It being the duty of YAHWEH to protect His king, so it is the duty of his king to defend his YAHWEH. Because the kingship is "priestly" the priesthood must be royal.[16]

Have we then been mistaken in reading the psalm as being about "the house of any and every pilgrimage", the common man's tenancy of the "substance" of a self? Hardly, for there is no diverting of its whole meaning into politics. The fervour is too intimate, the sense of mystery too vivid. The point of the other possibility is only to have us realize the third-party factor in its claim on inner integrity, its pressure on the longed-for "innocence". As long as the "enemies" are known such only on ground of ethics – as here – the psalmist's "enmity" can be guileless. When the ethical is overtaken by the tribal, the racial and the cultural, then its ethicism is suspect and the "enmity" darkly doubleminded. It points, then, to what became the crucial dubiety in "chosen peoplehood", the heavy burden of historic Jewry and Judaism. Deferring that destiny to CHAPTER FOUR and as a prelude to CHAPTER TWO, where for Arjuna "all my members written" held a strange and tragic fatedness, it will be well to stay longer with the Hebrew personalism of Psalm 139 and take further its soul–body unison in its reading of the human mystery. It is almost incarnational in its perception of the divine "knowledge" comprehending our human-ness, and of our alerted humanity creaturely at home with God. For these are the pronouns His "I" employs towards the soul as "thou", our several "I"s towards that heedful "Thou". Faith, on our side, is only pronounal because the body admits of the soul ever saying "I" in the creatureliness of mortal flesh.

IV

Mother is putting my new second hand clothes in order. She prays now, she says, that I may learn in my own life and away from home and friends, what the heart is and what it feels. So be it! Welcome, O Life.[17]

James Joyce tells of crossing a threshold out of nurture and into venture. Even his clothes are "new" as second hand – symbol of what his cast-offs require him to tell as the garment of his new autonomy, "away from home and friends". A mother's prayer is wistful about the hazards of a youth's loneliness as he defines his half-eager, half-apprehensive self against the newness of an unknown world. "Welcome, O life!" has at once a nervous and a passionate ring but his Ireland will haunt his hard escape from its clinging presence. There is a strife of alienation in his soul. His travelling body in its tale-telling clothes is the singular "house of his pilgrimage", the one constant physical fact of his life. Yet its only constancy is its relentless flux – a flux both material in the bio-chemistry of his frame and time-spatial in the geography of his exile.

The young Joyce's scenario has little evident kinship with the psalmist of Psalm 139. The one "presence" he would "flee from" is oppressively local and "God" is a large element in its being urgently "escaped". Yet, inside this contrast, there is one common feature. It is that "kingship" theme in the Psalm. Though rejected, it must still be a sufficient clue to the psalm's meaning. It points to what is true of us all, namely the fact of an autonomy in which "we live and move and have our being". We are all the subject-masters of our universe – subject in the unpredicatables of creaturehood yet "authoring" inside them with an authority that handles mastery.

Philosophies or faiths that so maximize the subjections as to find them crippling subjugation will come in the following chapter. Conceding their critique but not their veto on the experience of mastery, the present focus is on the mystery of human autonomy vested in the sensuous body where each holds presidential court in an individuation known as inalienable. Whether, in an old-style empiricism, we say: "There is nothing in the mind not first in senses", wisely adding with Kant: ". . . except the mind itself", or whether we opt in more recent terms, for some intuitive "expectancy" implicit in our human-ness,[18] we know ourselves as relatable, informable, addressable, conversable on every hand. We are endlessly furnished by occasions that issue into judgements, acquisitions, decisions – all tending towards the steady shaping of identity, drawing out its potential and disturbing its illusions.

All is centred on the body/mind/soul alliance that is the gist of personhood. That it enjoys a presidential quality, whatever the vicissitudes of poverty or chance, heredity and circumstance, can only be in doubt if it is first evacuated or renounced. Doing so will still have been its exercise. Such is the situation which pronouns transact. It necessitates them in giving them their personal coinage. In Biblical, Quranic and Semitic language, they speak in daily usage the language of "dominion" or *khilafah*, for which personhood is an acknowledged "creaturehood" entrusted with the care and answering functions of a benign creation, where *laborare est orare*.

Then the self as inwardly a "subject" in the nature of self-consciousness becomes, *vis-à-vis* its "empire", an "object" for itself, responsive and responsible to the private body and the inward mind wonderingly self-employed in the realms in which these mediate all meaning. Hence the farm and garden, hence the laboratory and the engine, hence the home and fief, hence the university and the state-house, hence again the temple and the sanctuary.

Such, for Piers Plowman's William Langland, was "the Field of Folk", where the "way to Saint Truth" was a spiral movement both "up" and "down", of whom it could be said: "Piers Plowman can no more disbelieve than he can disbelieve his own existence,"[19] which is to say that the world is credible because we are pronounal in it. This drama of personhood is only had as the script for an actor, in no way merely the text for a critic.

The Essais of Montaigne were significant for his time and place in his insistence on being his own self-analyst, despite literary conventions that disapproved. He was not indulging in self-love but rather ascertaining the significance of his inwardness to himself, be it "melancholy" or "expectation". The quest for self-knowledge was the first liability of selfhood in *assais*, or "testings" of its inherent nature, the very capacity of an "I" to say "me", the being named by its own pronouns. Unwillingness to be a self – were a mood of despair to propose it – would promptly prove a contradiction.

The pronounal self is thus an ever present tense in a continuum of tenses, past and future. The body dates itself in the flux of chronology from childhood into age. Memory, precariously or tenaciously, holds the flux in mind, giving a dimension of compound interest to identity alongside the simple interest of accummulated days and seasons. Recollection enlarges but also complicates our state of being charged with selfhood. The time-migrations in the pilgrim-house of bone and flesh embrace not merely what John Aubrey's *Lives*, writing on Thomas Hobbes, called "the minutes of his thoughts", nor yet George Herbert's "He (man) is some several men at least each several hour". They have rather to do with the "membering" (as Psalm 139 has it) of retrospect and the "membering" of anticipation – events with their sequences that are part of us since we were party to them or prospects that wait for us in the entail of what we have been. In earliest days, being ignorant of futures, childhood sees them only as endlessly open and lives in freedom from a past. That freedom is foregone when passing years accummulate their lessons and their fears. Potentials are no longer infinite and biography is prone to gather regrets or "struggle in the network of (fond) dreams".[20] Then our liability is for

19

mastering what is thus "written in the book" by all our "members", the impulses and patterns of our self-possession. For these, through all their vagaries, are the "substance" of our being, the ceaseless converse of our pronouns-personal, the "I" and "me and "mine" of our diurnal transactions, where consciousness has programmed the complexity of a calendar of years.

The time of the tent – reverting to earlier Biblical imagery – stems from the mortality of the body, its being the conscious field of the soul's expression. Our being temporal and our being physical are one and the same condition. On either count, the body is the nexus where all else obtains. "Bodies", as John Donne sang of them,

> Did us to us at first convey,
> Yielded their forces, sense to us . . .
> We owe them thanks . . .

His analogy following, however, does some violence to their proper dignity. Though "not dross", he saw "bodies" as "alloy" whereby "the gold" of the soul could be "minted" into coinage. Priest as Donne was, he had missed the deep sacramental truth of the body–soul partnership to which, in the sexual context, we must come in CHAPTER NINE.[21]

The "alloy" analogy is better than the "prison" favoured by Greek thought with its *soma/sema* word-play, but a "marriage" more truly captures the ultimate truth, seeing that either is intimate to the other, neither baser nor superior, by dint of their abiding mutuality. Only so could there be a judgement on vulgar eroticism, only so a case against mere aestheticism – the one defiling the body in the denial of soul, the other abandoning the soul for the glamour of the body. Psalm 139 was in no way sensuous yet a surpassing note of a wondrous "me-ness" breathes through every vein of its poetry. The "fearfully" and "wonderfully" of his making in birth abide in their "continuance" when adulthood knew "all of them".

It is when such "fear" and "wonder" no longer inform the human spirit that the body languishes into the sordid and the loveless. Like all metaphors, alloy language about the body needs a discriminating mind. In that things physical give currency in the sensible world to things spiritual it is sound enough. For the touch of a hand, the warmth of a smile, the lilt of a word, the cloud of a frown, the presence of a friend – all these are the interpersonal reality of soul with soul. Yet these transactions with the "gold" in no way inferiorize or relegate the vital partner, as if some separable "spiritual" was the only value in the exchange. That way lie all the distortions of a cold asceticism and the lingering fallacy of some charnel house to be escaped. Christian faith is even bold, in some sense, to find in "body" an eternal relevance.

Where else, we might ask, could such a lively awareness of "the thoughts of God" arise for the psalmist in Psalm 139 and elsewhere in the Psalter than through his sense responses, his dawn-ward, seaward, road-bound perceptions, his mind for metaphors from sands and wings and "uttermost parts"? "When I awake," he sang, when in my reverie I can no longer take more in, "I am still with Thee."[22] His sensibility exhausts itself in the wealth of reality read as "the thoughts of YAHWEH", legible via the faculties and energies of his mysterious body. He knows and confesses the plenitude of his physical being, pilgrim through place and time.

V

A twentieth-century heir to this psalmody of "Thou, Lord" and "I" in the person of Martin Buber draws out its social implications beyond where our psalmist left them. As far as v. 18, as we saw, other people did not enter into his ken, thanks to his intense preoccupation with YAHWEH. When they did it was only as "enemies" who needed to be "hated". In his now celebrated *I and Thou* Martin Buber argues that what is sublime theology in the psalm has to be taken as mandatory ethics in society. For the inter-pronoun situation between Lord and self demands a sequential inter-personhood in all our human doings as though "In Thy Book are all my relatings written". Divine personality underwrites all personhoods around us. For all are in "house in pilgrimage" no less than we ourselves, so that no "he" or "she" should be reduced into some "it" – no longer "frail flesh and blood". This contemporary Judaic case-making will be vital in the concerns below of CHAPTER FOUR.

What is immediately remarkable about Buber's *I and Thou* is that, while it stems from within the bosom of Judaic exclusivity, it reads an inclusive truth in human being. It betrays no concern for the Jew/Gentile distinction so crucial to him in other writings. God, who is ever to be "addressed" not "expressed", is the eternal "Thou" from whom all human bearings come. The "I" we all employ – out of our ineluctable individual being – is "the true Shibboleth of mankind".[23] What is addressed as "Thou" by an "I" can never rightly be reduced to an "it", or only so at the expense also of the "I" so doing. For, as Kant had it, no person can ever rightly be to another human "a means only". Reducing anyone to a mere "utility" role depreciates personhood either way, inevitable as an "I–it" nexus must be in day-to-day affairs.[24] Only in the conscious "thou" I hear addressing "me" and the genuine thou" I say in addressing others are our mutual identities transacted and possessed. Each "thou" so exchanged acknowledges what by its nature cannot become "It".[25]

Thus our inalienable singularity is known as always societal in a kinship of like inalienability known as the other. "The single one" – as Kierkegaard's existentialism likewise told it – is everywhere called to "the divine Thou" as gathering up and including all others. Buber is careful to avoid the less than personal term "the transcendent" which might imply some philosophic abstraction. He notes that "God is the most heavily laden of all words used by men". As diversely and even vacuously nounal it readily excludes all that can be heard only in the "Thou" of each pronounal "I".

Beyond such academic idiom, the psalmist in Psalm 139 would promptly agree. For his ardent "Thou" was his whole soul's poetry. Yet, at least in the context of his "I and Thou", Buber seems unduly – and indeed unHebraically – sanguine about how the pronounal usage "Thou" takes care, in itself, of the vexing ambiguity of the "God" word. For he writes:

> He who speaks the word God and really has *Thou* in mind (whatever the illusion by which he is held) addresses the true *Thou* of his life . . . But when he too, who abhors the name and believes himself to be godless, gives his whole being to addressing the *Thou* of his life, as a Thou that cannot be limited by another, he addresses God.[26]

The "Thou" in the historic life of Israel and of all the psalmists was rooted in what the Biblical tradition knew as "the place of the Name".[27] That "place", as many psalms sang, was the external world of nature, of spring and harvest, but more decisively, it was, the realm of history where divine "Thou-ness" had been intimately experienced. Buber himself gave memorable expression to this in his *Moses* where he expounded Exodus 3:14, not in the bare philosophic terms of a riddle: ("I am that I am") but of event and actuality: "I am as there I will be". In the deliverance of Exodus itself, YAHWEH was known "in the going" in terms beyond any prior guarantee, such as Moses knew his forlorn people would be seeking.[28]

A conviction of that order, placing "the Name" in a context of lived history, surely forbids the logic offered in *I and Thou*, namely that using the word "God" with a total intention of "Thou" in mind sufficiently identifies that "most heavily laden word". The issue of "divine naming" recurs taxingly in Islam as a later chapter must explore. For the New Testament the conviction about history as "placing the Name" passes directly into Christology and Paul's language as to "God in Christ", the giving into time of "the Christ in God". In no way can these be present, nor their Hebraic antecedents, in the anonymous one whom a self-styled "theist" engages in "God-address".

Must it not be acknowledged – beyond the Buber of *I and Thou* – that God can in no authentic way be "addressed" unless the "Thou" be in some measure "expressed" from within? To make the same point grammar-wise is to realize that pronouns, for all their central role, are always on behalf of nouns. The content of the divine Name will always be crucial in the worship that addresses its "Thou". The Qur'an would seem to leave the issue open by simply averring that "Allah has ("possesses") the beautiful Names so call upon Him by them," leaving to later theologians the burden of what they signified.[29]

Elsewhere in *I and Thou* – in his sometimes elusive pattern of discourse – Buber insists that selves "sunk in the world of *It*", or only saying *Thou* in mere ability to use the word, are truly in a state of "apostasy", where the I is "emptied of all reality", as only "defined by things and instincts . . . in the arbitrariness of self-will".[30] It follows that only in the honesty of the faith wherewith God is confessed as Lord are we "saved" from the degradation of ourselves and, from our part in the disorder of the economic realm which seeks wealth and of the political realm, the State, which seeks power. In his reproach of such degradation Buber has no less place for "grief" and "hate" than the psalmist of *Domine Probasti*.

This real inter-play of things religious and of things moral, however, only makes more crucial the "expressive" content we have in our "God-addressing" pronoun "Thou" in the intention of authentic worship. It would seem from his 1957 Postscript that Buber's *I and Thou* was some forty years in the making, if not in the writing. Perhaps only so did it attain its stature as a landmark in Jewish theology. For our pronounal purposes, the precedence belongs to Psalm 139 whence it stemmed via the long centuries of a Judaism deprived of land and Temple, and forced back upon its Torah and its Talmud, the scripted versions of its ancient "YAHWEH and Us", its "Us with YAHWEH".

Nature in its panorama and fertility, history in its experienced unfolding, were the twin schools of this communal persuasion. They were duly read as holding out a destiny whereby self and society lived their "I" and "We" in acknowledging God's eternal "Thou".

But nature, in the diverse measures of climate and terrain, is in no way a consistent constancy of mood or magnanimity. Nor is history a fair-dealer or a plain-speaker. Its vagaries are notoriously, monstrously unjust, in their fickleness negligent, it would seem, of all moral probity. There is a long crying in the streets and he who would be sanguine must not fail to calculate the toll of his journey. "The house of every pilgrimage" travels a road of many toll-gates. "Am I not grieved . . . ?" the psalmist protested to YAHWEH, wanting to side with Him against the "shameless" defaming of His Name. His kindred were often no less minded to protest against YAHWEH as men agonizing over what His Name could ever surely be.

There is need, therefore, to pass from Psalm 139 and its sublime celebration of birth and being, of body in the bliss of life, and take bearings from "the cellars of the soul",[31] from the dark incidence of human perversity and the stakes of poverty, adversity and tragedy so heavily laden against all humankind. Then what is only idyllic, or merely self-indulgent, in the wondering psalmist is more truly gauged and told in counsels of fatedness and frustration, calling for a different, a more sombre wisdom.

There is no place to turn more cogent and realist than the religions of India, the faiths we speak of as Hinduism and Buddhism. But, doing so, is there something more sinister in that "place of the Name" idea so central earlier? Is there something – as it were – "continental" in the diversity of religious verdicts, so that how we read ourselves and the world cannot fail to be chronically "controversial" also? Are humans incorribly "climatized" in the spirit as well as in the latitudes and weathers of the world?

If so, perhaps there was about Psalm 139 a possibility that never occurred to us earlier or – if it did – was resisted with embarrassing demur, concerning, that "mother's womb" where the poet had been "covered". We argued that maternity had made him "common man". But "motherhood" was then ensuring "godly seed", "YAHWEH's heritage", in line with "all our fathers". So, at length, "the sons of Jacob – offspring of Abraham", would come to feel, as "people of the covenant from the womb – the womb alone". We remember how outrageous it seemed, puzzlingly absurd, to Nicodemus to be told: "You must be born again". That would apply to "Gentiles" in their unhappy lack of "chosen people" status, not to "masters in Israel". The psalm's "Thine eyes did see my substance" might thus have a more to be suspected ring.

Yet it is surely wiser, truer, to return to the universal intention of the psalmist and stay as we began with universal peoplehood in one Lord. The issue will recur, inseparable as it is from religious pronouns. Meanwhile, to Asia "take we wandering steps and slow".

CHAPTER TWO

The Personal Interrogative – Arjuna and the Gita

I

William Morris, the Victorian artist, poet and high priest of the cult of household beauty, in his romantic Kelmscott village, Oxfordshire, seems a far cry from the ghats of the Ganges at Varanasi. He wrote:

> I won't submit to be dressed up in red and marched off to shoot at my French or German or Arab friends in a quarrel that I don't understand; I would rebel sooner than do that.[1]

How close he comes to the protest of Arjuna in the Gita, fated, he is told, to engage in battle with his cousins whom he recognizes drawn up in fighting array across the valley.

> As I see them here, my own kinsfolk
> Drawing nearer, so eager to fight,
> My limbs sink down, my throat is parched
> And there is trembling in my body:
> My bow falls from my hand . . .[2]

Down long centuries the parallel is uncanny, but there the likeness ends. There is no evidence of a kindred outcome. For Morris was an ardent socialist, refusing strenuously the perverted conventions of society. He demands the freedom of the rebellious spirit and knows his ardour to be authentic in the name of justice and truth. He will be no underling, subdued to the dark forces of ugliness, greed, folly and social blight. He is a romantic realist ranging his talents against the pride of the intolerable.

In his Indian idiom, Arjuna would be his soul-mate in the other clime and time, if only the fates allowed. The most celebrated of Hindu classics of religion holds its human hero to a vocation of surrender, by the will and through the succour of the gods, to a destiny of rigorous "duty" as the given clue to his existence. He must take his meaning from the caste in which, inexorably, his lot sets him, and in which he must attain to "desireless action" through the divine tuition coming to him by the grace of Krishna. The "salvation" to which, in these terms, he will come suffices to set at rest all the misgivings his untutored heart had registered at the first sight of what confronted him.

It is well to look for echoes of things common to the human soul across the distances of centuries and places – distances religions do so much both to widen and distort. John Milton's Adam had been bewildered no less than Arjuna by the horrendous "killing fields" of human conflict.

> O what are these,
> Death's ministers, not men, who thus deal Death
> Inhumanly to man and multiply
> Ten thousandfold the sin of him who slew
> His brother; for of whom such massacre
> Make they but of their brethren, men of men?

Milton's Michael then explained to Adam that the reason lay in the wilful adoration of "might . . . held the highest pitch of human glory . . . destroyers rightlier call'd and plagues of men".[3] The Gita perceives "destroyers" and "plagues" too, but to be allowed, not reprehended, in an order of things to be endured and – only so – transcended in the quest for attitudes that make them meaningless, or rather, the distressful meaning they seem to have becomes itself illusory. The Gita is thus worlds away from the psalmist of the 139th.

II

Yet it is no idle fancy that aligns them together. Each begins with the "I" and "me" of a private anxiety. The Semitic hymn, like the Genesis Scripture it shares, is starting with God, with YAHWEH, the "O Lord, Thou . . ." of the opening *cri-de-coeur*, while the Hindu poet is at first wholly inside a human arena, striving to resolve a dark *mise-en-scène* in front of him, on which deity will only later intervene.[4] It is characteristic of both Hindu and Buddhist traditions that their point of departure – even in some cases in a quite pragmatic way – is with the self as its own query-seat. Theirs is a "who and why am I?" not a "who art Thou, Lord?" For Arjuna the latter only arises when at length Krishna appears in his chief glory. Buddhism, for its part, as commonly seen, is content to be atheistic.[5]

However, the shared common pronoun "I" is the theme of their contrasted worlds and in either case is sanctioned by the mystery of native birth. For Hindus resemble Jews in that they become themselves by birth, not merely – as we all do – by the necessity of wombing, but by dint of our wombing making us who we are religiously. "From my mother's womb", as we saw with the psalmist, was by covenant and election the mandate of his identity. Thus no Jew ever has to "become" one.[6] For centuries, prior to recent, modern movements of neo-Hinduism, it was likewise with Hindus. Their faith-system does not "recruit" adherents: they belong in a sort of sub-continental tribalism, as holding the faith that goes with a vast territory where all other major religions have been imports or invasions from without, Islam most conspicuously among them. Thus, though in ways subtly different from those of Jewry, to be Hindu is to be Indian with a corroborating authenticity that others lack.[7]

It follows that it is sounder always to speak of "Hindus" than of "Hinduism", the latter being a device of outsiders as denoting something that is, in fact, essentially repudiating any particular identity, seeing that all "particulars" belong within the all inclusive *Brahman*. Every private *atman* is only individuated by *maya* or "illusion". It is vital to appreciate this Hindu theme before we can understand the serenity of "detached activism" which Krishna commends to the perplexed Arjuna in the Gita.

Its classic expression offers the paradox of a fully pronounal formula, namely the *tat tvam asi*, or "That Thou art" of Hindu faith and liturgy, affirming that each several *atman* is also the Ultimate Reality, the impersonal *Brahman*. Despite the pronoun "Thou", we must not think of another "Outsider" sharing the inner loneliness or solitariness our personhoods severally feel by virtue of what we will be exploring elsewhere as "the ego-centric situation". We have to think somehow of this "Thou" of ultimate reality as an infinite unloneliness where all inhere, despite unavoidable employment of a pronoun to denote "it". Inasmuch as no one can know "being me" as I do, each of us has to recognize that "all comes to a head in me", and – likewise – does so for all others, only as interior to them. In that way, each *atman* could be said to equal *Brahman* as participatory in meanings and awarenesses that belong with totality. It follows that Hindu *tat tvam asi*, in its discursive way, would have us know that when we register in our subjectivity the overriding claims of honesty in the recognition of truth, or wonderment in the presence of beauty, or obligation towards moral issues, we are taken up into what lays on us absolute authority akin to our interior "subject" status.[8] This might find analogy in the "definition" of music as "what kindles in us when we are reminded by the instruments". Is this classic theme in Hindu religion of *atman* equals *Brahman* and that "the soul is Reality", simply reminding us that all cognizance of truth, wonder, joy, duty and submission inside our subjective being belongs in, and derives from, what is for ever "beyond" and infinitely real?

If so, it is a profound religious *confessio* present – in some shape and measure – in every tradition. But can it well be hailed as "a liberation", a perception that saves us from the burdens and frustrations of life? Can it either justify or sustain the equanimity that – in the Gita's terms – will do "duties", as caste-enjoined and fated, in a liberated detachment that is "unburdened of its burden"? Or would the Hebrew prophet – had he lived in Hindustan – have said: "They have healed the hurt of my people slightly" (Jeremiah 6:14)?

For the equation "the soul is Reality" cannot fit our finite existence or apply to the empirical self. In view of transmigration, the human self may be destined to pass through many existences, in some of which the experiences of beauty, honesty and moral claim, characteristically human as they are, will not arise. They will take the self outside the range of those human discoveries which alone, as we have traced, impose their intimations of the absolute. "'Tis we musicians know" as Browning has it.[9]

Moreover, the equation is not, and cannot be, speaking of our empirical selves, caught as they are in the distraction of phenomena, beset in *maya* by the illusion of the finality these only seem to possess. Will not *maya* arguably rescind the case for understanding *Brahman* as embracing *atman* in terms like music, leaving us no option but to love it, or like aesthetic judgements being always *a priori*, making us only subjects of that which rightly masters us?

It is fair to ask whether the need for the pronoun Thou in the classic Hindu formula may not indicate that the personalism (ours) which alone can use it, is thereby reaching for a reality that is personal as the only feasible clue to what is reciprocal.[10] For the Hindu mind, however, *Tvam* is always understood as "impersonal", whatever the terms, either way, can mean. It is only in the phenomenal world, and thanks to our empirical selves, that we can ever receive those intimations of transcendence as a reality that thereby tells us how "beyond" it is. Can we ignore the long controversy of the religions as to "personal" and "impersonal" and not acknowledge that we, each and all and severally in our humanity, are participatory in a reality that holds us tributary in ours?

To ignore that issue would be, for the Biblical mind, a kind of treachery seeing that pronouns, human and divine, are duly and rightly reciprocal. For the Islamic mind it would be fatally risking idolatry. For, unless Allah is singularly addressed as the only and omnipotently exclusive Lord, false worships will ensue. It is, however, instinctive to the Hindu soul that whatever we can mean in religion has to be elusive and, as it were, categorically uncategorical. It had often been observed that religious pluralism presents no problem to Hindus. The gods themselves are in a flux of diversity and multiplicity. Reality is all absorbing yet endlessly differentiated, its avatars symbolizing but in no way binding its caprices and entities in their uninhibited fertility, responsive to what is nebulous or elusive on the human side of the equation. The very Krishna who, in the Gita, approaches Arjuna as a lowly charioteer emerges to be the utmost Lord, the supreme voice of sublime authority.

The aphorism that runs: "x" faith is what "x" faithful hold – though aptly said about all religions – is more congenially true for the Hindu soul. Theology should be about the religious life of humankind and avoid intellectual speculation and rational liability. It suffices if faith is lived, in the happy abeyance of intellectual interpretation. The ideal dogma is to be undogmatic. The only anathema is for anathemas themselves, not least those that the Semitic faiths have been urgent to reserve in defence of their absolutes.

To live and think in these terms (for there is no such thing as absence of mind) means that Hindus have an odd usage with their pronouns. The "I" and "Thou" of a Martin Buber[11] is strangely disconcerted or "disestablished" in that a personal deity (*Ishta devata*) to whom my "I" says "Thou" will be a personal preference, a for-the-time-being choice, doing duty in a viable, but in no way singular, shape for the transcendent reality, the "Thou" or "not Thou" of *tat tvam asi*.

The contrast with all things Hebraic and Christian would be pointed if, irresponsibly, we were to borrow the words of Exodus 3:14 and have them read: "I am being what I am being", and made to carry a Hindu-style *tvam* that was transcendent precisely in escaping all time and place and eluding all historical manifestations or evidentiality – the very realm of the credentials the Hebraic mind understands.[12] For, given the concept of *maya*, the Hindu mind is happy to renounce all relevance to history, natural or revelatory, of *tvam* as "Thou", unless personal preference opts that way and then, only inside Hindu perceptions of transcendence.[13]

It is time to return to a pronoun study of the Gita, but first to ask whether there are not "transcendental precepts" addressing us from an ultimately real, as well as transcendental otherness. If so, what must these mean for our human personhoods in what used to be called "responsions"?[14] We saw earlier Wilfred Smith's reading of "that Thou art" as our register of being "subject" to sublime authority experienced in the claim of truth for honesty, of beauty for recognition and of ethics for obedience. But, if we can think of these as "precepts" to which our sensitivity has to be responsive, must not the pronounal "Thou" that is their source and ground be moral and, therefore, no longer indefinable and "nameless"? Or, differently expressed, does our cognizance of ourselves as using "pronouns" Godward not suggest that we are being addressed from inside some mutual definition both of "us" and "Thou"? Could that ever leave us with free-ranging optionality about personal choices where we do business with the ineffable? Might we then be also falsely claiming, by implication, some variable definition of ourselves which would leave us no longer moral beings? Writing in *The Inner Loneliness* in 1982, Sebastian Moore observes:

> In the very heart and core of human loneliness is inscribed the divinity of its only possible partner. Therefore the greatest conceivable relationship is with that which intends my existence.[15]

We must learn to say and mean that "God is love".

III

To come to the Gita from this exploration of the Hindu mind is to entertain a conclusion with which it does not agree. Doing so, however, may be the sure way to take its central point. It would only be on the basis of some Bhakti-style devotion to a personally chosen deity as Lord that the Hindu could allow, if not share, the conviction just quoted. For that conviction holds to the goodness of desire as something we should gratefully trust, as proper to take us beyond things mundane admittedly inadequate to satisfy it. We might thus reach the ultimate reason for being "us" as found in being for "the other" that intended us for this very reading of desire, namely God as love. Such desire alone will lead us out of "the prison of ourselves" and do so authentically both as to the selves we are and the God we trust as the magnet of our "intended" being.

To come to the Gita this way has the advantage of posing a revealing contrast, namely that, for the Gita, human being, in our pronounal selves, is not of that order. The definition that has us in "desire-destiny", from and towards God as love, in authentic selfhood, has to give way to a destiny that situates us where desire must be forfeit to karmic duty and existence is circumscribed both by the incidence of time and the vicissitudes of selfhood. These teach us the wisdom of conformity to their exactions. Detachment from desire is the necessary condition in which we accept the destiny that inexorably belongs to our selfhood. The pronoun "I" is answerable to duty and only tangentially to "love" as towards the mentor-Lord who showed me what duty means and holds. So the Gita.

It may be well, before going further, to ponder why – supremely – we take the Gita for our guide to Hindu pronouns. "The Song of the Beloved" as the high peak of the Mahabharata, the great Epic of the legendary Bharatas, is the supreme devotional hymn of Hindu piety. As the saga of the long conflict between the Kauravas, with their blind king, and the Pandavas, it gathers to itself the quality of India's story from the invading Aryas through the ages of the Rig Veda to the times of its origin around the second century BC. Whether of single or composite authorship, the Gita's eighteen chapters form only a small fraction of the saga's hundred thousand stanzas, distilling a vast literature into a cherished compendium of Hindu religious quest. Sensitive spirits of whatever vintage find echoes of their own anguish in its lines.

We know already how Arjuna, one of five Pandava brothers, reacts with a highly intelligent dismay to the spectacle of futile war, as he surveys the two armies in battle array. From mutual slaughter no good can come. He is in no doubt about their valour or the legends they enshrine, but the kinships they share argue that there is no merit in their quarrel. Arjuna protests the violation of family and the dishonour of women. He would prefer to have death done to himself than to do death to some foe. Dropping bow and arrow down, he gives way to the bitterness of grief.

Krishna, still in lowly guise, reproaches him for cowardice. This Arjuna hotly denies, repeating his quarrel with the quarrel, and roundly insisting: "I will not fight." Whereupon, in Chapter 2, "the Blessed One" (oddly Hebraic phrase), answers his urgent plea for explanation as to why "fight he must", by expounding the teaching of the Samkhya school of philosophy. This differentiates between *prakriti* (the three *gunas* variously present in all humans and diversifying our personhood between virtue and misery) and *purusha*, or spiritual insight, which alone gives us to see through the *maya* which has us thinking that *prakriti* is the whole truth of things.

More crudely put, the "perishable" – what fights, suffers and dies – needs to accept that there is the "imperishable", the *atman* that is unscathed by all that action does and suffers, and, being inside the *brahman* that is all pervading, cannot suffer harm. In that realm there is no significant killing. Arjuna can properly fight because the *purusha* soul is indestructible, while *prakriti* is merely transitory and – whether in battle or other means – will die. Arjuna, in effect, will not be slaying his kinfolk, if he truly reads beyond the illusion by which he fears to do so. To think them slain, or himself their slayer, is to be void of judgement.

That exoneration – if we call it such – though to do so would be to misunderstand – is further underlined in Chapter 2 and Krishna's tuition of Arjuna, by the call to yogic "detachment". He must act without desire for glory or fame or success, proceeding free of longing. For these belong only with the "perishable" realm. This means that to speak of "I" and "me" and "mine" is never to come to the "peace" which rewards the abeyance of those misleading pronouns. There is thus no place for "mourning" and no room for reproach. Kshatriya – the warrior caste – have no option but that duty. Only a disgrace worst than death could wait on their disobedience. Their only "interest" has to be in action, never in its fruits. Arjuna's plea *in situ* for "inaction" is unworthy "attachment". He must allow the discipline in which he is not perturbed by sorrows, loses desire for joys and sheds all longings, fears and angers. To attain this he must not meditate on objects of sense. Desires, like waters entering the sea, lose themselves in what is never destined to be filled.

By Chapter 3, this has raised for Arjuna the painful question as to why, given this rubric of "detachment", a situation for action anyway represents itself. How can "desireless" duty present an invitation to action? The answer given is that, for us "perishable", this "law of work" is inevitable, stems from nature and is encased in history. That we cannot but act only reinforces the need to abandon desire in doing so. To enjoin this further, Krishna discloses himself as the avatar, ordainer of the caste order. Deeds and renunciation are not mutually opposed. While mental and physical functions operate (*prakriti*) the *purusha* self stays exempt and motionless. Such is the true asceticism. So far Chapters 3 to 5, with Chapter 6 an education into the skills that establish control over senses and mind, until the self is lost only in God.

This leads the argument of the Gita forward in Chapter 7 and onward into Bhakti devotion, in which the devotee is exceedingly dear to God and God is endeared to him. Here, significantly, there seems to be a far more "personal" quality to each in the mutuality of divine/human love where the Gita could, in its finely subtle sense, be genuinely "theist".[16] Krishna as Lord uses freely the pronoun "I" and tells of "the knowing ones" who seek him as revering "me" "with firm resolve". The meaning is developed further in Chapter 11 where, beyond all "contemplation", Arjuna is made aware of all-devouring omnipotence in Hindu terms, a sovereignty where "as into a flaming mouth" all creatures enter and pass into a "homage" where all time is contained and all history enacted. Arjuna can take up his own sword, disillusioned of all his inhibition, as enacting on earthly plane the design of the "all-Knower", doing sovereignty's work.

The remaining chapters of the Gita offer a miscellany of moral counsels, some having a Buddhist flavour, concerning detachment and right behaviour, the duty to subdue the passion and "darkness" in the human soul to the "purity" of *sattva* and, by ascetic devotion, strive to pass even beyond it by cherishing the supreme secret the ultimate vision has disclosed.

If we are thinking with pronouns (we can hardly attain not to do so), it is well to ask which is prior – the soul's realization of its human meaning or its vision of the sovereignty that is Lord. Writing in *Hindu and Muslim Mysticism*, R. C. Zaehner thinks the former.

> Self-realisation is regarded as being prior to knowledge of God: the liberated soul sees all things first in himself and then in God.[17]

To comprehend one's own soul – to be sure – via the body as link and clue to the material world but learning to stay unaffected by its deeds therein, is to realize that this recapitulates the relation of God to the world. This also transcends these "immediacies" to constitute the human soul's place of eternal repair and haven in the realization of a sublime indifference. By a sort of inter-analogy, the inner "me" of soul–self, via discipline and vision, counterparts, in its freedom from illusion, the divine "Thou" that is the ground whereby the truth, either way, is known to be so. The *atman* somehow "becomes" *Brahman*, when seeing *Brahman* everywhere and all things in *Brahman*, without *atman* being lost, provided that *atman*, through discipline and vision, is liberated from what ties it, in illusion, to the body. Only then do we have the clue to how the soul should read its mortal physicality.

Yet, confusingly, there are notes in the Gita that teach how "the Imperishable", before whom Arjuna lay prostrate in terror, is somehow greater than *Brahman*. Was the great poem introducing a new teaching here that took it beyond the Upanishads? Or is it that "the terminology varies quite inordinately"?[18] If so, either way, there may be occasion to draw its pronouns more confidently towards some measure of "God is love". It would not be fair to say that ambivalence in vocabulary might – for venturous exegetes – be the saving grace of the Gita, but its elusiveness may justify a hope to read it so.

IV

Given that final point in a survey of the Gita, namely the elusiveness of its crucial terms, and given also how far the loving prestige it carries has allowed it to be invoked for a wide diversity of readings, it will be well to be both cautious and enterprising in any response that brings pronouns and religions into debate.

One tack in being so could be to take up the theme of "fatedness" urged on Arjuna at the outset, the notion of some karmic necessity from which life, or duty, or caste, or time and place, or all these together, allow neither respite nor escape. It is a very contemporary, as well as an age-long register of human lot, and leads into the profoundest reaches of religious thought. It can readily be separated from the caste theme in Hinduism, with its sequences of soul-migration and the concept of predetermined roles or status in society that require to be mortally fulfilled. For, in more general terms, all human existence is compassed about by "necessities" so crippling when within awareness, so determinative when not.

They are of an order that has us asking with Prufrock in T. S. Eliot's poem: "Do I dare disturb the universe?" or the same poet's echo of Dante: "I had not thought death had undone so many."[19] In an endlessly vulnerable world, personal pronouns move among inevitable casualties stemming from circumstance at once harshly formative and remotely out of personal reach. Would not a social realist be urgent to ask out of what privilege and advantage could the psalmist we studied in CHAPTER ONE have attained his blissful theme?

There is always the implicit *karma* of the accident of birth. For we do not choose our parentage nor engage with why they came by us.[20] Or, that hurdle taken, did we enter a world that left us options or grimly fore-closed them? It is well known that "primal societies" yield no place for individualism, so that "what goes", through all "the rites of passage" and between them, is totally societal, denying not only all exemption but the very inkling of it. Or in more sophisticated settings, are not sociolo-gists convinced that puppetry is all we are fated to know, aware perhaps, if vaguely, that strings are jerking us but we quite unable to prevent them?[21]

Are we a species that "produces evil as a bee produces honey . . . suf-fering from the terrible disease of being human"?[22] What, then, should be said of the hive in which it happens so? Or of hive-history presently in its legacy? The Christian theme of "original sin", rightly compre-hended, has always understood our being "in Adam" as a situation, not of "inherited guilt" since at birth we had not yet lived, but of "inherited solidarity" in which there was a future of the past radically ordering the present in ways that we could not escape.[23] It has, we could say, many karmic elements about it, confronted with a world we could neither elude nor shape by our own devices, yet in which action was mandatory.

How many, in early or middle adulthood in the grim years of 1914–18, were an army of Arjunas crying: "I will not fight", grieving at the summons into massive slaughter, yet had their fateful duty, their dutiful fate, enjoined by concepts of "Kaiser und Deutschland", and "King and Country"? Was not the celebrated finger of Kitchener, pointing home that British legend, a sort of late-day Krishna demanding the performance of assignment? The poetry of Wilfred Owen grimly registered the irony of the intolerable in the ineluctable.

Political history aside, there are all the dimensions of "allotedness" in the incidence of poverty, ignorance and deprivation. There are, around us, the savageries of nature, with burning sun so far other than the mellow mists of temperate harvests. Could Wordsworth have been the poet of *The Prelude* in the burning heat of the tropics? What instinct could have led William Blake to set "Jerusalem" in a "green and pleasant land"? The psalmist's "How lovely are Thy dwellings" was hardly, in his day or since, a comment on geography.

It might be credible for a Thomas Traherne, in his rural Credenhill on a hillside in Herefordshire, to write of "something infinite that talked with my expectation and moved my desire" and thus be able to pen the poem we earlier noted. "I come His son and heir" rejoiced in the wonder of how

he "who nothing was" had arrived all wonderingly. *Karma*, had he
known of it, was rustic bliss ensured, far from the vultures and cobras,
the man-eating tigers of the torrid Indian scene. Admittedly, his adult
years were cast in the anxieties of the English Civil War but nevertheless
he had means to ensure "a good heritage".[24] "I come a *harijan*" would
more likely be the less than poetic self-discovery in the villages of
Tamilnad or Gurajat, with some dawning awareness of *karma* ensuing,
not out of "I that nothing was", but from an uncertain entail of earlier –
and less than benign – states of "me-ness" still carrying their momentum
forward into life's immediacies.

Unless we are to conclude that religious faiths draw their defining clues
from geographical factors of climate, culture and latitude in the one earth,
and thus have no viably common discourse and must be assumed to tally
with disparate and plural humanities, we must take due stock of how
those contrasting factors have conditioned our beliefs and the worships
they underwrite. This means that people of "election", whether of the
Hebraic kind in ethnic privilege or of the "fair seed-time had my soul"
vintage in "green and pleasant" climes, must have a mind for the perceptions faiths have, where cultures, born of scenes and story, present
harsher, sterner norms of reckoning with selfhood.

This means that readers of the Gita need to heed its counsels of disinterest or detachment as being the due pattern of the duty to participate.
Arjuna must take up the battle. So destiny demands. He must disallow
the emotions of futility and pity that hold him back. For their restraining logic can have no place in his will. Participation is all but
participation pursued in entire disengagement, such as to veto self-pre-
tentiousness or vested interest in the form of what might be called "the
assertive pronoun", the cult of private, personal acquisition of whatever
might arguably accrue from the situation. For those criteria were behind
the reasonings with which he had initially felt appalled by the prospect
of the battle. The pity he had then felt, the sense of a profane absurdity
which had bound him with his "cousins" seen inside the same emotions,
had misread what was also for them the same vocation to disinterest in
engagement, to participation as the destiny by which alone the self was
defined. It would almost seem that a karmic self-acceptance means
accepting to be "unselfed", if, by "selfed", we mean what pronouns "I",
"me", and "mine" intend in the ego-centric situations of hope, desire,
memory and the commerce of affairs. It is, therefore, urgent to appreciate what the Gita has in view in this paradoxical doctrine of
disinterested engagement, of detachment in participation, so puzzling to
many.

V

It is not difficult to recognize many areas in which a present/absent self might obviously belong. Mountaineering could be a case in point. When asked why they climb, mountaineers often reply: "Because the mountain is there." It calls to action in which there is no mercenary motive, no selfish intent, no hidden agenda. There is only the pure love of the task, only the challenge of the venture for its own engrossing sake like some journey to the pole or rounding Cape Horn solo in a yacht. These, though different from Arjuna's warrior role with its price in human slaughter, could fit the Gita's vision of commitment with no ulterior dimension.

Yet, authentic in these terms as mountaineers have been, there would seem always to have been attendant hazards of "desires" latent in their disengaged engagement – the self-interest of outdoing rivals, establishing records, gaining prestige and becoming celebrated. For the very prowess which tackles mountains for their own sake is highly susceptible to these concomitants. We head for a "both-and" situation in which the detachment is at once real and faulty.

The difficulty of the Gita's paradox becomes even clearer if we move from scaling peaks to decoding nature's secrets. The scientific enterprise has to be a model of disinterest. Clues must be pursued in complete detachment from what the researcher would like them to prove or reveal. They must be honestly followed where-ever they lead. Nothing in that way is more "karmic" than the exploration of matter in chemistry or physics. The summons for the laboratory technician makes a technical Arjuna everywhere – one who can never intelligently say: "I will not be tied to the clues".

Yet again the paradox returns. Little science ever stayed disinterested. Much of it from the outset was steered by vested interest, by investment with a view to gain, or power, or advantage over rivals, or products for merchandizing. The real presence of these factors did not obviate the honesty in the laboratory: they did stay to exploit its findings. The disinterest, we might say, was only tactical, subservient to a strategy it could neither exclude nor disown.

Exemplars multiply of the Gita situation where attached detachment (the way of pronouns in grammars) obtains. Imperialism in Gandhi's India would be an uncongenial one but there was in much "empire idealism" a genuine concept of ministry as duty. David Livingstone's "destiny" to geographical exploration was motivated – in an otherwise motive-less way[25] – by a will to end the traffic in slaves. Kipling's much derided "white man's burden" was no mystical load, and far more realist than John Lennon's empty lyric: "No need to kill or hunger, a brotherhood of man, Imagine all the people living for the sky".[26] There truly was in "the imperial dream" a veritable "mission":

> Clear the land of evil, drive the road and bridge the ford
> Make you sure he reach his own.

> And whoso will, from pride released,
> Contemning neither creed nor priest,
> May feel the soul of all the East
> About him at Kamakura . . .
> . . . think 'ere ye pass to strife and trade,
> Is God – in human image made –
> No nearer than Kamakura?[27]

However, the machinations and tragic manipulations of imperialism need no detailed exposition. The literature of anti-colonialism has made them heinous enough, with imperial power imperially corrupting in no less absolute ways than the domestic sort.

The Gita's prescript of disinterest could be signally echoed by the philosophy of Communism. Few partisans in political action have been more privately self-detached than the Communist recruit, who had to be ready to subject all to the Party, whose will alone decided all else. Such was the price of allegiance as notably exemplified by Frantz Fanon in his Caribbean dedication to Algerian Independence.[28] There was something rather Gita-like in his insistence on the necessity to hate, as the only option left by colonialism itself – the enormity which has contrived its villainy by first colonializing the mind of *les colonisés*. The necessity to resist meant a requirement to suspend all emotions of common humanity, or see "cousins" in the wretched "enemy". Any such emotions would be treachery to a latter-day kshatriya. Sartre's inescapable *être en soi* could truly cease to be an *être pour soi*, because it had passed wholly into an *être pour la partie*. However, the still haunting self-interest had only been transferred to "the Party" and been thereby collectivized" as a still more real attachment to desire. Collectivizing had only changed the name of evil, despite the evident elision of self-seeking by the self-eliminating partisans.

We seem to be left with the conclusion that, while there are many situations in which immersion in action often calls for selfhoods in total dedication to it, such abeyance of ulterior desire cannot well be action that somehow is no longer autonomous. Is there not a duty to discriminate between disparity of desires in always desirous situations? Mountains are not ascended by some neutral climber, nor are empires contrived in a fit of absence of mind. Does not the will *for*, or *to*, the action need to negotiate with the will in the doing? Detachment, in the Gita's terms, must itself be willed. Desire must somehow be ever present for there to be any urgent duty to suppress it. Situations on every count would seem to be requiring an alert critique of the desiring self, rather than its neutering.

Ought the reader, coming to the Gita, do well to agree that certainly life involves us in the necessity to act and that, doing so, we must learn that what *seems* real has something more real still transcending it, if not *sub specie aeternitatis*? There is clearly a moral duty arising from the sharp disparity, not merely the presence, of desirous situations. The will to obey could not, for Arjuna, be divorced from the will to choose. For the guidance he received from Krishna as to his first reaction to the battle array being illusory, was in no way illusory *in situ*. It was agonizingly existential, calling for action (namely joining the battle) which was now a different sort of action (from uninhibited belligerence) as overriding the initial disavowal of it. In this way, there was a decision the more radical in that it comprised an acutely felt paradox, a decision embracing but in no way resolving a dilemma. The Arjuna prostrate before divine majesty is the same Arjuna who despaired of the sanity of the world.

However loaded the dice or categorical the counsel of religion, we cannot forbear to act. There is no fugitive flight into permanent suspension of judgement. Before Arjuna's eyes the battle array is drawn. The conscience that rules out both cowardice and slaughter is not itself ruled out by karmic logic if only compliance with Krishna remains. Yet the map in the mind shapes a choice in the will. Krishna draws the one for the Arjuna who must bring the other. The mental and the actual, the karmic "wisdom" and the human deed are like the concave and the convex of one crescent shape. "To will and to do" come together. It is action, action alone, that is the sphere and occasion of the interplay we have traced between undesiring detachment and desirous commitment. Can we conclude that the Gita's teaching is that the merit of the former is necessary to sustain the right discharge of the latter? If so, then it follows that only what is innocent of self-seeking has the ability to be salvific. There is something – in concrete action – inside the will to serve that will subvert its yield of human good. On this count there must be a willed abeyance of desire. Yet these subversive wiles of sin in the will to good are to be thwarted, not by somehow exempting the will from its crucial part but by purifying of self-seeking the part it surely plays.

For the personal "I" as the only agent available is always dogged by the intervening claim of its "me-ness". The situation is readily illustrated, though in no way exclusively, in the distinction we must make in public action between the office we discharge and the person we are. How often the person can exploit the function to private gain. Hence bribery, embezzlement, tyranny and every kind of wrong. How often, too, we contrive to establish a personal nexus with an official in the hope it will serve to override the civic duty the office demands.[29]

Adapting a saying of Jesus in the Gospel, must we not aim to be able to say: "When we have done all, we are unprofiting servants"?[30] Was this what the Gita had in mind in enjoining participation with disinterest, detachment as the temper of sustained involvement? If so, it is strange the teaching of this "way" should have been in the setting of armed conflict where, for the perceptive Arjuna as a conscientious objector, it was the slaughter that called for the "involvement" of "abstention", the futility of combat that enjoined the action of exemption.

Could the theme of *karma*, then, be read – in some sense – *not* as that on which the self is ushered, caste-wise, out of a sequence of "having beens" where the present "I" has no aegis, but instead the self's arrival (as Traherne had it) by un-prefaced birth into a human scene where it enters on a proneness to wrong inherent in society as discovered to a readily corruptible soul? If so, it might be close to the real meaning of "original sin", where sadly but actually "experience" is always the antonym of "innocence", as William Blake, with a mind well tuned to things Hindu, would have us realize. It will be instructive to trace how this comprehension, taught albeit indirectly by the Gita, has registered in the modern Hindu mind and the "experience" of Neo-Hinduism.

VI

Does the foregoing approximate at all to the plea of the psalmist in Chapter 1, "Search me, O God and know my heart. Look well if there be in me any grievous way . . ."? We noted then how silent he was as to the immediacies of his context, his societal engagement. It is almost as if the song comes out of an immunity in meditation.

Such was in no way the lot of Hindus at grips with their Indian nationalism as world events began to suggest a feasible ending of the British Raj. It is evident that all explored in the foregoing about disinterested engagement applies to communal collectives, no less than to private selves. For corporate collectives are still more liable to jealousies and vested interests than are private selves, the more so when they insist that "communalism" is the betrayal of what is more rightly told as "nationalism".[31]

How did the Gita bear on the thinking of the Congress Party set on Swaraj, independence from Britain, in the complexities of the sub-continent? That lines were drawn from which there was no escape was evident enough. "Engage you must!" was the loud logic, however dismaying the likely price commitment would exact. But how could doing so be without "interest", given how strenuous the odds, how intractable the politics involved?

Despite the paradox we have studied in the Gita of a non-(soul) violence summoned to behave with armed violence, there were other areas of Hindu and Buddhist teaching to yield the concept of *ahimsa* to undergird the Gandhian theme of *satyagraha*, or soul-power, with which to "resist without violently resisting" the others' "wrong", identified not in themselves as "enemies" (pace Fanon) but in their behaviour as "inimical". While the Raj could not be tolerated or condoned, it need not be demonized as implacably malign. By the same token, *ahimsa*-style resistance deprived it of the excuse to respond with violence as if "enemy" were all the other allowed it to be, so that conflict could only be mutual and bloody. When it did retaliate in the usually violent terms (provided it was not Hitlerian) it would find itself nonplussed.[32]

It could be said, then, that Mahatma Gandhi enshrined in his person and his policy the teaching of the Gita in the contours – so different from Arjuna's "Kuru-field" – of the slow recession of British power in the sub-continent. Destiny disciplining desire and desire firmly within the discipline of destiny set the twin formula by which life and politics were pursued. "The bow did not fall from his hand." His practice of asceticism may have perplexed his British assessors but signalled to his fellow Indians the genius of his religion. Guided by the legacy of Ramakrishna Paramahamsa (1834–86) and Vivekananda (1863–1902), he contrived to diminish the worst features of the caste system and moderate the tragedy of "untouchability",[33] while his campaign for civil non-violence and the hand-loom strategy served to recruit popular zeal and imagination and galvanize abstract religious ideas into effective political action. When inter-communal passions erupted menacingly, to wreck the *ahimsa* ideal and disable *satyagraha*, the strangely unworldly device of fasting could, from time to time, avail – if only precariously – to pacify the partisans. It was a "weapon" alone made feasible by the stature his mind and spirit had achieved across the land.

That he died in 1948 by the hand of an assassin from within his community was evidence enough as to the controversy Hindus still have inside their Hindu identity on the endless issues of society and ethics and the "imperishable Real". Conceding the daunting multiplicity of all things Hindu, and the risk in any single focus, it is fair to read the Gandhi story and the Gita in the dual role of commentary and text, either to the other. It is true that the Hindu Gandhi had much going for him in the tide of world affairs[34] and that the Muslim mind-set precluded the achievement of a united India. But he had been kindled in a hard school and endured stupendous odds, to give supremely biographical form to the personal interrogation with which the Gita had anciently wrestled.

Ends and means, destinies and desires, are for ever urgently and deviously related. Disinterest and participation only make a paradox.[35] For some "me and mine", "us and ours" in the latter will always compromise the former. We cannot neutralize attachment, yet attachment breeds a will to violation and a treasonable growth of less than honest motives. Sincerity is to be prized above all in the transactions of our pronouns. We can never afford to discount it or to disallow its writ, but nor can we fail to be alert for its frailties. Whether or not the Gita was right in its enjoining of "desireless action" in its own locale, its point in time and social order, it told a perennial truth, namely that there must be a moral arbiter within.

There remains one final query to be carried forward into CHAPTER THREE. It might be curiously formulated by asking: "Is there divine *satyagraha*? Has the supreme Lord exemplified the unselfish work implicit in a divine destiny? For many, in many faiths, the query will make no sense, be laughed out of court. But, humanly, it presses. For the general Hindu mind, a warm theism is entirely right and viable, a personal devotion to an intimately loving deity, provided we ever remember that all such foci of our Bhakti love are only "expressions" of "the Imperishable" that transcends all particular character or concept, the totally "unidentifiable" Reality, where endless negations must also be said.

It would be sane and reverent to concede that the transcendent must transcend and be acknowledged *beyond* all the comprehensions that would, otherwise, exhaust – or even imprison – their theme. Yet this cannot mean that what we genuinely trust, with that proviso, may not decisively hold and authentically obtain. For if it did not, in some kind of apophatic theology, we would be engaged in sheer make-belief or playing with words and with ourselves. That is not faith which is fiction pretending not to be.

If "the Lord is by His judgements known", must He not be also known by His glory? It was by the vision of Krishna's "glory" that Arjuna was finally brought to the realization of his own selfhood in the Gita's terms of "desireless destiny". Must the glory that persuaded him not, then, be party to the meaning in which it tutored him? Would it be possible to think of the Real exemplifying, in duly transcendent terms, the destiny of divine participation in the human scene with no other "interest" but the saving benediction of our creaturehood? If, in that Gita-like "involvement" way, we could say that "God is love" would it not be the supreme "glory"?

CHAPTER THREE

"So Help Me – Who?"

I

D. H. Lawrence once spoke of Dostoevsky's characters as for ever "sorrowing their way to Jesus", and much in current agnosticism suspects the religious mind as deludedly bent on "finding consolation" in a world where, in all honesty, there is none to be had. Was it not the candidly ecclesiastical Dean Jonathan Swift who concluded in his mordant way that there was no happiness but by "the art of being well-deceived"? Faith, on that score, would seem to be our way of creating comforting fictions, the better for their purpose in being the less examined. Our burdens have us dream of one who bears them.

Unfaith, too, as popular writing amply demonstrates, is avidly in love with the fictitious and comforts itself by taking refuge in tales where it can both indulge its own exemption from reality and admire or hate itself in the proxies they provide. There would seem to be no monopoly of evasiveness in either realm. There is a *tu quoque* in the argument if we humans "cannot bear too much reality".

The two previous chapters in pronounal study have left us with painful contrasts and sharp questions. These are fit to bring to mind the plea that, in pledge or oath-taking, has long been a traditional formula – the "So help me God" of those newly charged with trust. And, if not God, then who? when realization comes that it takes more than I am to be me, more than we know to say "us" and "our". Such, doubtless, was the situation observers of the psalmist had in mind when they commented, dismally if not exultantly: "There is no help for him in his God" (Psalm 3:2) – to the poet in his faith the most shattering of all verdicts. In the bleakness of current secularity it is one we are accustomed to hear. Perhaps it is said with a wry smile, or heard with a smile of patient courage; and smiles – it has been said – were the beginning of language. "What then shall we say" to this helpless state of things, believed to obtain between source and suppliant, the psalmist's Thou and I?

"So help me . . ." the solemn rubric runs. What shall we understand to be the manner and the means in that puzzling "so"? And the "me" in the pleader – what part belongs with the self? Is all feasible "help" for ever only within, rather as a Taoist proverb has it: "The wise attain everything without doing it". The more severe forms of Theravada Buddhism insist that the Dharma teaches, but only the lonely self fulfills its wisdom. The warmer forms of the Mahayana tradition, however, tell of "agents of grace" readily responsive to pleas for help. If we want to ask conclusively: "Is there the Saviour?" we will need to come on Christian ground.

Between arriving there and holding that any "help" is a sorry or sinister illusion a great gulf yawns. All turns on the measures we have of the self-hood we possess. What we can predicate concerning "help" must belong to the predicament we perceive. It might be possible to reduce the "help" dimension to merely psychic benefits, in line with psychiatrists who advise that deeply devout people find resources of composure and peace of mind that others lack. Prayer then becomes a useful prescript for serenity and worship a prudent life-policy.

That would be to mistake the result for the cause. Moreover the help in question in the pledge-taking of the phrase is for action. It returns the parties to themselves, to the "me" who has the task in care and charge. To think that prayer has only a state of mind in view and not a labour of will is not to have the living situation at all. Then the implied exoneration, found in some inner peace, is in line with frequent assumptions about a clause in the Lord's prayer, if "Thy will be done" is read as a sort of resigned "Thy will be undergone". On the contrary, it has to do with action, with something attempted and accomplished inside the demands of the "kingdom" whose "coming" is to be served. We need, therefore, to keep both "help" and "me" in due harness, as a "salvation" "saving" me to recruit me and recruiting me that the "saving" may extend to all. Otherwise the pronoun I use never enters significantly into a mutual plural with humankind. There is no true "alright-ness" that is not ambitiously social, minding more than a private world.

In turn, in that way to see and know the source of "help" as steady inter-play with a self energized to be its instrument, will be the surest index to the nature of the God to whom the expectation looks. Only the theology by which we incur ministry in its name possesses a true worship. It is the way by which we escape idolatry, seeing that idols tyrannize only to enjoy adulation and never liberate from obsequious fear.

II

It would seem, then, that one hopeful way of addressing the "So help me who?" interrogative is broadly to review the Christian answer and let it be the measure by which to appreciate and assess the commentary upon it of other faiths, as a positive way of understanding the discrepancies. For faiths need to let themselves be sifted in the sieve of their traditional, mutual disparagements so that their dialogue is genuinely honest with the past of their relations – a quality which all too often it presently lacks or fails to deploy. If such open frankness can be had, we can hope to be freed from much polite obfuscation.

The Christian answer to "So help me who?" needs the mark not only of query but of exclamation. For is there one – and one only? Christianity, like all other major faiths of wide-world dispersion and long history, is massively diversified and multiform. Given its Semitic matrix, it may not be as deliberately formless and inchoate as Hinduism but, from its eastern ripening into "Orthodoxy", to its western Papacy, to its Reformed version, to its inner Quakerism and sectarian malleability, its permutations have been perennial and deep. Historians might well insist and theologians admit that we must speak of "Christianities".

So let it be, but at least its name is eloquent of its whence and whither. It has to do with the "Christic", and with "the Christic God". It tells a Messiah-had theology, out of a tradition long pregnant with the Messianic hope.[1] Only thus has it the language of "God my Saviour", as in the Song of Mary – a song whose range reached back beyond Isaiah and forward far enough to be the theme-song of a Marxist social vision, not to say the age-long celebration of the Incarnation.

It holds the meaning we must comprehend as eternally in God, historically in Jesus and confessionally in the Christian. The sequence – "Christ", "Christian" and "Christianity" – is evident enough and no matter for debate. Three nouns – original, derivative-singular, and consequential-historical nouns yield a governing adjective that speaks only pronounally.[2]

A right comprehension of Christianity has to be sought and found in its "master-narrative" measured and assessed by the roots from which it derived and by its adequacy for the human situation it claims to interpret and resolve. Those twin tests deserve to obtain in respect of all faiths. For all hold themselves bound into "master narratives", or in what some call "metahistories" which both originate and dominate what they have for their "salvation".

Thus the "master-narrative" of Buddhism is the saga of Sakyamuni, the prince emerging from the sumptuous shelter of his father's kingdom in North India, to seek the truth of the human situation and, through asceticism and an ultimately wiser discipline, to attain to his enlightenment, the vision under the Bo-tree. There is nothing "Christic" here. The impulse does not proceed from any sense of divine sovereignty, obligated to mortal history and in moral liability for the universe of things. On the contrary, it has no perspective of time in such custody. For time as essentially fleeting can house no ultimate reference but comes to be read as a dilemma to be escaped, a panorama of fleetingness to be fundamentally distrusted as offering what it can never afford. There is then no perception of a significant creation, nor of "covenant", nor of history as a scene of moral destiny for which a divine guidance exists whereby humankind may realize a genuine vocation. No personal frame of reference enjoys a divine society. Rather it senses a scenario all too liable to engage us falsely in an appetitive search it can never satisfy, a realm of desire it is our ultimate wisdom to forego as being, at worst a snare and at best a delusion.

For master-narrative, the metahistory of Buddhism centres on the Buddha-story as yielding the sublime wisdom of the Dharma, the "teaching" whereby the tormenting illusion of a wistful, desiring ego-hood may be forsaken into the bliss of non-being. For to prize the self, to love it, assume it valid, under-write it by ambition and – most of all – anticipate its eternal relevance as individuated, tells the utmost self-delusion, the direst folly.

The master-narrative of Islam is quite contrasted. Its metahistory shares with other "Semites" a confidence in creation. There is an intendedness about human history and a significant moral order comprising creature-hood in custodial tenure of the good earth and liable for the economic and social realms of a mortal tenure. Having these prescripts, Islam finds its master-narrative in the singular prophethood of Muhammad and his mysterious reception of the sacred Qur'an mediated to him by Allah as the prime textbook of revelation.

There is, emphatically, no Incarnation here and, by the same token, nothing "Christic".[3] The master-narrative is the story of a divine Lordship whose sovereignty is absolute, total, majestic and – by all these – inherently legislative and educative *vis-à-vis* the human world. It is held to fit us humans – recalling the point of adequacy to humans as they are seen to be – by virtue of such education as being our one obvious need. There is, in the diagnosis, an implied absence of basic contumely or radical perversity, which might need to evoke from divine sovereignty any other strategy than the one which final prophethood has amply fulfilled.

It follows that a powerful confidence coheres around the Islamic metahistory. "Religion has been perfected" inside the premises from which it springs and which it is seen to satisfy. "Truth has been distinguished from error" and "religion as far as God is concerned is Al-Islam".[4] Thanks to certain sanctions Islamic structures will supply and regulate, the human situation is firmly in hand.

The master-narrative of Jewry and of Judaism[5] has a clear kinship with that of Islam in the imparting of a divinely scripted Torah to a foundation figure in the person of Moses, but with a radical difference, namely that the Mosaic in Jewish definition is wedded to a strong tribal identity, possessed through a constituting event, cherished in an abiding communal memory, namely the Exodus from Egypt. These three elements of law, people and destiny combine in a trinity of land, ancestry and story to determine the character both of a religion and a nation-society. Thus the Mosaic contrasts remarkably with the "Muhammadan"[6] in that Torah, or law, is inextricably allied with place and race in a way that is not the case with Islam, where the undoubted Arabism of the Qur'an serves the incidence of revelation inside *manzil al-wahy*, or "house of inspiration", but only to have it avail for all and sundry in openly "international" terms.[7]

Moreover, the Mosaic reality for Jewry reaches both back into remoter history, and forward into the custody of its peopled setting by virtue of the Oral Torah. The antecedent is located in the saga of a semi-nomadic people understood to be in "promise" of the land where Abraham and his heirs sojourned, so that the Exodus of his progeny in the master-narrative from Egypt into Canaan was not innovative in its day but consummatory of a tribal destiny the great forebear had inaugurated.

Similarly in the forward direction, the Rabbis in their readings of their Moses enjoyed a prerogative whereby "the law of Moses" in its written shape could be duly developed or amended by interpretation with such readings ranking beside it in the guidance and "God-mindedness" of His Hebraic people. There are intriguing stories in the Talmud and the Haggadah of Moses consenting to be auditing, if not overruled by, the rulings found for him by the Rabbis. In this way the equal standing of Torah, written and oral, gave Moses his abiding contemporaneity and his proper community its high stake in his defining role. Thus it further confirmed the dual mastery the narrative exercised.

By a grammatical analogy it would be fair to see these master-narratives, or metahistories, as the "verbs" of the religions where the pronouns belong that call for further study in later chapters. For verbs in language are where the action is, while pronouns tell how disciples know themselves in the credence and the allegiance they bring.

III

Such allegiance, we must be clear, is itself constitutive of the master-narrative – not that there was never anything otherwise to narrate, but that the narrating came only via the believing. The term "actually happened" is always elusive, if not evasive, in these realms, where we are not in test-tubes and carbon printing. It has to be acknowledged that all faiths have variously massive liabilities for the histories which to them are "masters". For they have "mastered" them in a process we can only see as mutual. It is not that "nothing happened" or that it never happened so.

On the contrary, there were happenings indeed, but what they were is now irretrievably "versioned" in the forms we know. This in no way means that faiths are "fabrications". Nor does it mean that, given the will, their scholars are not perpetually liable to search out and explore their credences.[8] It does mean that the histories on which they turn – in being truly formative of them – have themselves been formed by a human wonder or hunger to tell the things they tell and hold the weal they hold.

To know it so does not mean that religions are merely "a faith in faith", if the term is meant as a gibe or piece of easy scorn. For "fantasies" are never a true estimate of religions, since these are structures and strategies for life. Yet they are, and cannot avoid to be, "a faith in faith" in that their warrant is intrinsically within themselves and their authority one of a willed reception in them. For that authority there can only be two fields of reference. These, as noted earlier, must be how apposite – both conceptually and imaginatively – their findings are to what we may discern as ultimately worthy of being worshipped, and to what we find to be the reality of our human situation. Inasmuch as these two criteria are already decided inside the religions by virtue of their being the faiths they are, it seems evident that they are not referable to any outside arbiter unless it be another religion. It is in this sense that faiths cannot help but be self-authenticating and, out of their founding master-narratives, also self-inaugurating.

That all have large problems of history in their origins is not in question. The story of the future Buddha's emergence from his father's palace lies now beyond precise historical documentation. Its truth stands in its meaning as the personal pursuit of reality. The account of what he encountered turned on determining what the faith holds concerning human frailty, infirmity and mortality – hence the sick man, the old man and the corpse. The event was in the reckoning to which it led, as was the forsaking of wife and family. They belong as facts-of-story because they tell the facts-for-faith. Even were they legendary their truth would be the same. They are not material for historical research that might somehow find them inaccurate. The "fact" is in the import.

The "history-situation" is not comparable in respect of Islam with its *mise-en-scène* entering squarely into the Qur'an via the *Sirah*, or prophetic course, of Muhammad. Yet, ultimately the things historically presented are the things religiously received. It is often held that Islam is free of the subtleties alleged to attend – and for some to embarrass – the Christology of Christianity. To be sure, there are various patterns in popular Islam of "miracle" and "marvel" in the birth and parenthood of the Prophet but classic, superstition-excluding, rigorous Islam is "mastered" by the belief in a verbal mediation of the Quranic text to an entirely illiterate recipient.

Thus the matchless Arabic eloquence of the Book constitutes the supreme "miracle" by which Islam is divinely vindicated.

Observers in no way hostile, but standing outside that decision of faith, know that large questions remain concerning Muhammad's antecedent habit of meditation, his intelligent contact with available theism, his inner processes of soul and mind in the onset of *wahy*, or the state of Scripture-reception. There are also large issues of scholarship around the factors in the defining Hijrah to Medina and the moral consequences it held for the identity of Islam. But whether or not Muslim duty and learning assume the tasks these impose, the essential "narrative" abides as the theme and ground of the faith. As in other religions what is held is what holds. It does so as a remarkable phenomenon of metahistory and only effectively as being such. For, otherwise, how would a single figure – this Muhammad – be understood and, faith-wise, established, as the finalizing "seal" of all revelation, bringing to its climax "the perfection of religion" and "confirming" all previous meanings?[9]

Furthermore, this truth-ultimacy comes to pass through a cultural geography whose crown of Scripture had little contact with the larger world. It is deeply interested in its local archaeology and the fate of its ancient tribes but of the vast areas – India and beyond, and the West via Africa – into which it was destined to spread it betrays no knowledge. There is, therefore, in its confidence in its inclusive human range and all-time significance a most striking expression of religion attaining-to-be. It surely makes a master-narrative that, for faith purposes, transcends particularist studies of this and that about its shaping, right as these may be in their place and context.

And these, in their lawful pursuit – whether inside or outside Islam – will be under the aura of the devotion of that perpetual *Tasliyah*, or "calling down of Allah's blessing" on Muhammad, that should follow each and every mention of his name.[10] For it is the emotional dimension of the metahistory, the way the role conceived is the role received – the Prophet possessed both in the story and in the soul. Such Muslim Islam – if we may so speak – in no way implies that there should be no academic Islamic studies wrestling with the hinterland of origins. For these are deep and radical. It does, however, mean that such scholarship is not dealing with "facts" that will elude or dismiss the fact of belief.

IV

There is, religiously, an identical situation around the metahistory at the core of Judaism. Large questions of legitimate scholarship play around the entire concept of "chosen-peoplehood", the figure of Abraham and his nomad years, the patriarchal feuds and legends, and the precise migrations and tensions of the Hebrew tribes. "The Books of Moses", as formula for the Pentateuch, would be naïve in the extreme. The narratives of the Exodus seem to have taken on aspects of the ancient creation-myths for which emergence from chaos was figured by passage through the slain dragon whose defeat signalled a creaturely world.

> Art Thou not He that hath cut Rahab (tumult) and wounded the dragon? Art Thou not He that hath dried the sea, the waters of the great deep, that hath made the depths of the sea a way for the ransomed to pass over? (Isaiah 51:9–10)

> "Thou didst divide the sea by Thy strength . . . Thou breakest the heads of Leviathan in pieces. Thou didst cleave the fountain and the floods. (Psalm 74:13–15)

The inter-association is clear so that the "dragon-myth" of creation serves to mythologize the telling of the Exodus. But the telling that way in faith-idiom tells also a veritable event. Ezekiel in his exile remembers Pharaoh as "the dragon" (29:3). The event has been sacrilized as definitive concerning YAHWEH and His people. It forms a master-narrative of supreme religious assurance which no siftings of archaeology, readings of rocks or probing of tombs can subvert, secure as it remains in the credenda of its people. As elsewhere in religions it is what what happened came to signify that constitutes its "historicity".

There was nothing totally unique to Israel – except perhaps its intensity – about the bond between land and people and that durable tie solemnized by a patron deity devoted to the tribe. African paganism has examples of this conviction. It would seem almost instinctive to the religious mind to hold together elements so vital to experience as the sky overhead, the womb and its siblings, the earth and its tenancy. In all cases, moreover, that sense of things is sharpened by awareness of those not belonging – "the stranger in the gates" and the menacing neighbour hard by with a similar version of their warranty. All such sacred identities have their "Philistines", and the Dagons due to be subdued by "us" and "Gaza . . . not in plight to say us nay".[11]

The Biblical force of such "we" and "us" will have to come in CHAPTER FOUR. For it stands among the most insistent and the costliest of human self-characterizations. The immediate point is that the burden of proof, as historians might seek it, as to the validity of all that traditionally underlies the stories told, is elusive or ambiguous. Yet, here too, the "So help us YAHWEH" that was ever its cry holds steady, undeterred by historical niceties as to whether there were Hebrew tribes always over Jordan and never in Egypt or why the Book of Joshua offers so bloody and so stylized a version of the entry or whether, again, the patriarchs thought of their theophanies as their annalists did. It suffices that an exodus became the Exodus and a living Moses the mysterious architect of their retrospect and prospect. All these Judaic things are religiously secure within the living being of Jewry in its Jewishness. For they are defining, in their own terms and character, what it is to have a master-narrative.

V

What then of the master-narrative of Christianity told, with the help both of contrast and analogy, inside the panorama thus reviewed stretching from the Buddha and the Bo-tree to Muhammad and his Hijrah? The threads in its fabric are supremely threads of thanksgiving. "Thanks be to God for His unspeakable gift" (2 Corinthians 9:15) is its central cry, its inclusive doxology.

With Jewry and Islam it belongs with a lively faith in creation and crea-turehood. It does not allow itself the Asian option for a fundamental distrust towards the meaning of existence. It does not greet the world as a theme of despair, a flux of transience that counsels tactics of wariness against the delusions entailed by the lure of youth, the horizons of fame, the glitter of wealth and the pride of ambition. It is alert enough to the real hazards of mortal humanity and the passions of human nature. But these do not disqualify the hospitality we sensuously know in the mystery of our aliveness and its entourage of worthy experience and available satisfactions – physical, mental, social and spiritual.

The Christian is one with other Semites in seeing the external world as granted into human dominion and, therefore, guided and governed by revelatory authority in law and prophet. It found, in its own generating story, imperative warrant to break out of the notion of particular tribal ethnic "privilege" on which Jewry depended. All humankind shared in an equal peoplehood under God in a single creaturehood where all separate identities had their own vocations to "chosen-ness" under a Lordship that had, with them all, the "covenants" of fertile nature and redeeming grace – the "God of only chosen peoples".

This Christian perception told its loyalty to the Judaic "narrative" of "law and prophet" precisely by the degree to which it allowed law itself to testify to the wrongness of the human world, told in how distorted humans had made their mandate to have the good earth in trust. It fully acceded to the Jewish reading of that distortion, which Jewry learned in the forfeiture of land and "promise" in the calamity of exile as brought upon them by their waywardness. It readily echoed the self-blame and self-reproach which had been at the heart of Jewish prophetic self-accusation when the Isaiahs and Jeremiah reflected on the dark history of their priests and kings and people, as "laden with iniquity", fit even to be likened to "Sodom and Gomorrah".[12]

The apostolic Church, more than merely heir to this deeply ethical tradition, concurred in its verdict of realism about the human scene because it had known in its own genesis, via the ministry of Jesus, the most telling proof of how authentic that verdict was. We cannot understand the emergence of the Christian Gospel and its instrument, the Church of those apostles of Jesus, unless we reckon with the prostrating trauma out of which it was born, namely the crucifixion of the Master and the utter despair into which it threw his band of followers. For that crucifying, inflicted on the mind behind the Beatitudes, indicated more aptly than any other event how perverse humanity could be. Did not the Gospel come to refer to it as "the sin of the world", whenever it summoned that world to "see the Lamb of God" as the one who had "borne it"?

So it was that Christianity came to pass as a living faith out of most desperate evidence of human culpability. The Cross around which it coalesced all its thoughts about Jesus of Nazareth – as the New Testament Letters clearly show – had evidenced the sinister pride of religion and the incredible obscenity of politics, hand in hand – the twin machinations of a "chosen people's" priesthood and a pagan world-empire, exemplars of God-centred ritual and imperial majesty. The Church clustering around its Lord's Gethsemane could be under no illusions about human perfectibility by dint of good advice or politically contrived "salvation". The cry out of which it had come into being had been the deepest pain of "O help us God". It was tragedy that gave it to understand what dimensions an answering God would need.

In its gathering conviction as to "God-in-Christ" it was not that the New Testament Church somehow overlooked or jettisoned the teaching Jesus or the preacher of Galilee – as some have alleged. On the contrary, it was precisely because of who the teacher Jesus had been that the crisis of his immolation by his time and place moved them so profoundly. The teaching and the suffering were all of one piece. Why else should they have wanted the Gospels that distilled the teaching in documents from which, ironically, centuries later, scholars would conclude that teaching was all we should ever look for from him? Indeed, there would have been no access to any "sermons on the mount" had it not been for a scribing Church loving them deeply out of its perception of his Cross as the ultimate in "saviourhood".

With its incisive wisdom and its gentle sanity, the teaching of Jesus had that other telling dimension in the givens of this world, namely its non-success. True enough, "the common people heard him gladly", but the optimal world proved not persuadable or amenable, and has broadly so remained. The efficacy of the inherent goodness and gladness of the teaching needed – and still needs – the partnering and confirming ministry of the Cross and its "work of grace" in the heeding soul. Such was the realism in Christian experience, both of the wide world of Rome and Jewry at its birth, and of the inner self in its reach for an honesty of will and deed.

It was in this way that the resulting faith believed itself to be in line with that necessary criterion of anything purporting to be "salvation", namely its having an adequate measure of the "distance" any "salvation" would have to cover in reaching where we humans are, the depths of sinfulness it would need to plumb, if it was ever to prove itself more than hortatory, more than accusatory, more than blandly "help". All that Jesus had truly said about "your heavenly Father knows", and "One there is who forgives . . ." and "no man with his hand on the plough and looking back is apt for the Kingdom" – all these and their whole context presupposed what Jesus *did* in the event of the crucifixion which was their climax and history's only sequel to the words. Is it not clear from the very shape of the Church's New Testament as Gospels and Letters that there neither was – nor should be – any cleavage between the teaching Master and the saving Lord? Insofar as studious surmise has made that cleavage, it has rightly reckoned with neither. The faith insisted on their unity and their patent inter-action – the word in the deed and the deed as the word – in a singular confession: "Our Lord Jesus Christ". The "our" pronoun belongs with CHAPTER EIGHT to come: the threefold names or nouns are the "So helped us God" of Christian conviction.

But why should they have reached that confidence, so formative of their very being and their communal mind? The reason surely lies in their heritage of Messianic hope, the Hebraic "expectation" – so variously awaited – which had to derive[13] from the whole Biblical theology of a created world significant to YAHWEH, and of a creaturehood, symbolized in Israel, divinely commissioned to "man-age" the world in the divine Name.[14] Having taken its own history as the crux of that creation-trust by virtue of election to covenant, and having undergone tragic frustration in their nationhood on its behalf, Hebraic faith had necessarily to anticipate some resolution of their tragedy on the part of the YAHWEH who had presided over it. Messianic hope was thus inseparable from Jewish being and identity. For, without it, Jewishness would have been implying either desertion or indifference on YAHWEH's part, either of which would have been lethal both to their destiny and to their worship.

Seeing, as we have argued, that the very career of Jesus, in his experience of rejection and apparent failure, had grimly recapitulated the dark shadows of Jewish story, how could his disciples have failed to cling to Messianic thoughts, the "help" there must be "in the Name of the Lord"?

Yet why should they find it in the place where it seemed most to be denied, in the Cross that most signally disputed it? The answer has to lie in two twin reasons, namely the fidelity of God and the mind of Jesus in his suffering and death. The first was rooted in their whole assurance as to "the faithful Creator" (as Peter's First Epistle had it, 4:19). The second stood in the paradox that Jesus had so "borne the sin of the world" that he had "borne it away". So, years later, John's double sense of the one word *ho airon* (1:29) – "he who bears, bears away, the sin of the world". In the meaning of the Resurrection, it came to be seen that "the world's worst" had been met by "God's utmost". In his Passion Jesus had "endured" in crucifixion – symbolically as to its focus, actually as to its meaning – "the wrongness of the world". He had done so in the love that cried: "Father, forgive . . . they do not know what they are doing". This, precisely, was "help", grace, pardon, "in the Name of the Lord".

It was not simply that "Christ died for our sins": it was how he did so, in the meaning of the forgiving, love-affirming, soul-commending word. Messiahship in God's own version could be recognized and give rise to that most definitive phrase in Christianity: "God was in Christ reconciling the world". Precisely in *"not* being overcome of evil" in the there and then at the Cross, of sullen resentment, anger, enmity or bitter silence, the sufferer had "overcome evil with good" and done so in terms as inclusive as had been the wrongness the human world had, in fact and symbol, vented on him in the Cross. All, so heeding, so perceiving, could know themselves present in the evil and hear themselves forgiven in the words he said.

The will so to know and hear translated into a theology finally Messianic in Messianically conclusive terms. Christianity had found, and been founded in, its master-narrative. Its Christology was born. The long antecedents, stemming from a good creation and a trustee-humankind and a history so far awry in wrong and shame and exile, had reached their climax in "the answer of God". "Help" indeed there was, this way, "in the Name of the Lord". A faith and a people could be born in its wake. "The Name" from which it came could then be more firmly and truly told by its light.

VI

Quite evidently, Christianity in these terms meets the two criteria we noted as feasibly required of any faith in its intrinsic character. There is no doubt as to its human realism. For it has at its heart the radical reality of the Cross. Likewise it may claim to have identified that which is supremely worshipable, that – as to God – which God most tellingly ought to be. It turns like any other master-narrative, on the faith that lives by it, so that it can only be commended and not proved, or rather its due proof is in the trusting.

The theology, then, to which it leads is where it also places humanity, namely "in Christ". Paul often used that phrase when addressing his correspondents in the several cities to which he wrote – "at Corinth", "at Philippi . . ." but the double "residence" was more than local. "In Christ" told of a soul-commonwealth, or citizenship (to be explored in CHAPTER EIGHT) the country of their hearts where they had found God also was, God in His Christlikeness.[15] Their "fellowship was with the Father" (1 John 1:3) because they could add ". . . and with His Son Jesus the Christ". Such was the logic of their experience of "the place" where God had been and would always belong, namely "in Christ". In this way, their Christology, in line with all they understood about creation, human history and Hebraic story, decided their theology. "God in Christ" would henceforth be their *confessio* with Messiah, this way, as its seal.

That the long centuries brought great permutations in the shape of this *confessio* is plain enough and is, for many, disconcerting as a veto on any claim to be definitive. Much diversity, however, can honestly be read as a shift in the centre of gravity of the faith as to "God in Christ". This has manifestly happened institutionally, ritually, mystically, in variants that can, nevertheless, be discerned as loyal to a core even in their aberrations. Debate will always revolve around the very notion of what is "aberrant" and what is "loyal". Those hazards are inseparable from the necessity of structures, both of mind and order, in which to house the truth received. Given patience, hazards can perhaps be weathered and patience has always been the pattern of the ever-present, ever kenotic Holy Spirit.[16]

The demand for institutional shape as needing to be singular, infallible and total has been instinctive to Roman Catholicism, the conviction that this "truth of God in Christ" could not have failed to identify where it could be reliably known, received and secured. For otherwise, on this view, its truth and grace would be perpetually at risk to the vagaries of time and temperament. "Church", duly authenticated, would be indispensable to "Christ", whose meanings could only be soundly had where they were duly warranted.

This was in effect to move the centre of gravity of Christianity, from where it had been first accessible, to the institution where alone those credentials were in keeping. Were these, in their very origin, not of a sort to prefer risk around them rather than monopoly with them? The shift in the centre of gravity in fact had many hazards of its own – its chance incidence in a capital city, its disputatious elements around Petrine promise, and the dissuasives in its own story. Incorporation and authority there needed to be, but there for their due place, always in loyal reference to "the mind of Christ", a mind always larger, richer, more patient, more gentle than their own, a "mind" in which other Christians might aptly share. Such sharing, by the same token, would remain participant with the fellowship the "centre" mediated, through, beyond, or despite all the "shifts" it suffered.

There has also been, both East and West in "Christendom", a sort of ritual "centering"of the faith whereby its sacramental quality is preponderant in liturgy and the devotions that belong there. There have long been Christians whose allegiance is essentially one of ritual practice, liturgical celebration and personal piety. These have their undoubted place and stem from the Lord's own Eucharist of "bread and wine", his "Do this in remembrance of me".[17]

As then, so ever, "He was known of them in the breaking of the bread". "Holy Communion" is at the heart of all Christian perception of the Cross. All our living has to be a "sacrament" of that redemption, sharing the Messiah who wills to be "all of us" in his collective fulfilment. Yet the liturgical expression of this "mystery" can become self-enclosed as "satisfactory" in itself, shorn of a deliberative, deeply alert and mental "presentation" of a whole self a living sacrifice in a "reasonable worship". Shorn is the more likely if the ritual occasion is emotionally reinforced by its own "theatre", a sacrosanct aegis venerated for its status as a guaranteed "channel" rather than inward "means of grace".

When such potentials attend on liturgy they may appeal to temperaments suiting themselves to "dim religious light" and thus frequently unready for the rigours of a lively *confessio*. If so, that shift from the centre of gravity calls for a livelier vigilance lest it need to say: "The Lord was in this place and I knew it not", in a ritual where "all was said and done". Rite needs to dwell in mind and soul alike and the kneeling to the sacrament tell a kneeling in the mind.

One vital realm where the Christian master-narrative can be ambivalent about the centre of its gravity is in the veneration of the Virgin Mary, so often seemingly supreme in popular piety. It is no vulgar crudity which needs to ask, in paraphrase of Paul: "Was Mary crucified for you?" The vocation to motherhood has its sure and sacred role in the Incarnation of the Lord, where it takes its necessary place in the credal sequence: "Incarnate by the Holy Spirit of the Virgin Mary, and was made man and was crucified for us under Pontius Pilate . . .". The Cross that Jesus alone "suffered" came in climax to the travail that alone Mary bore in what we may call "the womb of the Cross". Thus her stature only serves – never to displace – the living and the dying of her Lord.

So much was told by Mary herself in the meaning of her Magnificat, the song of a "servant" rather than a "queen", where the "blessedness" is of a grace given, not of a grace she will dispense. The salutation *plena gratia*, in point and context, is a sort of "congratulation": "How wonderful for you, Mary", making her "blessed" as a recipient of "high calling", not as a repository of grace in largesse she may confer on others.[18]

Christians, east and west, have long differed on how faith should inter-relate those two inseparables – the birth and the death of Jesus as the Christ. Should the Incarnation be read as a "deification" of us all through faith so that we partake, sacramentally through the Eucharist, in his divine being? If so, did his Incarnation never properly contain his Passion and how should the actuality of that Passion bear upon any "partaking of the divine image" unless forgiving grace be its very crux? Do we have our master-narrative only that "a child is born" when the ministry and its climax in the Cross were so far integral to how "a Son was given?" Will the "saving grace" of "the Word made flesh" brings us through to the Resurrection except by way of his Gethsamane? We do most right by his Virgin Mother if we stay close to her own mind, so evident in her own song, where "all generations" read best her "blessedness", lest Christ should have "died in vain".

It has been well to try for an open honesty about the variants of Christian presentation of "God in Christ". It could well be that historic sanctions make these well-nigh irreducible. Certainly a crude partisan-ship does them little justice. The very "centre of gravity" analogy suggests something that can reassert itself, being locked on to a magnet-ism where fidelities belong. Meanwhile there has always been a great and patient gentleness about the Gospel, a capacity to be wounded even in "the house of friends", and so, like the Cross itself, to survive all "con-tradiction". It is well that its professed custodians look likewise upon one another.

"Sorrowing their way to Jesus" was how we began as the habit, allegedly, of Dostoevsky's characters. "Quarrelling their way to Jesus" sceptics might say of his Churches since the defining Easter of their emer-gence from his story, the story they had greeted as the metahistory of their salvation. The "So help me who . . . ?" of the Messianic yearning in their ancestry had found its answer where, as they believed, world and "saviour" had come together. We have still to learn how significantly it used its pronouns, the "us", the "our", with which the answer found its proper language.

Prior to coming there in CHAPTER EIGHT the plan in four intervening chapters is to take due note of the pronouns in Judaism and Islam as a prelude to the "we" and the "I" in the New Testament. We carry forward the role of the "verbs", the founding "acts" we have reviewed in CHAP-TERS TWO and THREE, the "events" as faith-narratives possessed them, to make these in turn "events" of metahistory. After one chapter in the "thou" and "I" of sexuality, we can reach the Asian mind of CHAPTER

TWO in a penultimate chapter before taking leave of pronouns with "Faiths' Pronoun-Users Now".

All belongs, as the psalmist knew in the 139th, inside the perimeter of a finite, inalienable persona, the self we individually know as, at once, our only capacity and our constant tempter, or in the words of the poet-philosopher, Muhammad Iqbal:

> What is this world? – the temple of my thoughts.
> Its manifestation depends upon my wakeful eye,
> The horizons that I take in at a glance
> Are a circle drawn by my own compass.[19]

– a situation never more ambitious and never more precarious than when it wills to be religious.

Iqbal has caught in his lyrical lines what the religions are as we have reviewed them here – if, that is, we change his singular "I" and "my" into a collective plural. Their "truths" became "true" because the faith of faithful made them so. Each is a "construct" deriving from an eventful-ness, a personality in a situation – a Buddha, a Moses, a Muhammad, a Jesus – whose life-theme kindled or bestowed or attained a quality of recognition thanks to which it became the faith it was. There was always this mutual inter-action between "a perceived" and "a perceiving". Credentials were present because they were seen as being there presented, and the faith happened out of attending antecedents deep in immediate cultures, climates of mind and philosophies of nature, time and the world. "The horizons taken in" were the "givens" of the master-narratives: their "circle" was drawn by the compass of believing souls. What was there for cognizance was told in recognition.

It is this clear liability of religions for the religions they are that lays so large responsibility on how each employs its possessive pronouns.

> "You fancy you can be responsible to God,
> Can you carry the responsibility *for* God?"[20]

CHAPTER FOUR

Pronounal Jewry – God's Own People

I

"We Thy people" (Psalm 79:13) – the two prevailing pronouns of the Hebrew Bible and one of its most recurrent nouns, followed by the most loved imagery of a once nomadic story, "the sheep of Thy pasture", vowing to "show Thy praise through all generations'. The steady frequency of the "people" word – through narrative, psalm and prophet – tells both the cherished identity in Judaic covenant and the adjacent human diversities summoned to its recognition. But these are never in the same sense YAHWEH's "heritage" (Psalm 28:9) and are often denoted by "lands" as in Psalm 100 – the great poem that became the "Old Hundred" of English choral fame: "All people that on earth do dwell". More generally "all ye people" enjoins thanksgiving and heeding on the "tribes of heaven's choice".

The triad of history, territory and tribal birth as the fabric of this Hebrew sense of "we" and "our" was noted in CHAPTER THREE, with the ruling metahistory of Exodus from Egypt and entry into the promised land. If Jacob, wrestling with "the angel" and with his sense of inner crisis in the near presence of Esau, can take us (in CHAPTER FIVE) to the personal pronoun singular, the multitude around Moses at Sinai are the place of the plural one.[1] Even Paul, writing in his Christian fervour to Jewish and non-Jewish readers in Corinth, insists that "all our fathers were under the cloud and all passed through the sea". He thinks of them as "baptised under Moses".[2]

He is only echoing the decisive pledge in the Books of Exodus and Deuteronomy, and the high drama around it.

> And Moses called all Israel and said unto them: "O Israel, hear the statutes and judgements which I speak in your ears this day, that ye may learn them and keep them and do them . . . The Lord made not this covenant with our fathers but with us, even with us who are all of us here alive this day." . . . It shall be our righteousness if we observe to do all these commandments before the Lord our God. (Deuteronomy 5:1–3 and 6:25)

The concourse, or "congregation", to which Moses came down from out the blazing light of Sinai, bearing the Tables of the Law, was one which, by the triple sanction of birth, common journeying and the land-destiny to which it led, was meant to endure through all generations. Its generations, in turn, would be for ever both the custodians and the hazard-bearers of that status with their Lord.

Insofar as "You shall have no other gods but Me" was taken to mean "I will have no other people but you", it was a sense of vocation that could only be undertaken at the price of a human tension on three counts. As quite distinctive in its tenacious reading of its given credentials – ethnic, territorial and historic – it was destined to be painfully at odds with the human scene. Since, as we have seen, those determining factors of who, where and whence belong, in varying measure and by diverse reading, with *all* ancestral, local and memorable experiences everywhere, the Hebrew privilege in them was set to incur a threefold challenge from outside itself.

It is, therefore, only realist to seek an open and positive comprehension of the Jewish plural pronoun by way of this immediate and long-standing triple dilemma. Doing so will mean no disparagement but rather a proleptic sympathy with all that Jewishness has tragically undergone in implementing its own unique genius. All will to make it good has been fated, till this day, to wrestle with adversity and faithful hope in equal measure. No identity has been so honest, so contentious, so ardent with itself.

Given the same elements in identities on all hands, it is no surprise that the Hebraic is taken to task on three counts.[3] They have to do with (a) faith in creation, (b) this necessarily combative theme of Hebrew story, and (c) the inherent stimulus, if not to emulation, then to innate hostility.

On the first count, a doctrine of divine creation would seem to argue a divine intention for all humankind – an intention which the Noah narrative and the Noahid covenant readily acknowledge in the Book of Genesis, where "seed-time and harvest", after due ploughing and toiling, will reward all and sundry, however diverse their terrain, however contrasted their culture. Ought that inclusive potential to fertility ever to have been distinctively hallowed or further covenantalized *vis-à-vis* any particularity of land or race or story?

There has been a tendency – in which some Christian scholarship has also shared – to see the early chapters of Genesis, for all their grandeur and the sweep of their simplicity, as somehow only "prologue" to the arrival of an Abraham, with whom, it is said, the Bible truly begins. But can the good earth, the mystery of all that is and has come to be, serve only as stage-setting for a relatively private drama? Can we "hierarchise" what is universal? Must not a sense of nature have us confess that "God has only chosen peoples" in the plural?[4] The natural order per se would seem to put a question-mark around a separatism that has to speak of *goyim* and "Gentiles".

It might even be that such a posture denies to the transcendent order the corollary proper to it of human unity. In that event, would an exclusive human segment be making its worship a kind of idolatry? The secular Jewish notion – as, for example, in the thinking of David Ben-Gurion – of Jewry being "the choosing people" (i.e. reading their chosen-ness as their own self-electing genius) suggests that possibility. If so, any concept of a unilateral mutuality between God and one people must run plainly counter to two realities in universal human experience. The one is that all inhabit a created order yielding a human imperium where "materiality" is responsive to human devices of mind and will. The other is that, so pro-viding, God has, in a deliberate generosity, left its management in human hands. Biblical divine sovereignty graces the creature with the dignity of the conferment of a proprietor's freedom which He neither revokes nor manipulates.[5]

This realized human situation, implicit in the doctrine of creation, is – on both counts of feasible "technologies" and human entrustment – a uni-versal experience which is not *de facto* privatized so as to avail only in separated privilege. It is, of course, *de jure*, open to any people to take and mould their immediate share in terms of a distinctiveness responding to how they handle their instances of race, habitat and memory but not to read them by a unique theology.

It has often been noted, in the conflict of religions, that, soberingly, mathematics, chemistry, biology, human anatomy and the rest, take no stock of religious frontiers, but obtain consistently across them. They have a fidelity to their place in the order of the world, so that it can only be a sentiment to hold that the rain falling in Judea has a special benediction or that the dawn which broke over Jacob at the ford of Jabbok had not broken over all the Amorites. The creative will that upholds all that exists awaits from each and all the consent with which to rise into the privilege of being human. It will be a kind of "idolatry" to think to say that what idols are to God, "Gentiles" are to Jewry, as of a worship that lacks its truth.[6]

Worships, we must frankly say, are often *not* of "the same God", inas-much as the predicates by which we make God "subject" vary widely and darkly. Yet "the same" God must be, as their multiple "addressee" if we duly reckon with the inclusively human order we discover in His creation. Whatever devolves for faith and worship from Abraham and Jacob, from Moses and Joshua, from Samson and Elijah, must first return to Adam and share the privilege he first knew in the help-meeting of Eve.

II

Turning to what does devolve, we encounter the second aspect of the Hebraic collective, namely the combative quality of the ancient story once "the promised land" is in possession.[7] Allegory drawn from "being strong and of a good courage", though long approved also in the Christian tradition, cannot conceal the sharp features of genocide and enmity. The actual history, could we know it, may well have been less sanguinary (for the Book of Joshua is highly stylized), but perhaps, not. At least that is how the annalist thought it to have been. The compassion the sages came to feel for the Egyptian corpses on the shore, was not matched for Sisera and his stricken mother in the majestic strains of the Song of Deborah, one of the earliest pieces of surviving Hebrew poetry. How could it be? For these were a people summoned to national heroism and caught in the strife of tribes, invoking the kindred succour of their "Lords of hosts".

When deep pathos comes into the annals it has to do with the interior conflicts in the house of David. Not fully till the supreme prophets of the exile anticipated and endured, do we reach the supreme ethicism of things Hebraic and the will to know YAHWEH as their great accuser rather than alone their doughty warrior-lord. Meanwhile, "the Philistines be upon thee, Samson", tells the familiar scenario, from the praise of which John Milton was by no means immune, finding in his "Agonistes" one who

> . . . on his enemies
> Fully revenged, hath left them years of mourning
> And lamentation to the sons of Caphtor
> Through all Philistian bounds . . .[8]

– a sentiment much to the mind, millennia later, of Vladimir Jabotinsky whose radical Zionism breathed fire in his novel named for the old protagonist of the Gazan legend.

There was nothing exceptional about this martial strain in Hebrew history in land entry and contentious settlement. It was only reciprocal. Its role in the story has often had the deep reproach of the Jewish conscience. For there was always in later centuries the warning of the Mishnah Torah that

> He who destroys one life, it is as if he destroyed the whole world and he who saves one life as if he saved all mankind.[9]

However, it could always be claimed that the exigencies of survival might override all else. There was a readiness for anathema in the very sense of destiny and a school of intolerance in the conviction that could – in that later Talmudic tradition – plead "an argument for the sake of heaven".[10] "The hand of them that hate us" came for so long to occupy the Hebrew mind as a legacy from the legendary years on either side of Moses and Joshua. That it should have been so stemmed from the deep faith that – as a twentieth-century Rabbi had it – "The Jewish people are the base on which God's throne rests".[11] It was an awesome mystery to sustain.

It is fair also it ask whether the "dwelling alone" sense of themselves could have been quite so absolute as their annalists declare, given how far and frequent the bonding of people, place and past with sundry other identities, as explicit in all human experience. And, further, how indebted may Hebraic rituals have been to Canaanite religion, how obligated Moses to Egyptian mentors, how affected the populations by their adjacence even to their "enemies"? Chemosh among the Moabites was seen as "acting in history", Marduk likewise, and the deities of Babylonian epics. In all these, history was read in terms of divine acting inside national fortunes.[12]

Parallels are by no means equations and there is much entirely *sui generis* in what matured into the ethicism of the great Hebrew prophets – a stature that deserves to work backwards to hallow the contrasted matrix from which it sprang. While the mystique of absolute particularity abides, it is only right that it should not divest its history of wide connectedness and "neighbouring" on every side.

Whatever finality archaeologists and historians may reach as to the extent and quality of this inter-action in the long Hebraic story, there is no mistaking the constant instinct either to suspect it or repudiate it. Solomon may have reached the apex of Hebrew monarchy in ready rapport with Hiram, king of Tyre but, for all the fine Lebanese timber in the very fabric of the Temple, the ancient story never lacked prophets and seers to castigate those who let themselves be seduced and risked the menace hidden in the alien *baalim*. The mighty Samson may have successfully defied the rules but never had to encounter an Elijah on the height of Carmel. The moral and racial antiseptic had to be upheld. It found a symbol in the ever vigilant "order of the day" for the returnees from the east to Jerusalem. The good leave of the alien Artaxerxes was monitored by the rigorous Nehemiah.

We can defer till later the social and ritual sanctions of this psychic separatism so evident in the history and politics from Joshua to the exile. Reproach of contaminating relationships became the stock in trade of prophets and the perceived bane of compromising kings, and a sure clue to history. Steadily, and seemingly inexorably, identity became for Jewry a deeply preoccupying onus. The "we" of plural consciousness carried an all-engrossing liability, not merely – as with other identities – that of existing and surviving, but, more anxiously, of matching the summons of something *sui generis*, a destiny making for a corporate *agonistes*. They had been called to be "the performative people of YAHWEH". The onus meant perpetual self-scrutiny and unresting self-appraisal, ethnic, ethical, social and – therefore – political but, somehow, more than all of these, eluding attainment and perhaps also comprehension.

III

A people and a culture, immersed in general history at a cross-road of the earth, with such a conscious *raison d'être*, could not fail to draw upon itself the perplexity and the unease of humanity at large living within its intriguing and bewildering range. Hence the third point, listed earlier, in its nexus with the human world, namely to kindle emulation or, more likely, arouse a countering resentment.

The former, of which certain prophets seem to have been well aware,[13] could be explained by the corollary of "chosen-ness", namely that it was always "on behalf of" humanity at large. There can be no certainty as to when this perception came into currency, though annalists held Abraham's individual call a theme for which "the nations would bless themselves" – the meaning being active, i.e. their coming to realize it so. This could hardly be without Jewry itself alert to that vicarious aspect of the unique identity.

Moreover, it provided a sort of alibi for a distinctive standing with God, or a mitigation of what might seem otherwise inordinate. Could it be that "Israel" – inside the inclusive human created order we studied – was a sort of "pilot scheme", a test-case, a tutorial to the rest of humankind as to due custody of all the sundry ethnic, climatic, cultural and economic potentialities of human habitats and kindreds? If so, that would obviate any great necessity for "Gentile" umbrage or demur.

However, it would do so only on one proviso, namely that the special vocation might come to be shared by all who willed to rise to its cost and dignity. Since it is the business of all teachers to make themselves no longer such to their pupils, their proper discipline tending to their own redundancy, the taught should attain to equal them. There could be no point in "pilot schemes" that never concluded, or tuitions that required to be perpetual.

Unhappily – indeed tragically – it was this logic the Hebrew genius could never concede. It had, for its own exoneration, the plea that the role could never be foregone, nor its mission finalized. The *sui generis* reality of Jewry required to be perennial and that – for the sake of a humanity never fit to be exempt from its ministry. The age-long *pro bono publico* quality of everything Judaic could never be rescinded.

This resolute "loyalty to the loyalty" of vocation could not fail to ensure that, in the absence of emulation, a latent resentment would follow or that, possibly, some will to emulation would persist as the very form that resentment – as if by compound interest – would decide to take.[14]

The next chapter is due to study intimate personal aspects of the burden of Jewish existence of which Joseph, coming in his "coat of many colours" to seek out his brothers, became forever the vivid paradigm as the victim of a brooding and vehement hatred. In the long and in the round, anti-Semitism has always been a painful mystery to the Jewish people, an inexplicable malevolence defying all logic in its continuity and arrogance. Many Jews have concluded that the "Gentile" world is incorrigibly bigoted, implacably perfidious.

That Jewry has incurred a hostility of rejection unparalleled in world history is tragically plain enough. The factors in a phenomenon so long endured have been complex and controversial but that the tragedy has made "all Jews victims"[15] is not in doubt. The conclusion is inescapable, namely that it is the people most given to "chosen-ness"[16] who are the people most darkly and fiendishly harassed and persecuted in recorded history. That the two factors are compellingly allied is neither to exonerate the one nor to denigrate the other. It is simply to register reality.

Plainly the plural pronoun we are studying holds the double mystery of its uniqueness as both "elect" and execrated, "chosen" and victimized, a "people dwelling alone", not only in divine society but in human persecution. The utmost proof of that "dwelling alone" in the victim role was the twentieth-century Shoah concerning which Elie Wiesel could write: "Once upon a time there had not been a holocaust."[17] Through all the vicissitudes of the centuries, it could be said that Jewish existence has been experienced and, indeed, defined, in costly relation to the burden of its being "people to God". It was the burden of its own cherished, never to be relinquished, destiny and of the minding of it, rude, sanguine, contemptuous, fickle, mildly tolerant or fanatically hostile, of a world around and outside – a world prone to be triumphalist in its disdain if not guilt-laden in its better conscience, confused in its own ambivalence when not primed for its sadism. The high privilege of "peoplehood with God" exacted the long tragedy of "unpeopling" with humankind at large. It was an education in a supreme paradox – that of enjoying "wantedness with YAHWEH" and enduring "unwantedness" with mankind, and either forever in the context of the other, so that the inseparable burden turned on the dignity of separation.

IV

It is the abiding inter-play of these that constitutes the story in the Jewish psyche and lies at the heart of its conflicting choices. The land story and the land necessity that defined the metahistory in the origins would seem to argue the place of statehood, the role of things political. Jewry became decidedly a "national" reality. So much David ensured and Solomon symbolically glorified. Yet they did so to fulfil founding patriarchs who had been tribal nomads and had survived nomadic perils by finding sanctuary as refugees in Egypt. Though prospective of their entry, they had received their Torah outside "the promised land".

Their high peak of monarchy was relatively short-lived, always jeopardized by vastly more powerful empires. It finally succumbed to Greeks and Romans, despite the brief ardour of the Maccabees. The Jewish Revolt of the first century CE brought tragic dispersion on their own heads, when Rome held them a *religio licita* and their future in fully ritual and social terms could have stayed secure[18] Were the Zealots wisely Jewish in demanding that only fully political terms sufficed their genius?

When finally under Hadrian the land dimension, in habitation, tragically ended, a supreme irony around the land-power clue to self-understanding ensued. The long centuries of diaspora condition demonstrated resoundingly the survival quality of the Jewish tradition. Torah and synagogue, Talmud and the sages, proved more than adequate, sanctified by Sabbaths and enshrined in dietary customs, to perpetuate an invincible Jewishness despite the utmost odds.

Then had this landless, stateless durability in fact disclosed the true nature of Jewish being?[19] How, in the face of this near miracle, could the indispensability of "the land" continue to be argued? At worst, the anti-Semite would continue to guarantee Jewishness, if only out of the bitterest constraints: at best a Philo, a Maimonides, a Spinoza would achieve a noble Jewishness.

Plainly, the land could be no longer the *sine qua non* of authentic Jewry. Nor could non-Jewishness be held at bay by power-wielding that was wholly out of reach. In any event, was not diaspora the very arena for vocation, the means, discernibly, whereby destiny for "the blessing of Gentiles" could be the better realized? The privations of the powerless, the state-less, might be harsh and wearying, but the supreme assets of spiritual virility could surmount them. The Jewish people could be their own all-sufficient "homeland" all the more a haven for having no frontiers to guard, no political crimes to incur. Forlorn ventures of Messianic zealotry gave tragic proof of their futility.

How Jewry should read itself set the centuries from David to the heroes of Masada against the longer centuries, we may say, from the sages of Yavneh to Theodor Herzl, by virtue of the contrasted logic read in them. The watershed between them was the Fall of Jerusalem and the loss of the Temple, which together in grim drama posed the hard alternative. For, if the land was truly "for the sake of the Temple", the forfeiture meant life without its priesthood.

That cruel hardship coincided with the rise of Christianity and, with it, the sharpest pains of Jewish diaspora existence. For Christianity, from the beginning, posed for Jewry the ultimate question, namely whether a cherished "peoplehood with God" could ever be opened to a comprehensive access – that "whosoever will" of Jesus himself – unrestricted by accident of birth or land or language. The dilemma here for Jewish priority and Jewish self-perception was all the keener for the fact that the Christian opening out of such access had been entirely a Jewish initiative.

Later factors, Greek and Latin and other, would come into play and clues like the Logos theme take up the Messiah language of the Semitic mind.[20] Such initiatives were implicit in the openness but the decisive step of "Gentile" inclusion was taken by the original Jewish apostolate, with the Gamaliel-tutored Paul of Tarsus the symbol of its meaning in his own biography.

Coming a bare quarter century before the watershed of the sixties of that century which asked Jewry to face forfeiture into diaspora of its land-known self, the Christian revision of its peoplehood proved at length too hard to take. The risks of a hospitality with such meanings for its very self were too heavy to accept. The new reading of a "Jewry" no longer a "segregating" of those already there, but an "aggregating" of those who might accede and "become" the community of circumcision widened into one of baptism, was more than – at that juncture least of all – its considered mind and heart could admit or undertake. The Christian Church would inevitably resolve itself into a "Gentile" faith-community in which the founding Jewish dimension would slowly diminish.[21]

All the bitter complexities that followed in the long centuries stemmed from this fundamental situation. What could have been experienced as fulfilment came to be shamefully cast in the teeth as "supersession". Stretching from Tacitus and Tertullian to late modern times, the long late-antiquity and medieval centuries took out their spite and scorn on a Jewry, grimly maligned for an obduracy that was inwardly no less, no more, than the tenacity of a people loyal to their own reading of themselves.

It is important to realize that the long tragedy was outside the New Testament tradition which, in its handling of the Cross, had always read in its meaning "the sin of the world" and *in situ* always invited into its forgiveness all whom it had "concerned". The perversity through the Christian centuries that used the Cross as a licence for hatred betrayed its whole significance. By a grim paradox the perpetuation of Jewish privacy was partnered by the perversion of the very Gospel that had occasioned its most crucial reckoning with identity.

For the perverting trustees of that faith ghettoized the people whom the ghetto ironically enabled more ardently to be themselves, intensifying their inner meaning by the reality – and the climate – of their affliction. Given all the passions and recriminations that have been engendered bitterly around the heavy guilts of Christendom, it is vital neither to contrive extenuation nor devise false ease to conscience but rather to keep all else inside the inclusive issue Jewry faced in that first Christian century. The self-definition it then made in the context of what proposed radical new venture had its own logic. It needs to be exonerated from how modern anti-Jewish bigotry has minded a long suffering people to read and fulfil themselves now. The "we" and "us" and "our" of Jewry – thanks to all that anguished history – are pronouns sometimes too laden to bear.

So some at least have made eloquently plain. Personal Jewish pronouns on their lips are abidingly weighted for such users by the entail of that crucial point of history. Dimensions in a few personal exemplars are to come in CHAPTER FIVE. All that they – and their Christian "others" – have to handle grows out of that defining point. The Jewish self-exemption from what Jewish/Christian apostles then pioneered meant that Jewry could only disallow, and be disallowed by, the sequel in the Christian Church. Either saw the other as only "wayward" or "deceived".

The cleavage concerned the very definition of both Jewry and Christianity as exponents of "divine peoplehood". From that shared tension all else followed – the "possession" of Jesus; the presumption about a Bible, now "old" and "new" in its cohabiting "testaments"; the relegation of ritual laws in the "open sacraments" of baptism and communion; the blame and shame circling around the crucifixion; the hostile "imaging" of Judas and of Caiaphas and the Pharisees; the endless quarrel about Messiahship fulfilled or falsified or for ever futurized.

Thus the age-long onus of being Jewish was kindled into new intensity by the emergence from inside it of the Christian Church. That new intensity was circumscribed and desperately aggravated by the long centuries of perversely Christian antipathy and guilty disesteem, leaving to Jewry what late nineteenth-century incipient Zionism could only read as the intolerable alternatives of death by persecution or demise by assimilation. Not even "the Enlightenment" proved either secure or hospitable enough to undo the bitter logic drawn for so long from the malediction of a Christendom perverse.

V

How Zionism read the Jewish pronouns in the wake of an "emancipation" construed as deep betrayal proves only to have accentuated the ancient controversy as to the proper destiny of "the people of God". It is essentially the primal debate renewed but with all the added anguish of those Christian centuries and the reading – as Zionists saw it – of the inveterate animosity to Jewry of the non-Jewish world, despite the obvious undoing of such a conclusion by the ever more evident "homeland quality" of diaspora in its vital, if ever paradoxical, role in the sustenance of the Zionist "solution".

To explore this subtle tangle is to discover new and painful measures of the art of being at once both a plural and a "singular" people. For it becomes more and more evident that the total politicization of Jewishness entailed by Zionism draws the Israeli dimension of Jewishness inexorably away from any "specialness" and steadily into an entire similarity with the rest of nations. It may pretend to have only "Defence Forces" and thus no "army", but it is expertly equipped with nuclear power, an efficient spying agency, secret police and diplomatic finesse, like any other national State with the same qualities of pragmatism in the service of an ideology.

Doubtless there were some among the Zionist pioneers who never assumed it could be otherwise, but there were also many who anticipated and proclaimed a complete "innocence". These had not reckoned with the inevitable consequences their aspirations held for what the Balfour Declaration curiously described as "the existing non-Jewish population". Only on the assumption of a territorial vacancy could there have been a dream of "innocence". At the outset political Zionism either ignored the awkward issue or allowed the first ventures to remain ambivalent. To avoid provoking fear among the population they held it dormant among themselves. This may have been opportune but it was never realist. The event has proved that Zionism committed Jewry and, in measure, Judaism, to a decision – that for "the land–State" "solution" – which crucially compromised the vision of its "chosen-ness". It did so, moreover, in terms in no way extraneous to its intention but grounded in its policy. They would be incurring – and paying – a heavy moral price in the very reading of their identity.

But they were also reaching a bitter verdict on the human situation in that early Zionist thinking concluded, or needed to conclude, that humanity was insufferably hostile to Jews, incurably anti-Semitic and altogether incapable of dependable co-existence with Jewry. It needs a certain effort of mind now to realize what a minority verdict this was. Largely, too, among diaspora Jews there was a sense that it was a wild

and wayward conclusion – one, indeed, that jeopardized Jewish participation in sundry nationalisms as relaxed and effective citizens. Against
the logic of these, thinkers like Theodor Herzl had to invoke some of the
harshest caricatures of the anti-Semites concerning abject, fear-ridden
underlings by the stereotype the Zionist case sought to make of them, but
only out of a past tradition it had left behind.

Did a right-minded Judaism need to categorize the human world at
large in such dire terms, so that the notion of "host nations" represented
a dangerous delusion and an ignominious fate? There were, indeed,
pogroms in Poland and Russia, and persecution a constant risk, but was
it not a Jewish writer who gave to the world the song inscribed on the
Statue of Liberty inviting the homeless home?[22] Was the alleged choice
between persecution or assimilation really the only option – as the
Zionists argued, so that, neither being acceptable, despair about diaspora,
and with it, despair about humanity, was the only conclusion? If so, was
"the dwelling alone" this argued a wilful "aloneness", one that in
despairing of fellow-humanity would the more urgently need the human
neighbourhood its thesis decried?

The most terrible irony of all was that, while this "logic of human
despairing" antedated the rise of Nazism by some forty years, the
Holocaust came all too grimly to vindicate it. Hence the crucial role the
Shoah has played in the justification of Zionism and the entire case for
Israel as a nation-state. It is certainly true that the state embodies whatever reparation there might be and that, had it existed in time, the Shoah
might never have happened. It is also true that young Israelis, brooding
on that defencelessness, have incredulously asked: "But where was our
Army?"

Yet, overwhelming as the agony has been, is it legitimate that the
Holocaust should be read as vindicating the original logic of despair, the
despair which said – and is still prone to say – "Jew-love is the only love
Jews know"? Elie Wiesel's warning that if "the survivors" were really to
be avenged of the millions dead, they would have "to burn down the
whole world" could only have been drawn from an unbearable anguish
of soul, never from a seeing mind. For then the burning would have to
feed its fires on the cemeteries on Mount Scopus and in the deserts of
Egypt and on the tokens everywhere of the human cost, paid by many, for
Israel's ultimate existence.[23] It is only in the utmost inter-humanness that
grieving can be understood. If despair of humanity has to be total, no
unilateral escape from its implications can ever be communally contrived.

Was that, then, the inner fallacy of a "go-it-alone" Zionism – failing to
see that we always need fellow-humans and are always liable to trespass
on their humanity grievously when we dismiss its relevance to ours?

It follows that the supreme venture of a long century of Jewish initiative in renewed self-definition in Zionist terms holds at its heart a deep and grim tragedy. In the abstract of a territorial emptiness – where it would never have been the thing it was either in effort or in costliness – it could have been hailed as supremely self-fulfilling and an admirable success. Ensuring the tragedy its very success would enfold, no territorial vacancy availed, least of all in the locale where every historical emotion required it to be, a locale with a hinterland ripe for brooding dispute.[24]

Paradox is the constant burden of the story. The "prosperity" pledged by the psalmist to all Jerusalem's "lovers", proves to the most ardent of them a deep adversity. The will finally to eliminate the desperate unwant-edness of Jews issues into a new and insistent renewal of it as the sequel to the very quest and the logic of the form it took. Yet that form – as nationhood in "land" – seemed to Zionism the ultimate lesson bitterly taught by the experience of the long centuries. "Dwelling alone" in that form and fulfilling that destiny would kindle emotions and inflict wrongs precisely calculated for ever to obviate the hope of fulfillment. Yet if Zionism cherishing that goal was never a viable option, had the goal not been tragically implanted in their souls by generations of persecuted jeop-ardy or bewildering assimilation?

These harsh paradoxes in their bitter incidence as narrative are steadily enacted in the immediacy of here and now. Zionism, *in situ*, has so divided a mind about what its vision is and how that vision relates to Judaism as a profound religious faith. How is Judaism to be understood by the surrounding world when deep and violent incursions into "Palestinian" camps and cities, forbid them from all normalcy and co-existence? Why must there be Jewish settlements even in the Gaza Strip to generate enmity and make occasion for inter-provocation? Why does a 500-strong arm of Jewishness have to entrench itself in Hebron, a nest of hostility in a city with 260 Arabs to every single one of them? To be sure Hebron has the famous tombs and bitterly remembers a massacre of Jewish Hebron folk in 1923. Yet is there need to carry memory into remorseless pursuit of hatred? Could not the "rest" the Jewish Sabbath so long ordained domes-tically, abating a world forever avid of its means and ends, not extend to inter-human politics and call a blessed halt?

The question of the integrity of Judaism in fee to Zionism was always present in the relentless policy of "settlements", throughout the oscillating periods of negotiation, Oslo-wise and since as well as before. These seemed designed to forestall whatever might come from negotiation by creation of "facts on the ground" which would be irreversible, whatever governments in their diplomacy might explore. And meanwhile, such endless exploring ensured time and leisure for their continual creation.

The careful pragmatism has paid long dividends in enabling the current mapping on the ground of Palestinian pockets, some hardly even

"Bantustans", girdled with barriers, and girt with a network of roads that ensure free Israeli mobility and due Palestinian confinement. The economic and agricultural viability of these hapless enclaves is perpetually dependent on Israeli "will and pleasure".

It may be said that these sorry exchanges of power with frustration and despair are only the exigencies of a conflict situation, willed on Israel by Intifadas of the irreconcilable. Yet these, in turn, stem from abortive hopes, sickened by the manifest failure of good faith in political diplomacy, where – if only forthcoming – the will of the "terrorist" would be gasping for its necessary "oxygen", now so freely supplied.

The question must be asked whether the burdened mind of Zionism has rightly read the divine mind as perceived in the ethics and the destiny of Judaism. Have its success and its deep Palestinian quandary over-reached the mission in which it "conjectured the purpose of God" – of YAHWEH as its "choosing" God?[25] For its whole enterprise seems to have intensified rather than eased the burden and pain of Jewish exceptionality. Sadly, in the Palestinian context, there is a deep legitimacy in that old "unwantedness". It is a legitimacy entailed, not by the very presence of Israel (for Palestinians have a tradition of hospitality), but by how that presence pursued its politics both prior to and after partition. Israeli politicians may duly insist that their politics were made inevitable by Palestinian inhospitality. Is that, however, a plea that Judaism could honourably make?

Zionism as sharpening, not resolving, the Jewish dilemma is oddly illustrated by Israel's tense relations with the United Nations. In the palmy days of the late forties and of Abba Eban's eloquence, the United Nations (albeit still a very partial congress of nations) was the supreme disposer and, to this day, what juridical warrant there is for the existence of the State of Israel depends on UN Resolution.[26] Subsequently it has come to be seen as a nest of prejudiced sentiments. Its sundry Resolutions have been contemptuously ignored or defied. Peace-making on Israeli ground is no part of its mandate. The UN that once gave it being has become an entity which it is liable readily to loathe.

That being Jewish in the prevailing Zionist form accentuates rather than heals the pain of Jewishness is curiously evident on sundry fronts. The reach of the American/Israeli Public Affairs Committee into the making – and the debating – of United States policy is well known. It readily claims to align its own immediate interests with the wider manoeuvrings of national policy, thus enlarging the range of responsive suspicions and enmities.[27] It is almost as if Zion must arrogate to itself the manipulation of all affairs seen as even remotely threatening to itself. Everything becomes urgently and exclusively self-referential so that a psychic isolation is the more entailed. Israel expects the Jewish diaspora to be eagerly its sponsor and only silently its critic. Insofar as the wider Jewishness conforms to that rubric, it is involved in a partisan mood extending into still larger realms of inter-human tension. Happening in the name and for the sake of Israel, this only sharpens the problematics of Judaism.

It must be recognized that all, with Zion and Zionism, is *in via*, "on the way". Its deep ideology must be given time. The odds have been too great, the hazards too cruel. Yet inexorably the means irreversibly define the ends, unless the ends, if only clearly asserted, could still redeem them. Again, it must be true that the complexities belong with all nationalisms and should not be uniquely reproached in being Jewish. Was not Israel set to normalize the Jewish meaning and by nationalism emulate the nations at large? Did it, then, as some have held, quite deliberately "secularize" itself, "choosing" to be no longer "chosen"? If so, then it cannot escape the reckonings inseparable from that reading of identity. Yet how should so choosing belong with the unique "people of God" or is that vocation thereby irreparably surrendered?

VI

Brevity in all the foregoing does scant justice to issues of sharp complexity. At least it indicates the present tension in Jewish pronouns plural, the usage of "we" and "us" and "ours" in Jewish terms. Judaism, as a "hereditary faith", takes its name from its ethnicity,[28] but its bearings, thanks to Zionist readings of its nature, have been deeply re-immersed in human confrontation. Politicization, as it were, has "internationalized" Jewishness in very different terms from those of the long centuries. To have again a Joshua and a David means no longer the seven tribes of Canaan but a whole ecumene of human interest, entangling with the world of Islam via Arabism and caught into the web of the global investments of the current super-power. By dint of "holy places", it tangles with the stresses of world Christianity. It is embarrassed and pragmatically served by the total endorsement of a Christian Zionism giving it a false authenticity, while the conscience of the rest of Christianity can only deplore its hardness of heart. For many in the post-colonial independence of Africa and Asia it seems to incur the reproach of a renewed imperialism riding roughshod over "native" rights and hopes.

In all these stressful ways, Joshua/David *redivivi* find themselves in a globally related enterprise that, in re-possessing an ancient territory, risks dis-possessing Jewry of the self-definition it reached, beyond all local, territorial bounds, in the ethicism of its great prophets, the prophets who cried:

> Woe to them that join house to house and field to field, until there be no
> room, that they may dwell alone in the midst of the earth. (Isaiah 5:8)

It was cruel of that Isaiah to echo so pointedly the "dwelling alone" theme
of the Pentateuchal text. But then he was capable of likening Jerusalemites
to the people of "Sodom and Gomorrah". A contemporary conscience
might surmise that he was anticipating the "settlements" that have so
effectively created a patchwork of land-possession capable of being
coalesced into ensuring one nationhood and precluding another.

In those campaigns of Joshua, which so fascinated the Biblical studies
of David Ben-Gurion, the stakes – according to the Book's narratives –
were starkly militarist and local. Zionism could reasonably claim that it
had been obliged to achieve itself *vis-à-vis* an impulsive adversary in less
than adequate control of its own counsels, inept and imperceptive of the
full dimensions of its tragedy. Should we be blamed for winning or repair
where they have blundered, a realist Israel might ask, or perhaps even read
"their luck" as a sign of "the good hand of the Lord" by the logic of a
Nehemiah?

But if, in such terms, "God meant it unto good", there was no Joseph-
style providence discernible that might incorporate all alike, the wrongers
and the wronged. For there was no Joseph mind to be vicarious in terms
of a shared redemption. The "we" of "us" and "ours" was only the more
to be asserted in confrontation, legitimized by a successful vindication of
a competitive identity.

Jewry and Jewishness, to be sure, are more than and other than the
attainment of Israel but their definition everywhere has to be seen as
conditioned by it. The State has symbolized more than it encloses and
speaks for what does not migrate to it. The diaspora which it both disowns
and represents is known by it even when at odds with it.[29]

It follows that the Jewish personal pronoun plural, this soul-language
of "we" and "us" and "ours", lives in a tension between religious nationalism and witnessing by a religious destiny. Writing in 1981, the leading
Jewish theorist and scholar, Jacob Neusner, urged that "to be a Jew just
by religion" would be no valid or viable option.

> Without Zionism, religious conviction, forced to bear the whole burden by
> itself, would prove a slender reed.[30]

Yet he found the Zionism/Judaism nexus an embarrassing one, seeing "the
Jewish problem solved by Zionism" as only "the Zionist problem
addressed to Judaism".[31] Addressed it certainly remains and with equivocal and ambivalent answers. There the whole burden of Jewishness
belongs. Was Zionism in political form a dark aberration, an ultimate
betrayal? Was it a necessary "spiting" of the "Gentile" world, a sure

therapy for Jewish self-hatred? For Jacob Neusner, Zionism has recaptured the ancient myth of land and covenant, whereas for such as Hermann Cohen "our promised land" was "the moral world as it unfolds through history",[32] meaning the gentle ministry to humankind of a Jewish particularity serving all by its unique characterization of ethical value, demonstrating the meaning of being "people unto God". That "land of promise" could only be sullied, blighted and betrayed by political, military, aggressive reacquisition of a tract of "holy ground".

Not so the consensus of Zionist will, perceiving a humanity finally set against a Jewry which, therefore, could only assert itself in the counter form of a decisive nationalism of its own, thereby relinquishing, in part if not in whole, the other "promised land" of exclusively religious witness and exemplary destiny.

For that role, Judaic prophethood, the benediction of the Sabbath and the wisdom of the Torah, thoroughly equip the "just a religion" theme. Whether or not concurrent Zionism can somehow serve it, or only inexorably repudiate it, turns precariously on the ever more embittered tragedy in which Zionism is presently locked and on the Judaic values by which it might be redeemed. "Just a religion" may seem a diminishing version of identity, foregoing the politics of sovereignty, of land and power. Yet the toll of these is the price they exact – a price that forfeits the elect vocation in the jeopardy of an ever compromised success.

All personal pronouns plural have their singulars. How the individual Jewish mind has read the "Gentile" world or coped with the pros and cons of diaspora or Zionist definition has to be remitted to CHAPTER FIVE. The private spirit is the surest refuge of the public hope, the sharpest mirror of the common image.

CHAPTER FIVE

The Self-Encounter in Judaism

I

Literature has few narratives of self-encounter more dramatic in their incidence, more mysterious in their meaning, than the Biblical story of Jacob's "wrestling with the angel" prior to his rendezvous with his estranged twin brother, Esau.[1] According to Genesis 33:4, Esau "ran to meet Jacob and embraced him, fell on his neck and kissed him and they (both) wept". How do we read "the tears of Esau" – a man impulsive, generous, fondly expectant, careless of ambiguous byegones, ardent for reconciliation? Those "tears of Esau" would take their place in the saga of Messiah who alone could dry them, thought the sages.

What, though, of "the tears of Jacob"? The sages answer: "Because Jacob understood that Esau's embrace was a trap more dangerous than his hate." Musing on the story, Elie Wiesel remembers how his master, Saul Lieberman, often warned him that the Jewish people "lost more souls through seduction than through persecution".[2] Of the place called Peniel where he had met "the angel", Jacob cried: "I have seen the face of God and my life is preserved . . ." and "the sun rose upon him". Even so, tradition preserves from it an irreducible wariness of the suspect world drawn from the same human womb.

The ancient story captures the strange, abiding paradox of Jewish existence, singularly visited by the divine presence engaging intimately in the depths of personal being, yet instilling – if not requiring – a posture of distrust towards all else outside that privacy with the one people's YAHWEH. What must it mean in the inwardness of the Jewish soul to carry the privilege of that distinctiveness and, when the latent antipathy became reciprocal as the inevitable non-Jewish reaction, to bear the burden and the liability?

The question arises directly from the unique peoplehood explored in the previous chapter. Indeed, except for purpose of reflection, the separation of the plural and the singular pronouns in the vocabulary of Jewish faith would be quite arbitrary. For the "we" and the "me" are always inter-active, Jewish and the Jew. Yet only Jacob "wrestled" at Peniel to find in sharply biographical experience, "the new name" that, long centuries later, denoted the recovery of Zionist nationhood on the west side of Jordan beyond Esau's territory.[3]

There was, at its bestowal upon Jacob at the fording of Jabbok, a strange and abiding ambiguity. "Israel" properly means "God prevails", or "May God rule", yet Jacob becomes the subject of the verb. It is he who prevails – but is his "prevailing" over Esau or over God? Is it that "God let himself be coerced by Jacob's violence"?[4] The question might be no more than the puzzle of an ancient tale, were it not somehow capturing the whole mystery of Jewish identity – this ambivalence between what is gained from God by sheer tenacity of soul-intent, figuratively in Jacob, and what is also bestowed as a divine conferment of "status with God" ever to be enjoyed. "Thou art Jacob: thou shalt be Israel". Thus to ask who prevailed in the encounter is to be moved to say: "Mysteriously both." Their victory stood in an entire partnering of divine granting and of human acquiring – the one by the initiative which the other brought to pass.[5]

The whole Judaic ethos of the "cripple crowned" is inaugurated and epitomized in the Peniel story. The supreme destiny would be the perennial hurt. CHAPTERS THREE and FOUR have traced the historical factors in their "people" terms and the collective sanction of Jewry by the triad of Lord and land and legend. The task now is to find the meaning of this membership in the private self as memory and meditation have told it from within. How is the essential personalism of all "I" language felt and told from inside the distinctive "we-ness" chartered by Jewish corporate self-belief? What of the implicit Jacob in the explicit Israel his progeny became, "the children of Israel" from their great progenitor?

That its intense distinctiveness belongs within the human whole is the first and crucial point. Jacob, the quintessential Hebrew, remains a truly human figure, the tangle of his story such as any family could match. The destiny of Jewishness – the Genesis 32 story seems to say – is out of the fabric that is common to us all, not that "election" is self-induced but that it is self-received, something not "of them" but certainly "through them". For, in being reciprocal between their Lord and them, it could not have been had without being given, nor given without being taken. "We life's pride and cared-for crown".[6]

There are many perplexities around Jacob's encounter at the ford of Jabbok – a strongly flowing river at that point and time, thrusting through a gorge of precipitous banks on either side. The narrative has to be read with many layers of meaning to unravel.[7] There seems to be a play on the word *ye'abeq* "wrestled", and *yabboq*, the river, used nowhere else. Did the danger of the crossing mean some deity of the river needing to be overcome as the ground of a deeper fear in Jacob's heart? Or was it that crossings and thresholds are always fearsome for the first time?

Or is Jacob now encountering what is more awesome still – his own sense of guilt, the deep apprehension with which he comes, after twenty years, to rendezvous with his estranged and unpredictable brother? Why does the "someone" (*ish*) who wrestles with him prove to be "an angel of divine theophany" and finally the Lord? "The God of his fathers", of his cruelly cheated father, Isaac, is confronting the schemer in the accumulation of his success when all that his busy wanderings have attained stands precariously at risk and nemesis may be justly at hand.

Characteristically, Jacob is not so fear-torn as to lack a strategy. He sends his families ahead, with sequences of flocks as presents, planned as instalments to blunt his brother's anger and argue a cumulative appeasement. Then, in deepening alarm, he is alone. Night falls – night when "ghosts of the past" come abroad till dawn summons them away as "the day breaks".[8]

Jacob "wrestles" with the truth of himself he has too long disguised to himself, in conflict with the assailant. The struggle lasts as long as Jacob clings. Only when crippled is he asked his name. "And he said: Jacob" – the name his very voice had disowned in the sacred presence of his blind and dying father. In that moment of his real identity – which the vision had demanded to be told – came the "Israel" re-naming as – we must assume – the "victory" he had won in that home-truth honesty about himself.

The "name" of his assailant he urgently demands to know. Answer is withheld. For the Jacob he remains might be tempted to use it for his own devices.[9] Yet answer is implicit. The "Un-nameable" has been encountered "face to face". The place is called "Peniel". Symbolically "the sun rises upon him". The tryst with Esau prospers, thanks to the elder brother's generous soul. The still calculating Jacob refuses the offer of "protection", suspicious of the "surveillance", or "safe-conduct", implications it might carry. He is happier to keep his own distance and be no brother with a chaperone.

What has happened to the "I" and "me" of Jacob/Israel in this second "inaugural", this Peniel beyond Bethel, of his self-awareness as his Lord's protégé? The narratives still use the birth-given name. It is Jacob who persists through the vicissitudes of the Joseph saga, the drama of a providence that will lead into the sojourn in Egypt and lay the ground-plot for the Exodus. It was Jacob who sent Joseph to enquire after his brothers to set in train the tragedy of the blood-stained coat and the bargain with the Ishmaelites, a Jacob who "heard that there was corn in Egypt", a Jacob to whom, chastened and disconsolate, the brothers returned from their encounters with Joseph. It was a Jacob who, at the climax of their settling in Egypt, "blessed the Pharoah" (Genesis 47:7 and 10).

Yet, intriguingly – as the documentary tells it – "Israel" it is "who takes his journey into Egypt". At Beersheba, "in the visions of the night, God spake unto Israel" (46:1–2) twice using the name Jacob. It is "Israel" who blesses Joseph and his sons (47:31 and 48:8f). So, too, long years on, the psalmists celebrate the dual story of how "Israel came out of Egypt, the house of Jacob from among a strange people" and "Israel was His dominion", the strange ambiguous phrase,[10] enfolding the double sense of status granted and a dignity enjoyed.

II

If there is for every personal "I" and "me" in Jewry something of the Jacob/Israel pattern as theme for patient exploration in this chapter, the "Esau-element" is part of the story. In the Biblical scene, he seems to disappear, being only recalled where tribes and ancestors are retold or where transit to "the land of promise" traverses "Esau-lands" (Deuteronomy 2) or the obscure Obadiah finds a target for dire reproach. There is always this nexus of a past story – a story that has inexorably to do with brotherhood human and familial and carries thereby dimensions of guilt and estrangement that live in the fabric of memory like the knots that, surviving into the wood of carpenters, stay evident in their handi-work.

Thus Malachi, carrying "the burden of the word", and stressing how the Lord protests His love of Israel, has to admit the question to his thoughts, musing on the puzzle of "this love". "But was not Esau Jacob's brother?" (Malachi 1:1–2). True he was, but the Lord continues: "Yet I loved Jacob and I hated Esau . . ." From that divine stance the Jewish psyche perpetuates the "Esau-connection". It is perennially renewed in the Hebraic concept of the *goyim*, the "Gentiles", the people outside covenantal privilege with YAHWEH, who must always be the other party for Jewish self-awareness as "a people dwelling alone" (Numbers 23:9), in an "alone-ness" responsive to "you only have I known".

Yet the single "birthing" abides. Jacob is bonded with Esau in the pater-nity of Isaac. They together share as progeny of Abraham, whose backwardly widening ancestors can be read enclosing all humankind. What Esau represented to Jacob of kinship inalienable, all humanity represents to his conscious legatees. There is always "the non-Jew" correl-ative to the experience of Jewishness, the other party inseparable from the identity.

What follows is, has long remained, an urgent task, a heavy burden, an often desperate equation. These cannot be foregone except by self-renun-ciation. Nor can they be borne except by the costly travail of identity. In a subtle and burdening way, the Jew "needs" the non-Jew, the "Gentile", even the anti-Semite, not to be inwardly known (for the elements are positive) but to be outwardly confessed (for the distinctiveness is of the essence).

The paramount truth of a common human-ness as known through all singularities is underscored by the fact that the denominators Jewry always invoked to affirm its distinctive destiny belong comparably to all ethnic and territorial particularities. The previous chapter studied the three Biblical factors of people, place and past, memory, racial ancestry, local terrain and its historical story as held in corporate legend characterizing the Hebraic self-consciousness. There are numerous examples of similar bondings between the "who" and "where" and "whence" of all human cultures and annals.[11] Many have their traditional "Esaus" against whom to define themselves via conflict or enmity. The Biblical narrative of "chosen-ness" was unique for the intensity and great range of its influence, but not otherwise.

Even the intriguing note of almost apologetic demur concerning it, on the ground of – otherwise – being insignificant, is not unique. Where Deuteronomy, foregoing all vain pride, has its Moses say:

> The Lord did not set His love upon you, nor choose you, because ye were more in number than any people, for ye were the fewest of all people. (7:7)

the Welsh of Wales could follow suit. The poet R. S. Thomas, to whom "the verse was particularly dear", found it "encouraging for a small nation such as the Welsh, recalling their valour in the past".[12] It has been open to all and sundry peoples, only given imagination in their souls, to read a destiny in their story and self-sanction in their memories.

The point is underlined by the Biblical borrowing of R. S. Thomas – preaching at the time to his congregation in Manaton – seeing that the theme of "election" has been so far and so often coveted by other tribes and histories. The idea has proved eminently exportable – a fact which has only added to the Jewish ill-at-ease-ness, holding that imitable it can never rightly be. For to have it, like some first edition, "out of copyright" would be to forfeit its reality. Exceptionality must stay exceptional lest its mystique be lost.[13]

Yet emulated, in claim if not in truth, it long has been. Abraham Lincoln, addressing New Jersey Senate, could guardedly describe his Americans as "the almost chosen people".[14] Less circumspectly, Oliver Cromwell talked of "God and His Englishmen". Time would fail to tell of peoples and places, from "Holy Russia" to Afrikaaners of the Vaal, reading divine "election" in their "hallowed earth" and their open destiny. It is just this feasibly comparable claim that must interrogate the utter uniqueness of the "we-ness" that first gave it passionate currency.

Even they seem at times to have conceded a people-land-and-Lord situation everywhere also.[15]

Yet intensely distinctive it remained and it remains, and the fidelity has remained a costly destiny – one for ever captured by a tragic irony. The very people whose ritual gave history the "scapegoat" were made themselves one in the long crimes of history.

Had not the Jacob role in the ancient story deeply disadvantaged Esau, leaving a gnawing sense of guilt on the one side and of resentment on the other? Jacob's attaining of the birthright could not be undone. For Isaac's solemn bestowal was irrevocable. By the same token, neither could it be forgotten. What the one singularly enjoyed, with the other could only rankle. There was about the very being of Jacob as Jacob a quality of latent enmity known to have been aroused.

With very different antecedents, the pattern was renewed in Jacob's own offspring. Joseph, son of ever-cherished Rachel, distinctively his father's favourite, kindles the antipathy of his (thereby) disadvantaged brothers. There is a sense of burning fury as "this dreamer" comes to rendezvous beyond Dothan where they are feeding flocks. "Let us see what will become of his dreams!" All unaware of the "providence shaping their ends" they send back to Jacob the blood-stained "coat", symbol of their felt inferiority, to carry its grim message of "Joseph presumed dead" to their stricken father, their bitterness wending its dire token home to its origin.[16] Their deception and revenge were damnable but they had known themselves provoked.

The Joseph saga was an inter-Jewish story and, on every count, a far cry from anti-Semitism. Yet explicit "chosen-ness" spells implicit disadvantage – one that is not dispelled by the sincerest avowals of the inclusive benediction that "chosen-ness" can hold, is meant to hold, for all and sundry. For, if "the Gentiles" are for ever only clients of its benediction on them, the inferiority persists, indeed, may be subtly deepened. As long as the privilege cannot be shared, or aspired to, or multiplied, even cliency – for all its potential treasurehouse – only the more dismays.[17] "You only have I known of all the kindreds of the earth" will seem like Isaac's vow to Jacob.

The Esau-factor in the patriarchal story turns solely on the matter of Jacob's cunning in deception and defrauding – aspects quite absent in the Joseph cycle where the guilt is all the brethren's. But, keeping that distinction clear and operative, the story still has a bearing on age-long history. All guilt apart, there is a situation of sustained unease, whether or not an evident guilt is present. Where some are dispossessed by others, the "others" will fear to be dispossessed in return. The sense of a perpetual anxiety about where and what one is, and why, will stay with every claimant to advantage, however come by. If

> It was the force of conquest; force with force
> Is well ejected when the conquered can . . .

as Milton has it in *Samson Agonistes*, and as Samson knows.[18] In the privacy of the devout Jewish heart is the endless negotiation of mind and spirit with exceptionality. For to ignore it, secularize it or repudiate it, while in no way to escape the meaning, is to forfeit its very insignia. And always around the negotiation, observing, blaming, despising, or simply existing, will be the perpetual jury of "the Gentiles". And "Gentiles" remain the great unresolved paradox of "the people dwelling alone" and perennially never left alone in a gregariously, precariously, inter-pronounal world.

III

"Gregarious" and "precarious" are apt enough to tell the private experience of Jewishness, contradictory though they may seem to be. For Jewry has always been immersed in the world, whether in its ancient, formative locales, or its exiles and diasporas and never more so than in modernity. The beaches of Tel Aviv and the commerce of Brooklyn are no less Jewry than the haunts of Mea Shearim and the settlers in Hebron. The sundry social and communal organs of separatism – the Sabbath, dietary laws, circumcision and the ghetto – make their point and play their role only in the common scene and for the reckoning of the excluded. Such is the manner of all register of human differentials.

By the same token they spell precariousness and sharpen the likelihood of its incidence. It is evident that the same ghetto where Jewry might shelter was the ghetto that deepened their need for it, inasmuch as it attracted the enmities it was set to nullify by a withdrawn docility. Its strong psychic necessity was in direct relation to its futility. Yet, without it, short of rethinking hallowed norms, a true existence stayed in jeopardy.

The irony is only heightened by the fact that "Gentiles" employed the ghetto also, to sustain their will for suspicion or disdain, finding these arguably justified by the image it carried or they wilfully assigned to it.[19] Examples are endless of this – ever mutual – situation. At random, Walter Benjamin, recalling his boyhood, writes:

> My clan lived in these two districts with an attitude that combined dogged-ness and self-satisfaction, making them into a ghetto which it regarded as a fief.[20]

His youth had been spent in a Reform community in Berlin; in maturity he found ever greater difficulty in identifying with his Jewish traditions and moved, still Jewish, into a wide cosmopolitanism in which active, political Zionism utterly repelled him.

Of a quite different order was the ardent prose of Zvi Kolitz purporting to write a "diary" out of the Warsaw ghetto after the Nazi invasion. Though long taken as authentic, it was only so as a *cri de coeur* from a defiantly Jewish self-affirmation. "I am proud to be a Jew," he wrote, "not despite the world's relation but because of it . . . Being a Jew is an art . . . I am happy to belong to the unhappiest of all peoples in the world."[21]

The age-long ghetto pattern of Jewish separatism had several economic factors in its rationale, stemming from usury laws and money-lending but there is no doubt that the psychic ones were dominant. There was this element of defiance in the very timorous imaging of an identity ready to be discounted and discern its real glory thereby. Reciprocally, as vividly depicted by Shakespeare in his *The Merchant of Venice*,[22] non-Jewish society was reactive in its lowest, most vulgar terms. A mood of impervious pride on the one side, even in soul-searing rejection, fostered a malign willingness to minister to it on the other. Even if anti-Semitism was not latent on other scores, it was – as it were – embryonic in the very climate of such co-existence.

Jews were suspected because they were thought to be powerful and despised because they were perceived to be weak.[23] The "powerful" quality could be attributed in sinister ways concerning manipulative skills, or hidden devices, or otherwise in the very tenacity with which Jewry sustained what was so evidently "weak" in their vulnerable condition. From this too often came mentalities brooding on vigilance as a duty excluding all venture into understanding. What divided was a gulf of mutually perceived conspiracy, more enervating on the Jewish side in that the odds were so unequal – a factor which, by the same token, only excited its characteristic inwardness the more.

The legend of animosity from Jewry for the non-Jewish world was fed from many sources all of which, in sundry ways, made its burden greater on their spirits. It was all too easy for ill-will to reach back into Biblical sources and castigate even the superb ethical monotheism of the Hebrew prophets as being no more than a "monolatry" originally harnessed to bloody conflict, dislodging through conquest the peoples with other worships, so that claim to exclusivity was close to the barbaric.[24] The calumny ignored how the ultimate prophetic monotheism always reserved its sharpest reproach for a near-idolatrous Israel/Judah. But it served to suggest a long tuition of the world in militant intolerance.

More darkly still there was the animus against the Jew from the Christian "possession" of Jesus and of his being "the Christ" and of how saving events had transpired, indirectly by the "betrayal" at the hand of

Judas. There was not only the "Jew-excluding" "monopoly" of "Jesus the Jew" – only recently ended[25] – but, even more bitterly the anti-Semitism that, however fraudulently, could found itself on the Passion story.[26] The poet, George Herbert, might read only Christian self-condemnation in "the sin of the world" (following the Fourth Evangelist) but widely-nursed enmities were not so minded.

> Thou who condemnest Jewish hate
> For choosing Barabbas, a murderer
> Before the Lord of glorie –
> Look back upon thine own estate,
> Call home thine eye – that busy wanderer –
> That choice may be thy story.[27]

The long and tragic story of the travail of Jewry under the malignity of anti-Semitism is well captured in the medieval legend of "the Wandering Jew" – Ahasuerus was he called? – who allegedly told Jesus on the Via Dolorosa to "move along faster" when he stumbled. In retribution, he was fated to be unable to die until Christ's "Second Coming". He sought death ardently, trying poison, falling off a high cliff, emulating Empedocles leaping into a volcano, but all to no avail.[28] If "the Wandering Jew" is a figure of pathos only in being a figure of virulent scorn, all that he represents either way in the deliberate "teaching of contempt" or the easy assumptions of discriminatory prejudice serves to underwrite, with due realism, the exploration we have in hand – how the burden of Jewishness, in the privacy of the soul, has known its weight.

IV

The term "the final solution" has often been applied to the things concerning Jewry, whether by Zionist visionaries or by agencies of hate. It is wiser to conclude that none exists. We can discern a pained and sharp diversity of interim responses coming from how the "I" and "me" and "mine" of Jewish existence tells itself today. All have their biographies. They oscillate under the pressures even for those who most intimately represent them. At best they have a pilgrim quality, at worst an angry doggedness. For everything is "on the way". Jewish thinking long ago abandoned any Messianic naïveté of a literal sort, moving towards that of "a Messiah who may always be awaited because he never comes". It may be that, reading representative minds in the Jewish world of pronouns, we may envisage how the ancient destiny may finally escape or fulfill itself.

Attitudes might be examined under five heads on the way to where hope may ultimately come – at least for purposes of present study. The five are: soul-perplexity, the "Sabra" mind for national assertion, enduring in tenacity, a mutual scrutiny with Christianity, and abiding in diaspora.

One moving document of the first, a soul-diary of anxious wistfulness, came at mid-twentieth century out of Tunisia. Albert Memmi published his *Portrait of a Jew* in 1963. It offers a frank, often almost despairing, portrayal of Jewish experience in a world seemingly devised to bring home "the malaise with which you realize you are a Jew".[29] Thanks to "an anti-Semitic universe", Jews are never free to live their Jewishness with spontaneity, unable to be themselves without always being made to know they are "heterogeneous". They inhabit a world of hostility and exclusion, shaped by a culture of counter-distinction that inevitably sees them as "problematical". He knows that he contributes to his own burden in that, as and where he is "accepted", he is somehow no longer acceptable to himself. He senses that he is denied acceptance on his own terms.[30] He is perpetually conscious either of rejection or of condescension, to which he can only respond by resignation, surrender or revolt.

Thus he registers something irreconcilable in his very soul, there being a mutual "necessity" of "Jew" and "non-Jew". Anti-Semitism only perpetuates the intensity of what arouses it. Memmi applies the familiar analogy of colonialism colonizing the mind the better to colonize the territory. Just so the non-Jew mythicizes his "Jew-other" the more to make him so. Yet the identity, so reinforced, is what the true Jew is the more urgent to affirm.

Living with this angst, Albert Memmi finds relief neither in assimilation nor in Zionism. The former conspires to have the Jew make his Jewishness invisible. Thus "Gentile" goodwill "rewards" him, "saves" him, only by denying him. Recalling the rabbis about "the tears of Esau", "good intentions are a snare". As for the State of Israel, Memmi found no solace there. It may have availed in a pragmatic way to restore Jewish pride in "auto-emancipation", but its cost to the mystery of Judaism makes its political goal elusive.[31]

The widely esteemed and prolific scholar Jacob Neusner published his *Stranger at Home*, in 1981. Though a quite different document from Albert Memmi's *cri de coeur*, it describes comparable perplexity, stemming both from the stresses of diaspora and the painful ambivalence of the Zionist "solution". "Why I should be a stranger where I think I should be at home?" he asks, "whether in Jerusalem or in Providence, I cannot say."[32] Anti-Semitism sees Jewry as "a pariah people", and diaspora existence "a perilous siege", which produces all the evidence of a siege mentality, and so tempts Jews to lay more stress on being Jewish than on being human. He asks himself whether Judaism could persist without the unnatural conditions of persecution.[33] Yet what if it be the very destiny that evokes the unbearable tribulation? As for Zionism has it not cost a tragic "Gentilising" of its Jewish makers? For it accepted the premises of European anti-Semitism all too perversely.

How tragic it must be seen to be that the Shoah comes so far to under-gird the self-awareness of diaspora Jewry, especially in America.[34] The Holocaust grimly affords a desperate dimension by which – at ever receding distance – Jewishness is affirmed. Thus puzzling paradox is everywhere. It cannot be said that American Jewry is "in exile".[35] Zionism, therefore, is at a painful tangent to diaspora problems. Moreover, it leaves ever at risk in practice, the ethics of the "Zion" it espouses in such "Gentile" terms. How far are having a land, and not having a land, definitive of Jewish existence?

Yet, either way, Neusner insists that his Jewishness has to be categori-cally distinguished from all other human beings. Is it, we may ask, for this reason that – as he has it – "western Jews live as slaves in freedom"? The ambivalence of Zionism is caught in his phrase: "The Jewish people is my homeland". The State of Israel can be described as "an act of daring and defiance, an act of spite in the face of history". Yet it must also "serve as surrogate for the holy place (the Temple)".[36] Statehood was a necessary gesture but the problems it created – and perpetuates – mean that a peren-nial dilemma remains. There are diaspora Jews who think that they can readily belong in general society without too much Jewishness, whereas Zionism held that "emancipation" was always a mirage only covering and distorting the sure prospect of de-Judaization.

Two mentors are impossibly limited evidence despite their eloquence. At least the sense of perplexity is plain. Neusner's critique – with admi-ration – of the Zionist venture well prefaces the second category earlier listed as vibrant nationalism, that of the Sabra on the land and, exem-plarily, of David Ben-Gurion on the prow of statehood.

V

For in the Zionist, shedding all misgivings, we have a lively pride of personhood, passionately emancipated from earlier generations of unwar-ranted Jewish subjugation, utterly disavowing inhibited self-hatred or self-apology, ardently rid of the "Gentile" surveillance, consigning the ghetto to the ignomony of history and, as yet, creating a new and tragic dimension of unwantedness in its chosen locale. Sabras, those born in the land named for the toughness of the cactus tree ruggedly defying sun and wind, symbolize the temper of most of those who came in successive *aliyahs* and fathered them. They had the temper of forthright pioneers like Vladimir Jabotinsky and Max Nordau, who shed their European names

and read their enterprise from the beginning as inevitably forceful, invasive and irreconcilable with the aspirations of "existing population".[37]

They were unashamedly displacers and primed for a pioneer assertion
of their Jewishness, as of right and honour, renewing the prowess of a
David. They were roundly dismissive of the ideology of "creative diaspora" and ready for the dilemma they had their Judaism incur at their
hands – or, if not ready, happy to stay unaware. The old legend of "the
Philistines" could suffice to characterize any resistance their Zion might
encounter, confident that he who understood them must love them. Jewry
had at last awakened with a will to destiny by strength.

One exponent of this version of the Jewish "me" comes in the novels
of Moshe Shamir in such imaging of "settler" life as *He Walked through
the Field* and *My Life with Ishmael*. If he had to die, unlike ghetto-ed
ancestors, he would die on his feet, or more happily, live as old Nehemiah,
with "a sword and a trowel" or a spade and a hoe. Virility was all. The
use of force had lost its evil savour. The only lesson the "Gentiles" had
for the Jew was that "sovereign statehood" was the answer. The only
"Messiah" was their corporate activism, with maximal internal self-
reliance and minimal external relations.

Moshe Shamir's stories breathe the temper of Haganah and Palmach,
the Zionist forces. *My Life with Ishmael* writes of "The Unfinished War,
The Unrecognised Justice, the Unheeded Call and the Inevitable Sequel",
oblivious of how all the adjectives could be equally Palestinian.[38] "At no
stage and not for one second did we have any hesitation about the moral
aspect" his sabra hero, Aharon in *Beneath the Sun*, cries:

> I cannot stand to the side. I must be in everything . . . I have to be master,
> so that I myself should exist alone in the world. Orchards? nonsense – these
> are my very limbs.[39]

Where such writers told their Jewish identity in tales of lived fiction, David
Ben-Gurion lived and defined them in the fires of battle and of government. His *Recollections* are eloquent index to the master-mind of achieved
Zionism – one who told his manual love of land by finally retiring to his
holding in the Negev. So tellingly did he make his own the "Israel" naming
of Jacob at the ford of Jabbok that he not only had it bestowed on the
nascent State but even disavowed the very title "Zionist". With him it
denoted those non-immigrating Jews who – still at odds with the word in
their diaspora – presumed to invade the monopoly of Jewish self-definition now firmly lodged in the Israeli State.[40]

For Ben-Gurion, the old theology had it wrong. It was "the people
Israel" who had "chosen YAHWEH". Their sense of covenantal destiny lay
in their innate virility – a virility which return to the land made real in the
only terrain where it could, and should, obtain. Jewish faith was in the

physical existence of their nation whose land was the only place where it could be authentic, for ever emancipated from the ghetto, persecution and assimilation.

He was happy enough to see "the Arabs" as a servile "labour force" who had never done anything in or with the land, perennially desolate from the Roman age and Jewish dispersion. He read his Hebrew Bible for study of Joshua's campaigns and remarked:

> Recently I was asked whether, in moments of stress, I commune with God. I shocked my interlocutor by asking him back: "Does God have a telephone?"

He saw Arab nationalism as "a cultured pearl", imitating "the real one". As an artificial thing, it had no political nexus with the soil and, at best, was no more than the peasant's love of working plot.[41]

His whole personality, we might say, extolled and exemplified what he called "that exceptional virtue, *halutziuty*, pioneering".

> It is the soul of every man . . . of which only few find expression . . . each of us may show himself hero and pioneer with the best . . . the magnificence has come to pass for which the people waited for generation on generation.[42]

Jewishness had at length re-achieved itself in the only arena where it could be its authentic self – a national State in a heaven-ordained land. All Jewry should flow thither as the true and final harbour of their destiny. The "I" and the "me" of the person in Ben-Gurion had written in valour the meaning of the Jewish "we".

VI

This meant incipient quarrel with diaspora Jews in their – perhaps benevolent but still absentee – versions of Jewry, their merely "cheque-book Zionism" and their liability to interference well devised. It was, no doubt, latent in the very downrightness of Ben-Gurion's reading of "the high calling". But, querying his ardent pragmatism, could less resolute, more reflective minds approve themselves as the fabric – one the more hesitant precisely in reaction to minds like Ben-Gurion – best described as a tenacity more Job-like than those we studied earlier? The fertile writer and symbolic survivor, Elie Wiesel, most powerfully represents them.

In his sundry novels and stories and more recently in the two volumes of his *Memoirs*,[43] he gives voice to a radical despair which, nevertheless, holds on to what might be called a fidelity in spite of itself.

> Flooded by suffering but anchored in defiance describes a permanent conflict between us and the others

It is the Holocaust that desperately afflicts his soul, not only the enormity of the Nazi will for a total annihilation but the anguish of how to perpetuate the memory, seeing that to have neglect overtake it would be to kill the victims again. "Faith in God" has to be "in spite of man and perhaps in spite of God" also. For, as a student told him in Russia, "We are Jews for spite". In such travail of soul, God or YAHWEH Himself is "of all characters in history the most tragic and He too needs redemption".[44]

Without the intolerable memory, a determined collective memory, the Jew would not be a Jew, indeed would simply not exist. Yet how, within resolute identity, should he live for ever unrelieved of "the most ancient collective prejudice in history?" The instinct to find it all foreseen at Sinai, as the Talmud might, with anti-Semitism stretching back to ancient Edom, brings no consolation. To be Judaic is to live without respite. The only solace is the mystery of a prodigious survival, for ever wrestling like Jacob and for ever leaving Egypt with Moses, for ever renewing the dream with David. With "study, marriage and good deeds", no Jew can let end in him the long lineage from which he sprang, one with a people who count with none and count only on themselves. Abraham of old had known and shown that Judaism means separation.[45]

Elie Wiesel seems to be searching for a language that has words to explain the burden of a tortured silence. His anger is "inside faith and not outside it". For "it is only permissible . . . to accuse God, provided it be done in the name of faith in God". "He – God – has no need of a name to be present."[46] For so deep a tenacity the conclusion is clear. It is that a Jew can only be a Jew in the meaning of his Jewishness – a passionate verdict the more decisive in its being almost a tautology.

It follows that Elie Wiesel has no mind for a Ben-Gurion style surrender to the finality of Zionism. He pays the State of Israel the ambivalent tribute of remaining a non-immigrant. On the one hand, had it existed before 1947 Auschwitz could not have happened and it was proper in 1967 for diaspora Jewry to be lifted on a tidal wave of solidarity. Even assimilationists saluted its symbolic "miracle". On the other hand, however, though he would not wish to live in a world that lacked a Jewish sovereign State, he could not make its Jewish priority "exclusive". For, even in memorializing the Holocaust as a tragic debt in surviving, Jewishness must strive for universal human-ness.[47]

Strangely, perhaps, his forbearing to reside in Israel – while always a coveted visitor – justifies him in avoiding to sign protests against its policies. Challenged by the reality of Palestinian tragedy and the injustice inherent in the invasiveness of Zion and the policies of Israel, he agreed to visit Israel to enquire. His encounter with Golda Meir only evoked the exigencies of a confrontational scene. There had to be torture and imprisonment without trial. For open court procedures would jeopardize the lives of the vitally needed secret agents in the "alien" community. He can only conclude, enigmatically, that "Jerusalem is something more than the shadows that inhabit it".[48] From the ghetto scene in Sighet to a world-figure eminence in letters of self-agonizing study, Elie Wiesel attains to enshrining in a living prose the entire contemporary paradox of "a people dwelling alone" desperately immersed in the struggle both to continue – and to cease – doing so. For if, as Ben-Gurion alleged, "Zionism was the Jewish re-insertion into a creative stream of human history", whereas "in free and prosperous countries it faced a kiss of death",[49] it proves *in situ* yet another shape of deep unwantedness, the inevitable sequel to the pattern where "both Israel and Esau weep", as once they did by Jabbok. It is the genius of Elie Wiesel to have told the tears and not betrayed the faith.

VII

The tenacity Elie Wiesel exemplifies has to conclude that only God could resolve the God-question. One whom he could only regard as a Jewish renegade believed that, in Christianity God Himself had, in fact, resolved it. Simone Weil wrote:

> God Himself solves the problem of God . . . The Cross mediates between the infinite goodness of God and the brutal necessity of the world.[50]

"By no means" he would earnestly respond. That two so different Jewish minds should together relate the issue where it best remains – in God, creator Lord – signals how deeply Jewish and Christian meanings meet in common burden. Sobered by all the foregoing, our quest for how the pronouns are felt in Jewry has to take up its fourth dimension – the inevitable, and often unsustainable, tension with Christianity.

The literature is vast and ever growing. How should Jewish community relate to a Christian "take-over" of Jesus, the language about an "old" Testament, the warrant for any "new one", the attribution of the Holocaust to the Cross of Christ,[51] the mythology of "the traitor" Judas, the dubious Christian palliative that purports to ease relations with some "two covenant" theory,[52] the problems it still leaves, and the toils of what queries the Jewishness of Zionism for ever caught in those of anti-Semitism. The catalogue is endless. The present concern can be only for two examples of how, remorsely, the Christian factor weighs on Jewish reckoning with being Jewish.

The life and thought of Franz Rosenzweig (1886–1929), passionately enshrined in his *The Star of Redemption*, embraced a deep negotiation with Christianity and an emphatic distancing from it. He fulfilled the first condition of any bi-lateral inter-faith duty, namely to feel the other's appeal keenly enough to want to belong. His converse with Eugen Rosentock-Huessy and others allowed him to wrestle with the heart-meanings of Christian relation to "God in Christ". That genuine attraction was halted, and finally broken, by the strong "undertow" of Hebraic loyalty, more truly told as a profound "overflow" of Jewish ethnicity where "God in general", "the Creator . . . constricted himself into Creator of the Jewish world and revelation only occurred to the Jewish heart".[53]

The Jewish Torah, in the keeping of the Jewish "people", he likens to a "radiant sun" whose "rays" may be diffused by Christianity and Islam – a theme he seems to have drawn from Solomon Formsticher (1808–89). Thus Christians come to God by way of Jesus from their native "paganism", whereas Jews have no need to do, for they are already "there" in the loins of Abraham. It follows, enigmatically, that Jews will never "cease to be chosen" while Jesus continues to be Lord. The two faiths are that far at odds with each other.

For Rosenzweig, Jews are racially and metaphysically distinctive, touched by divine YAHWEH. His mystique of racialism proved contentious with other Jews, who disavow that an eternal people must stay biologically untainted, or in "the eternal self-preservation of procreative blood".[54] It could be, ironically, that Rosenzweig drew this emphasis not only from his Biblical source but also from the German folk-theory of Nietzsche as a people making their own concepts of right and wrong, and self-espousing the faith of their identity.[55] Perhaps the suggestions is unfair. For there was a great pathos in the setting in which Rosenzweig wrote his classic work – one of ill-health and privation. But, precisely from his intense awareness of Christian faith, he had contrived an eloquent document of Jewish re-affirmation in the sharpest personal terms. Whatever corporate "rebirth" Jewry at large may seek or find, "the individual Jew" is "there" in "the great Here . . . in the mystery of his first birth", and "Abraham's loins".[56]

Martin Buber (1878–1969), with his long years, Jersualem home, and role as a Hebrew guru, was a thinker of a very different cast from that of Rosenzweig the tormented. Yet he toiled with many of the same issues and reached comparable conclusions. Firmly, if less passionately, he held to the "exclusive faith-relation of God with Jewry", as what could only be constituted with a single people as "a theo-political act".[57] He derided the Christian idea of peoplehood to God not made "concrete" in a particular piece of earth and its "folk". He held to the hereditary quality of Jewish faith as the only ultimate monotheism and to any "identified" Messiah as "Messiah betrayed".

His major direct treatment of New Testament faith was his *Two Types of Faith*, in which he sharply contrasted Christian "believing that" and

Judaic "trusting in" (*pistis* and *emunah*), noting how Christians need to "become" while Jews were "born". Having "God through the Son" was to lack the immediacy Jewry enjoyed through the unique "covenant", as their "primary certainty of God". Buber insists that Christians are left to a rigid individualism because they lack the sanction of an inviolate peoplehood "indwelling with God" in the history of unfailing generations.

He is ready to concede that both abide in their mysteries and can acknowledge each other at least as being contrastedly in them. It was this sentiment that found voice in his celebrated *I* and *Thou*, a remarkable essay in those pronouns of personhood, noted earlier, in contrast to all "I"–"it" nexus. Its most remarkable feature is that it prompts the query whether, as a deep "human" study, it has not somehow transcended the sharp "Jew/non-Jew" contrast argued in other works – unless it be that where "Thou" meets us through grace, "grace" has some restrictive sense.[58]

Since it is in saying "thou" that I become "I" and since love is responsibility of an "I" for a "thou", this can hardly be the case. It would, therefore, seem that we have to take Buber's *I and Thou* as a profoundly and humanly inclusive treatise of those precious pronouns. "Thou" said takes us beyond all "thingification" (the "I"/"it") which spells manipulation, exploitation and calculation (though "hate" is an "I"/"thou" relation also). Buber's thought is here close to that of Kierkegaard about "the single one" as partner in reciprocity, though Buber thinks that Kierkegaard's only worthy "Thou" was God.

This true inter-human intimacy of self to self is the paradigm for God/the human, Person and person. Had not Robert Browning earlier said the same – "Face my hands fashioned see it in myself"?[59] though Buber would not finish the quotation. For him, God is addressed but not expressed. It is first "the leap", and then the "act", of faith to live in the I/Thou. In such divine communion we needs must return to the "it". For without it we cannot live, but whoever lives with "it" alone is not human.

It is no strange thing that the thought of Martin Buber – in this dimension so close to the New Testament[60] – should have been much admired and loved by contemporary Christian theology. It would seem that living the glad risk of "I"/"Thou" our personhoods hold the vital decision within themselves – all tribe, territory or tradition apart, an "election" in the "covenant" of its own making in the common realm of earth.

VIII

The fifth dimension, as earlier suggested, of Jewish personalism – the one scouted by the theory and practice of Zionism – can, for present purposes, be more briefly handled. For its logic is so widespread and pragmatic. It is that of diaspora and of keenly undertaking the risk of assimilation that it holds. CHAPTER FOUR noted the irony, for Zionists, in how far the survival power of scattered Jewry, stateless through long centuries, queried the case that told it as ignominy and compromise. The philosopher Philo and the historian Simon Dubnow and multitudes of unknown faithful had been proud to claim that "their homeland was the Jewish people", and that however and where-ever, the Jew could never be separated from his Jewishness. Torah and the synagogue and the ethos of family, of memory and of perennial irony like that of Marc Chagall's paintings – these could finally suffice. There was no need to reckon the non-Jewish world implacably hostile. For, as and when it seemed so, Jewry proved imperishable.

Diaspora could be read as itself vocation, a scattering for benediction, salting the populated earth. If a recovered Zion based on land-necessity and power-wielding served to comfort that vocation, so it might thankfully be, but one need not pay that reassuring symbol the tribute of immigration thither. The United States could be found a Zion too.

To be sure, endless personal problems remained. The Rabbis – Orthodox, Conservative, Reform – would be anxious about the haemorrhage of inter-marriage. The Sabbath and dietary laws might be at steady risk and the perpetuation of loyalties through the generations a precarious duty. But all these would only interrogate what "being Jewish" was and, in the measure that ritual and social norms receded, their essential moral meaning could be the more essentially sifted. The very immersion in the "Gentile" "we/they" situation could shape, from minimal to creative, the practice of Buber's "I/thou" engagement with humankind, leaving the essence of Jewishness to define itself.

Yet all such achieving of still separate genius would not resolve the ultimate issue of "the universal" and of "the necessity of Gentiles". What of some Jewish readiness for "shared elections", for an authentic interior retention of "chosen-ness" which no longer enjoined upon humankind an exclusive recognition? For this remains the deepest issue around those Hebrew pronouns "we" and "us" and "I" and "me".

The secularity liable to attend the assimilation option may readily neutralize the separatist impulses that beset religions, but it does so only at the price of forfeiting the sense of wonder and of reverence towards the mystery of human being. The crucial awe and sacred destiny, rooted in Jewish self-regard, must never be forfeit. Yet can it not be held without an ethnic exclusivity, without requiring that there must be "Gentiles" who may not share it? Are these, then, in turn, to go for that strange "two covenant" thesis to perpetuate a new exclusivity of their own in which to have no part or place for Jewry, so partializing the universal grace of God?

Such a *modus vivendi* might ease relationships while doing no justice to their honesty. Perhaps the task for Jew and Christian alike is to realize that we can hold to "private covenant" and "open grace" as specially ours in interior possession, without external corollary that dispossesses others. Then we might loosely resemble old Walt Whitman standing on the ocean shore-line and saying: "All this is rolling in for me!" Indeed it is and he needs the whole of it to have it so. But he has the whole only in its being – in its wholeness – no less accessible to all, who in their turn cannot exclude him. Every "I" and "me" is warmed by the same sun, the whole sun, which in every privacy stays universal.

The analogy is far from solving all problems.[61] Yet it tells faiths that our faith-pronouns exclusify their cherished meanings only in our inwardness, the inwardness out of which we can only commend them outwardly where we must think them to be for ever offered.

Given the age-long Judaic self-perception this must be for Jewry "a hard thing", so long has exceptionality seemed to need due recognition as a status "whose being was to be perceived" such. Even so, Rabbi Abraham Heschel had a voice and pen with the deepest Jewishness to undertake it. In *Man is not Alone* he reached for the sea analogy but in terms of the sea-shell to the ear where we hear "a perpetual summons from the waves".[62] His central theme – for which he has been much reproached by other Jews – is that of "divine pathos", that "fellow-feeling" the Hebrew prophets like Jeremiah had with YAHWEH, from which they knew that YAHWEH reciprocated it in a *unio sympathetica* with humankind. Here Heschel is certainly of one mind with Hosea concerning "the Most Moved Mover", for whom the creation was/is a liability of unfailing love.

His thought is deeply lyrical and ready for paradox. He could enthuse about (the State of) Israel as an "image of eternity" and ignore the sombre politics of a state-told Zion. Even so his conviction about divine love, identified in and with our human scene and anguish, brings him very close to that in which, for their part, Christians are steeped and which they find translated assuredly into "God in Christ".[63]

The "I" inside the "we" of religious identity, the singular the plural will shape, the plural always propounding what the personal becomes – these are the inherent elements in the drama of religions, nowhere more tense than for the Jew in Judaism. For Jacob at Peniel, to have "seen the face of God" gave him the new name of "Israel". With it, the Rabbis thought, he still remained suspicious of "the tears of Esau". Now, only when "the tears of Esau" are understood and trusted will those of Jacob be dried.

CHAPTER SIX

The Muslim Personal Pronoun Singular

I

If Jacob at a place he called "The Face of God" finding himself re-named "Israel" graphically symbolizes the personal dimension in Jewry, then perhaps the shedding of sandals for ablutions before ritual prayer is the "marker" of Muslim individual identity where personhood comes home. There are few more intimate actions than washing one's own hands and feet, arms and face, and doing so in obligatory preface to *Salat*. Taking off shoes or sandals re-enacts what was commanded to Moses as he interrogated the mystery of the "bush aflame".

> When Moses had fulfilled the period and was travelling with his family, he had sight of a fire on the side of the mountain of Tur and he said to his family: "Stay here! I see a fire: perhaps I will bring you some word from it or a firebrand for you to warm yourselves." (Surah 28.29)
>
> When he came up to it there was a voice calling him and saying: "Moses, I am your Lord. Take off your sandals, for you are in the hallowed valley, the valley of Tuwa. I have chosen you. Give careful heed to the revelation you receive." (Surah 20.11–13)[1]

Footwear outside the mosque portals are the enduring symbol of the will to hallow and be hallowed in the approach to Allah and the ordered sequences of the prayer-rite.

The origin in Moses is clear though there are other interpretations of its meaning – the baring of the sole in the presentation of the self; the excluding of the dust and tread of the market and the highway; the break with merchandise and traffic till – no less symbolically – the sandals are resumed.[2] The Sufis were capable of exotic attributions of meaning when, for example, soles of donkeys' leather could signify the stupidity of human wisdom which the contemplative wisdom laid aside. All rationale apart, an exercise in self-awareness was clearly under way, a focus of intention made.

It is this dimension of "the singular" in Islam, the personal believer, which we have here to explore. A succeeding chapter undertakes the pronoun plural, the "we" and "us" and "ours" of Islamic structure and community.

That it is legitimate to distinguish between "singular" and "plural" in Islam is evident enough from the classic division, in both the Qur'an and the career of Muhammad, between what was Meccan and what was Medinan, provided that we do not read that watershed arbitrarily. For there were plural things in Mecca and singular factors in Medina. Nevertheless, the broad contrast between them is clear. In the former, individual recruits came persuadedly into Islam and only tentatively developed any corporate community. In the latter, Islam strongly emerged as a structured society eminently equipped for solidarity and cohesion. The Hijrah, or emigration, from the one city to the other was the great Rubicon of Muslim identity.

It would be fair to see that singular/plural quality, coinjoined in the Hijrah by individuals personally set towards intense collectivity, as also discovered by each and every Muslim in the act of ritual prayer. For, when in concert in the mosque it is powerfully corporate, the unity of the many is deeply experienced. The mosque carpet is likely to be patterned in serial, successive rows of individual prayer-mat sizes for separate occupancy, at once both isolating and inter-associating the participants – all identically "doing the prayer" yet in the immediacy of their own bodily movements that take the unison of one rhythm. The art of *Salat* is at once both privatized in each and every self but in terms that all identically share. At times when mosque attendance is not mandatory or possible, a solitary Muslim creates his/her own, where-ever the ground is made a "mosque" by dint of one's physique at prayer.

II

We can defer further exploration of this ritual self-identity to ascertain the profound sources it has in the Islamic faith. Doing so takes the course of thought at once to the *confessio fidei*, the *Shahadah* – always recited with the personal pronoun explicit in the form of *Ashhadu inna* . . . "I bear witness that . . ." It is not formally uttered with the plural verb. Its two sufficing themes are that Allah has no "other", and that Muhammad is "*the* Apostle of Allah".[3] It is from the utter unity of God and the intense singularity of Muhammad as the final "messenger" that Islamic personalism derives.

Tribal deities sponsor collective – but rival – loyalties. To cry "Great is Diana of the Ephesians" is to have one's citizenship for pride and protection. Doubtless, a private Ephesian is able to indulge the sentiments but in the setting of the province and the city. Worship and ritual confirm a public image and a collective identity. There have, likewise, been many times when the cry *Allahu akbar* has performed a similar service for Muslim emotion, as and when Allah has been made the virtual patron of Muslims only.[4] Such aberration, known in all faiths,[5] cancels the force of the *Shahadah*, seeing that such patronage, in being isolated to its proper partisans, is no longer universal but "one people-possessed" with the assumption clearly implied that other peoples, excluded from His range, have their adopted patrons who defy Him – a service the Philistines entrusted to their "Dagon" in defiance of the Hebrew YAHWEH.

That "there is no deity but Allah" cancels all such pagan possibilities. Allah's unrivalled sovereignty clears the air and the world of all patron-competitors aiding and abetting tribal rivalries. A God ready to be tribalized can never be divinely universal. For the worshippers have violated the meaning of unity on the human side, by acts of tribally private exclusivism. It was one of the major features of Islam in its first history that, in unifying heaven by the truth of the Oneness of Allah, it came to unify the tribes whose divisive deities were dethroned.

The same unifying of worship as belonging uniquely to Allah also served to liberate the mind from the divinization of natural phenomena, where wells, oases, peaks or landmarks were held to be the abodes of "powers" needing to be placated or recognized. The Quranic affirmation of the trusteeship of humans over nature revised that earlier chaos of fears and spirits into a cosmos potential of *khilafah* or "dominion" at human hands.[5]

The figure of the Quranic Abraham may be significant in this regard. For he was a great iconoclast, repudiating the worships of his clan and coming to be found *khalil Allah*, "the friend of God".[6] Was it – as some Hebrew tradition holds – that Abraham became bold to be a nomad because he understood himself summoned and guided by a personal Lord, a "travelling" God by whose call he had been freed from tribal bonds both ways – his own and those of his people's pagan patron? Islam was deeply impressed by that precedent, though – via Meccan and Medinan factors – exempting itself from the "seed" concept of the founding patriarch's lineage via Isaac and Jacob to which the Hebrew faith was uniquely party.[7]

But the supreme relevance of divine Lordship as the *Shahadah* told it lay in the way in which it awed the individual believer by the unmediated encounter of this sovereign, solitary Lord with the personal Muslim, always – in this context – dramatically "on his/her own". Intermediaries, pagan and tribal, agencies located in nature or figured in landscapes – all these partialized and diversified the divine dimension. The private self had several, even bewildering, liabilities to negotiate in "fear and trembling".

Muhammad's message banished them all in the singular "He and me" of personal devotion.

The most frequent pronoun in the confession: "There is no deity but . . ." is *Huwa*, "He" – known by the grammar of Arabic as "the absent one" (i.e. not the speaker nor the one addressed). In life and piety Allah was no "third person", but the overwhelming *Huwa*, "the One". The formula *la ilaha illa Huwa*, "there is no god save He", occurs some thirty times, first in 2.163. Rarely, as in 27.87, do we have the more direct form *la ilaha illa Anta*. "There is no god but Thou", on the lips of *Dhu al-Nun*.[8] Doubtless the steady use of *Huwa* rather than *Anta* was due to Meccan Islam being in a witnessing, affirming task *vis-à-vis* a stubborn pluralism, so that "None but He" was the only form of statement. That, however, in no way made Allah an abstract "third party" in believer-consciousness.

On the contrary, "He" was an all-absorbing awareness both ways – His of each of them and theirs of Him. The "there is none but He" was often followed by one or other of the divine Names, or varied by the use of *ghair* "none other than He". The word "Allah" occupies some seventy columns of the Qur'an Concordance. Only at 20.14 in the setting of Moses at the "burning bush" do we have *La ilaha illa Ana*, "There is no god but I", echoing the great "I am" of the Decalogue. Muslim witness to the divine unity was all the more fervent for its being so urgently made in the setting of a wilfully obstinate resistance. This, in turn, surely sharpened the loyalty with which it was upheld, the experience from which it derived and the commitment to which it summoned each of them. For all the fervour that cried – in the plural – *Iyyaka naʿbud wa iyyaka nastaʿin*, "Thee it is we worship and Thee to whom we turn for aid", the private surrender was at the heart of it. The senses, as we have yet to study, that conduced to Islamic inclusion in community, were themselves rooted in the deep personalism of individual Muslims. Both were consequences of the divine Oneness. It was the religion of the singular pronoun.

III

As such, it had the corollary of the intense singularity of Muhammad as "*the* Apostle of God". The Arabic of the *Shahadah* in its second clause admits no other reading; *Muhammadun Rasul Allah*. *Rasul*, grammatically, is *mudaf* and *Allah mudaf ilaihi* – the state of "being joined" and "joined to".[9] To say: "An apostle . . ." would require a different form. That Muhammad was held to finalize a long sequence of preceding messengers is true enough, but none had the inclusive range or the ultimate station he possessed. He was their culmination and had the stature they had only foreshadowed and never reached since they were awaiting him – a situation inclusive all the way from Enoch to Jesus.

Believing that Allah was thus uniquely possessed of this messenger held profound significance for the Muslim disciple. It was a state of things that seconded the personalism drawn for him from the unity of God. Loyalty to Muhammad had logically to be undeviating, given the finality with which he was endowed. Each separate Muslim could find deep corroboration of being Muslim from this conviction. This was the more so for the original Meccan – and so Arab – followers. He was of their kin, used their native tongue and spoke on behalf of God in their vernacular. It was, therefore, possible – precisely because of his unreachable eminence – to find inward participation in those aspects of identity so manifestly shared. It was not only from the side of the individual recruit that this was so. Muhammad, in the Qur'an, presents these aspects as his clear credentials as *Al-Rasul al-Nabi' al-Ummi*: "the prophet-messenger who is from among the – as yet – unscriptured people".[10] Thus his descriptive was one he shared with them, reciprocally they shared this "scripture-awaiting" state with him. It powerfully reinforced the private sense of each. When, years later, Islam spread beyond Arab and Arabic confines this initial bond could no longer obtain in literal terms but the Qur'an's status as being Arabic helped to perpetuate it outside Arabism.

The steady, devout recital of the *Shahadah* meant that each and every Muslim, making personal witness, concerning "the Apostle" was not likely to be swayed into some alternative allegiance to Shu'aib or Salih or Hud, "minor prophets" who had been sent long before to now forgotten tribes. Nor did the finality of their own Muhammad allow them to cherish a Moses or a Jesus beyond the parameters of how their own Qur'an allowed these to be understood. Thus Muhammad's status commanded undeviating loyalty and so confirmed the self-assurance each individual Muslim might enjoy. He powerfully sustained their Muslim status in his own. Later we will find the poets and the Sufis devotionally celebrating Muhammad's role in their heart-allegiance.

It might seem that the Shi'ah schism in Islam, so soon after Muhammad's demise, disproves this reading. However, it never impugned the status or finality of Muhammad. The issue for the Shi'ah was the caliphal succession and the shape in which Muhammad's Qur'an and *Shari'ah* should be "exegeted" and perpetuated. These concerns were deeply intensified by the tragedy of Karbala' and the immolation of the Prophet's grandson and the other enmities to the partisans of 'Ali, in conflict with the Sunni Umayyads in their Damascene régime. In their own terms of the Imamate and *Ta'wil* of the Qur'an, the Shi'ah held themselves undeviating from the finality of the one Muhammad.[11]

IV

In line with the unity of Allah and the finality of the Prophet, there was a third factor contributing to the singular pronoun in Islam, the "I" as "me" and the "me" with "mine". As with a refrain, the Qur'an is insistent that "God calls no soul to account except for what is its own", and "no burden-bearer bears any burden but his own". It cannot be that these prescripts intend to exclude all vicarious suffering, all human vulnerability at the hands of other humans, all responding, burden-bearing compassion in such perennial situations. For if they did they would be destructive of the essence of religion as human mutuality both in exposure and responsibility. They can only sanely refer to human guilt in misdoing and perversity.

As such, they indicate the inalienable nature of ethical responsibility in Islam, which is another result of its rigorous unitarian theology. Just as there are no patron deities to undertake tribal protection, so there are no alibis to assume ethical liabilities or to intercede for wrongdoers. In classical Islam – as distinct from folk Islam – the veto on mediation is absolute, unless by direct divine permission which, it is believed, is never granted or granted only to Muhammad.[12] It follows that we humans have no demonic or angelic agencies calculated to take off us the guilt we individually incur.

This feature of the Qur'an reaches back into the theme of CHAPTER THREE above, with its burden as to the possibility of "saviours". Their exclusion from the reckoning marries with the salient emphasis of Islam, namely that the divine bears on the human scene exclusively in terms of prophethood, law, messengers, education, direction and reminder, all of which complete the orbit of the Qur'an's perception both of history and revelation. Given that we are "taught" away from "ignorance", "guided" away from "erring", weaned away from "forgetfulness" by "reminder", and "organized" away from randomness, it follows that evil-doing can in no way be attributed to social or psychic factors as alibis for our tutored selves.

Our guilt is our own – the more reprehensible in that the volition, which always remains at the heart of it – for Islam sees the will as what distinguishes humans from inanimate nature and chemical processes – is thus eminently our own.[13] So the rubric had to be: "There is no burdening of a burdened that is not his own burden" (lit.) in Surahs 6.164, 17.15, 39.7 and 53.38, reinforced by: "God does not call any soul to account but for its own" (Surahs 2.286, "We" 6.153, in the passive 2.223, cf. also 4.84).

This strictly personal accountability of each several soul for its wrongdoing is the more exacting inasmuch as none are immune from the wiles of *Iblis*, in Satanic scheming to undo them. It is part of human responsibility to be alert and vigilant against such machinations. Surah 38.82–83 puts humans under Satan's power to subvert their souls from the right, except "the sincere of them as God's servants". Snares and temptations are real and multiple. Not even prophets are exempt from the guile that would "cast false words" into their uttering of the given Scriptures. Ordinary believers undergo wiles against their probity and allegiance but are in no way thereby exonerated from the liability to achieve *ikhlas*, "sincerity" and *taqwa* "integrity", or *pietas*, as the Latin is.

Theology in Islam never fully resolved the problem of free will and determinism, in the light of Satan being permitted and our being culpable. That irresolution in no way diminished the overriding Muslim sense of personal wrong as "non-transferable". There was always the perhaps enigmatic word *'Alaikum anfusukum* – "Upon you your own selves" – in Surah 5.105, where the meaning seems to be that an inner integrity of "self-charge" will make "the believers" (there addressed as such) immune from beguiling ways in the "erring" folk. It is a principle of personal self-handling in line with the overall Quranic view of an entrusted humanity in *khilafah* over the created order, of which the personal body is the first and last arena and the condition of all other *isti'mar*, or "empiring" in society and the world.[14]

If there is, in ethical terms, a "downside" to this emphasis on moral individuality and its exposure to guileful external pitfalls, it must be a failure to include the complexity around all personal integrity in the workings of society, of environment and the entail of history. For all too often these compromise any private ability to do the right, entrapped as all are by "Adamic originality" – to adopt a Christian concept about which Islam has always been reluctant.[15]

When Paul, for example, spoke of our "being in Adam", he did not mean some hereditary factor for which we were guilty before we began to be or to act. He meant, rather, a human situation into which birth introduced us, where factors were already at work from a long past and from which we could not expect to be exempt, since they were part of the on-goings of history. We "inherited" them, not as a moral incrimination but as a circumstantial condition spelled out by history. In this sense we were all "in Adam".

The positive aspect of this realism as to the human context is that, duly sobered by it, we can set ourselves to undo its collective hurts, insofar as in us lies. We need not take up some Hindu view of inevitable caste-casting of our lot, or of role-fulfilling inevitably assigned to our frustration. That may be, in part, the picture. For "in-Adam-ness" is no "easy ride". Yet it is a quite partial one that vision and energy may indeed escape and transcend.

As and when they do, we realize that "no burden-bearer bears the burden of another" is drastically untrue. Some sense of collective suffering for others because of collective vulnerability will supervene. This will not abrogate the Qur'an's ruling in respect of guilt. It will override it in respect of the redemption that only comes where evil is "borne" so as to be "borne away". Society is always vulnerable. What makes it so is often at the door of collectives in which individuals, at best, have played an anonymous part, and at worst have contrived, behind "causes" and "interests" and "dividends", to conceal their own personal guilt.

Then it is no longer possible to isolate a private guilt or to indicate a personal innocence. All is too tightly inter-involved and collectivized. It is not always possible to inculpate persons severally, nor to exculpate our individual privacies. There are many evils where an assumed or pretended "innocence" is part, or proof, of the crime. The Levitical principle "Thou shalt by all means rebuke thy neighbour and not bear sin because of him" (19:17) may apply about concealing the fact that goods are stolen. One is not free from "bearing the sin" because one has merely deplored the evil face of capitalism or reproached the practice of "ethnic cleansing". In the contemporary world we have to accept the multiple, complicated forms of social wrong and undertake collective liabilities around our private doings, sincere as these may be and, for their part, law-abiding. Do we have to be responsible to divine *Shari'ah* and not also responsible for it, if sincerity of conscience belongs with it? *Ikhlas*, or sincerity, has to be inclusive if, truly *'alaina anfusuna*, "upon us are our souls".

At once this sense of things widens what, truly, is "burden for us" in being "our burden". If the very concept of guilt has to be, in measure, seen as inevitably collective, its personal burden will no longer mean only what I did with my own hands or where I walked on my own feet, but in what society and forces of history involved me, through an indirect, or even unaware, connivance I could not escape or honestly deny. Also there will be room for all those blessed burden-bearers – mothers, martyrs, activists and faithful ones – to whom we owe much "carrying" on our behalf. *'Alaina anfusuna* is a far-reaching verdict.

Given this larger reading of the private Muslim in Islam, there will be vivid point in its traditional eschatology, where hands and limbs and tongues consent to the deeds their owners did, the words their users said. Its vision of post-mortem interrogation draws out the witness from the bodily selfhood, so dramatizing the doctrine of self-liability in a most decisive way. If "culprit" means "guilty and ready so to recognize", it will let bodily agencies concede the part they played, when, otherwise, they would be schooled to evasion or denial. In its portrayal of "the grand assize" with its emphasis on souls only "chargeable for their personal own" the Qur'an is sharp and rigorous. Whether the collective issues we have noted suggest any less incisive verdicts, or any probationary eventuality, we cannot tell, nor stay to wonder here.

V

We began with the leaving of the sandals in the precincts of *Salat*, though it seems unclear during the Meccan years when the ritual art of prayer found its familiar shape.[16] However that may be, there was an exacting awareness of "a self as a self" in the very preaching of Islam on Meccan ground. The summons to faith was made and heard in a context of sustained hostility. Muhammad's preaching had "foes in his own household". His guardian uncle, Abu Talib, did not in fact adhere to his faith, though protective of his person. Others of his own kin were relentless in their rejection and the art of calumny. They sensed a threat to their vested interests as a focus of pagan pilgrimage and to the prestige of clan and city. Muhammad was suspected and accused of "troubling the house" and importing subversive counters into their society. He was hard-pressed to assert his integrity and the divine warrant of his mission. His following was only precariously gathered, initially few in numbers and modest in standing, with some exceptions like the redoubtable 'Umar.

Thus it was no light thing for followers to accede. Meccan Islam was no easy option set among discursive minds, as on some idle Areopagus, ready to give philosophic ear to "some new thing". There was vitriolic Abu Lahab, "father of the flame", and his venomous wife (Surah 111). The new preaching, though claiming to reach back into the city's "pure origins", had hard going against entrenched resistance, in no way mollified by notions of its past. Its present was resolutely pagan, a mentality for which – at best – Muhammad seemed to be "calling from a long way off" (Surah 41.44) and – at worst – impugning a proud establishment on its own sacrosanct ground.

The reasons that ultimately led to the Hijrah to Medina have to be read back into the whole thirteen years it brought to climax, as a story of unyielding confrontation about word alone and the meanings it brought. The costly personalism of the Meccan recruits is then evident enough. They took risks in ostracism, malignity and persecution to which the Meccan Surahs bear ample witness. *Ashhadu*, "I bear witness" – concerning Allah's being "One" and this upstart His "apostle" – was a matter of courage facing clan tensions and family ruptures. It brought to a strongly tribal society a new dimension of individual initiative only conviction could avail to take. This Meccan Islam, as non-coercive, a verbally persuasive thing, appealed to personal will and individual conscience, eliciting what response its credentials could.[17] That was

Muhammad's first tribute to his hearers. As and when they responded they shared his vulnerability and the implications of his preaching-strategy, innocent as this was of all coercion. In ultimate paradox, as we must see in closing this chapter, the Hijrah which radically changed that strategy, also evoked from each and all *Muhajirun*, the "emigrants", their supreme occasion of personal decisiveness.

It is often observed that the absence of "clergy" in Islam both reflects and fosters this strong personalism, in that all are the "officiants" in their own right in their own *Salat*. There is no vital "sacrament" over which another presides or on whom each believer trusts for "ministry" they do not themselves transact. To be sure, the "clergy" elsewhere, assuming we understand rightly their office, are replaced in Islam by the legists, the *fuqaha'*, the exegetes and the lawyers, whom in their private ignorance the faithful must trust or from whom they must extract some "lay" sharing in the issues of *ijtihad* around interpretation and liberation from things anachronistic and hidebound.[18] A personalism that is only devotional, precious as it has to be, is less than complete when circumscribed by a punditry it cannot amend or challenge. Despite the large efforts of the *Salafiyyah* in Arab Islam and the *élan vital* of figures like Muhammad Iqbal, there are still many hurdles to be taken in an ordinary Muslim's quest for rights of "private judgement" – a claim often muted or halted by gathering perplexities suggesting it is well to conserve rather than initiate.[19]

Nevertheless the symbolism of Muslim *Salat*, addressed by preachers duly to be heeded, remains the strong, direct, physical and ritual sanction of Muslim individuation in which the body's pliability of arm and limb and movement corroborates the one identity of faith and person, the "I" as Muslim in this Muslim "me". The concluding greeting each sends around the circle centering on Mecca: "Peace upon you and the mercy of God", in being a token of over-all incorporation, tells each that they belong.

VI

As if to intensify these features of a personal Islam, the ultimate measure requires that we go to the long Sufi tradition. For there an urgent – some would insist a wayward – Islam reaches towards something like an Asian sense of the precariousness of all personhood, the fragility of self-in-body as almost forbidding a confidence in one's reality and driving self-owner-ship into burdened questioning. Then the personal pronoun is highly interrogative, pondering queries akin to those of Arjuna in CHAPTER TWO – if with a differing resolution. Who am I and whence and why? The assurances we have discussed, drawn from so firm a single theism and the lofty status of the one Muhammad, gave a distinctively Islamic shape to these leanings into mysticism, yet making them also indebted to its wider reaches.

Disputed as the Muslim "seekers" of the Sufi Orders were, they were able to draw much warrant, and solace, from the Qur'an itself. Foremost among their usings was the theme of "refuge" as it found voice in the last two Surahs. There the pronoun "I" could find vent for its fears and apprehensive doubts, the inner anxieties of its outward stresses. The words mirror the mental world of pre- and early Meccan Islam, the world Muhammad's meanings had in mind.

> Say: "I take refuge with the Lord of the daybreak, from the evil of what He has created, and from the evil of the enveloping darkness, and from the evil of those who bind their spells, from the evil of the envier in his envy." (Surah 113)

> Say: "I take refuge with the Lord of men, the King of men, the God of men, from the evil of the whispering insinuator who whispers in the hearts of men, from jinn and men." (Surah 114)

A'udhu (the pronoun is hidden), "I seek refuge", speaks out of the core of personhood dubious, for whatever reason, as to its security, circumstantial or psychic. *Ta'widh*, the action, lent itself readily to the impulses of the Sufi mind. Other Surahs confirmed it when – using a synonym *malja'* or "shelter" – they said that there was "no refuge from God save in Him" (9.118). But how was refuge to be sought? If it was *from* the burden of selfhoods *per se*, rather than from what was feared from others, might it mean some discipline, even technique, of withdrawal from the acquisitive selfhoods of the mercenary world? If so, might the "seeker" aspire to emulate what might have been Muhammad's own practice of *tahannuth*, prior to the onset of Qur'an recipience on Mount Hira'?[20]

"Refuge-seeking" had clear Quranic precedent in Noah (11.47), Mary (19.18), the Prophet (23.97–98). It readily became the theme of a Muslim pattern of studied *dhikr*, or "recollection", enabled by rhythmic recitation of formulae like *Ya Allah, Subhana wa Ta'ala* ("be praised and magnified"), any of the Names of Allah – *Ya Karim, Ya Latif*, or attributes of Muhammad as divinely loved. The sense of the praying self was heightened in the very urgency with which "the Other" was invoked or "brought near" by ardent plea.

The great masters of Sufi discipline left to their Orders, the community of their disciples, *Awrad* and *Ahzab*, manuals of devotion that provided a pattern of liturgy outside the obligatory *Salat* as the *du'a*, or "petitioning", of "seekers" duly graduating into the status of "initiates", in the paradox of the abeyance, and yet the attainment, of "desire". For "desire", as in all mysticism whether or not aware of the Buddha and his Dharma, was the key to all else. "Desire not to desire" had been his ancient formula but the Qur'an told of "desiring the face of God". This *ibtigha' waj-Allah* (2.272, 13.22, *et al.*) was the posture of *Zakat* in the offering of alms and the practice of all due obedience as not done out of self-pleasing or private pride. But might such ultimate "desiring" of God in the inmost heart demand deliberate "undesiring" of all private indulgences well calculated to impede or supplant it?

The Qur'an had strongly warned against *rahbaniyyah* as against Islamic norms (57.2) and a mere Christian "invention". Yet it had seemed to approve "monks" (5.82) as "free of pride". As early as Hasan al-Basri (642–728) Muslims of like mind began to develop ascetic patterns of life as a means to abating human passion in quest of "the face of God". Whether Christian and Persian precedents played their part is in dispute, depending to a degree on whether the assessment aims to make aspects of Sufism completely "native" to Islam and right by Islamic norms, or whether it purports to defend a "pure" Islam by attributing such trends to alien influence.

Whatever factors affect the scholarship involved in the sources and growth of Sufism, there is no doubt that it carried a major significance in heavily weighting the personal pronoun singular among Muslims. For it pre-occupied the individual discipline with the state of the heart. It made *ikhlas*, or the search for it, a conscious "accountancy" of selfhood, a reckoning with "the springs of thought and will". So doing, it could well isolate – in measure – the private soul from the scrutiny of orthodox norms or orthodox custodians of these. When the latter reacted out of their suspicions or their vetoes, the private Sufi was the more "lonelified", the more moved to dependence on the *aqtab*, the "masters" as the axis of their disciplines and mentors of their following.

In that event tension grew between practitioners of *du'a* in their *zawiyas* or "corners", and the "official" *'ulama'*. The canonical duties might then be at stake, if mature Sufis reasoned that Hajj, the mandatory pilgrimage, availed nothing as a ritual in "desiring the face of God" if the wayfarer to Mecca was "far" in heart, or if he were "near" the going would add nothing. To that degree did Sufis become capable of disputing the claims of "orthopraxy". For, in respect of the Hajj, it must be remembered that *Labbaika, labbaika*, the pilgrim's cry at sight of Mecca: "Here I am, here I am where You willed me to come", told a communal, impressively plural obedience for which a private Sufi was boldly proposing to substitute a personal régime.

As with all explicit or implicit separatisms, Sufis in Islam enjoyed the warmth and fervent succour of their communities, whether as partially

"monastic" or – more usually – the guilds and fraternities that also clus-
tered around trades and crafts. In these, choosing often to convene on
Thursdays, the eve of the hallowed Friday mosque-prayer rite, they could
do the rhythmic chants in unison and forge the links that bound them as
confirmation of their "pronounal existence" as it could honestly be
described, their self-attention to self-transcendence.

Part of the technique lay in the art of story-telling to which, as chroniclers witness, they made massive contribution. Tales abounded of pious,
wandering souls, the Za'balawis of their world,[21] sought for their wisdom
but often elusive to their client seekers. These were masters of wit, heroes
of the odd dénouement, the sudden turn of fortune, the outwitting of the
gullible, who proved so intriguing in the telling as their reputations
spread, so educative in their humour and their guile.[22]

The philosophers, however, were able to take the basic "desiring qua
undesiring" further into psychic *pro* and *con*, the intellectual interrogation of the "I" and "me". One noted example comes from the Ruba'iyyat
of Jalal al-Din Rumi (1207–73), founder of the Mawlawiyyah Order and
one of the greatest of all *aqtab*. In two quatrains he captures the entire
dilemma of self-alert selfhood.

> Awhile, as wont may be, self I did claim.
> True self I did not see but heard its name.
> I, being self-confined, self did not merit.
> Till, leaving self behind, did self inherit.[23]

His point is that, when we speak of "being ego-centric", there is – as we
must explore more in CHAPTER TEN – a clear and often unrealized ambiguity. Do we mean the ego-centric situation in which, as bodily
constituted, we all experience the "I" that is "me", or do we refer to insistent self-interest and cupidity, to amoral pursuit of our own lusts and
claims?

Rumi is well aware of this and says that he followed the usual habit of
seeing himself only for himself, though he had intimations ("heard its
name") of a different way by which he would not be thus "self-confined".
Realizing the "unselfish self" he was called to be, he "left" the old self
"behind" and came to "inherit" a true one.

His poetry has neatly and tellingly captured the entire issue of selfhood
discovering its true destiny in an "unselfing" which is given back a "true
self". "To love life is to lose it but to lose it is to find it" is how the Gospel
has the meaning.[24] The issue between religions will always be in what
terms and by what inner event or decision is the discovery made of "false-
self-ness" and "left behind" by what crisis? At its surest and deepest, this
was the question that Islamic Sufism, in the care of mystics and poets,
sought to resolve.

106

They had first to know the situation for what it was, to recognize what they did and meant in finding themselves using a personal pronoun. They were awakening – we might say – to relationality in highly conscious perception of its mystery and its serious depths. This might be through their instinctive Muslim "Allah awareness", or their quest for intimacy with the persona of Muhammad. By and large, their Qur'an guided them to a sense of sin as being in misdeeds committed or from which they could easily plead exoneration, as in the familiar human language about having "done nothing wrong" when under suspicion. Actual doings were then the things at issue.

Sufism came to perceive self-accusation or exoneration in terms of character rather than things done. What am I? more than What did I? That anxiety, we could say, was close to the point earlier made about "original sin" and the tendency to confine the concept of one's evil to empirical deeds of one's own to the potential, or actual, exclusion of one's being part of a more embracing wrongness to which one contributed in ways that legalism could not identify or indict but of which honest conscience must be reproachfully aware.

In this way the quatrains of the poets and the prayers of the disciples were sharing, in their Islamic idiom, something of the temper of Psalm 139: "O God You have searched me and known me . . . see if there be any way of evil in me . . ." A much used and widely circulated manual in this sense was *Taharat al-Qulub* of ʿAbd al-ʿAziz al-Dirini (thirteenth-century CE) – "Purity of Hearts". His Arabic had a literary quality of prose-poetry and musicality that are hard to capture in translation.

> O God, my plea is my need (*hujjati hajati, ʿruddati faqati*) all I have to offer is what I lack, my intercessor is my tears, my treasure my weakness. O my God, a drop from the ocean of Your glory will suffice me. So have mercy on me, provide for me, pardon me and pardoned me it will be. Breathe on my sorrow and make glad my stress and strain (*hammi wa ghammi*) by Your mercy, O most merciful of all.[25]

Al-Dirini and numerous other writers in this mind for penitence and petition developed a language that used classic invocation of the divine Names to bear the more explicit weight of their yearnings while retaining a telling brevity. They used short phrases that carried, in one, an ascription of praise and a plea of heart, with a soul pithiness that made still more pointed the conciseness of the traditional Christian collect.[26]

Thus a much-used manual known as *Al-Fuyudat al-Rabbaniyyah* of ʿAbd al-Qadir al-Jilani, "The Overflowings to the Lord", prays in a sequence of "descriptives":

> My task is that I put my trust in Thee, O Thou on whom every trusting soul relies, O Thou in whom the fearful find shelter. O Thou on whose grace

and the beauty of whose customary ways hang all the hoping ones. O Thou
to the power of whose might, the greatness of whose mercy and righteousness, all anguished ones appeal . . .[27]

In this way the urgency of private needs was joined to an expectant
theology drawn from the divine nature, the attributes of Allah being
crucially related to pronounal situations in mortal wistfulness, pleading a
pronounal heeding in the "Thou-ness" they ascribed to Allah.

It was in this way that Sufism filled out in warmth and fervour, as well
as frequent anguish of heart, the meaning of "Thee it is we praise" in the
ritual of *Salat*. They also brought home to their souls the truth so often
formally expressed in the third-person terms of *Allahu akbar* and *La ilaha
illa Huwa*, "There is none but He". Responsiveness to the realm of nature,
as well as to heart-need, entered far into this articulate awareness of what
doctrine said. Thus:

> O Thou by whose command the heavens and earth abide.
> O Master of Covenant and promise, Lord of majesty and power.
> O Thou before whom everything bows in awe.
> O Thou whose signs are clear proof for the observant.
> O Thou whose signs are in the horizon.

It was a devotional theology which also embraced in its terseness an
implicit intercession as briefly comprehensive as its words of adoration.

> O Thou who art ever aware of what Thy servants need.
> O Thou whose hands are stretched out in mercy.

To say: "O Thou whose word is always apposite" was to leave the hope
of prayer with the response of God. In sum, it would seem fair to say that
the Sufi tradition of praise, penitence and prayer intensified the personal
pronoun singular in Islam to match both the deep crisis comprised in
human selfhood and emotional experience of the One Lord.

It was, therefore, no coincidence that it also generated – first in Arabic
and later in Persian, Turkish and Urdu – the sublime poetry which gave
shape and beauty to their insights. With the poetry came ventures of
philosophy probing in abstract terms the theology of unity and the issues
of the self and the mind-in-body riddle. The classic theologians with their
Aristotelian sources, like Ibn Sina and Al-Farabi, had stoutly wrestled
with the problems of rationality, of freedom and determinism and meta-
physical theology. More elusively, the Sufi ones, like Abu Bakr
Muhammad Ibn 'Arabi (1165–1240), famous from Spain to Damascus
and beyond, reached for ideas of – and means to – a unitive "theosophy"
of mystical knowledge seeking to overcome the pronounal duality of the
personal "me" and a divine "Thou". Thus the "unity of Allah" would no

longer be a "stating about" but, somehow, an inter-indwelling, a *hulul* transcending empirical norms of "me here" and "Allah there, beyond".

This theology, horrifying to classical unitarians as *bidaʿ*, or "heresy", represented the extreme point of Sufi sophistication and, though enamouring for like minds and gathering a subtle following, proved too remote from simple devotees, the users of Al-Dirini's manuals, the cherishers of Rumi's quatrains.

The Sufi notion of *ittihad*, or the unitive state of absorption into God, had, however, been dramatically told in all its inherent ambivalence, in the career of Abu al-Mughith Husain al-Hallaj (858–922), the cordwainer of Baghdad. With him, antedating Ibn ʿArabi by three centuries, the pronoun *Ana* "I" acquired a tragic significance in a martyrdom that turned on two vital and related aspects of Sufi perceptions of Allah and the private self. These were the theological issue as to the meaning of divine "unity", and the place of mystical "absorption" (if attained) in the private/public order of society.

Al-Hallaj remains one of the most perplexing personalities in the Islamic story. He fascinates historians and psychologists alike. His long and intimate association with Sufi *dhikr*, in ascetic quest for divine intimacy, brought him into controversy with both orthodoxy and Sufi associates. He puzzled the latter when he doffed his Sufi garment to register that he did not withdraw from social protest and civic moral concern. Thus he highlighted the ever open question: What was mystical "absorption" for? Was the experience one that should be perpetual or should it inspire a return out of it, perhaps like the pendulum an "in and out", so that its fruit had social impact? It was to remain a vexed question both inside and outside Muslim mysticism, as germane to all self-interpretations, in theory or *in situ*.

The social concerns of Al-Hallaj came into his fate but it turned still more on whether he had said (and, if he had, what he meant by) the words: *Ana-l-Haqq*, "I am the Real". Was it a claim to entry into Allah so that somehow the pronoun "We" replaced all "Thou" and "I"? If so, his heresy was notoriously plain.[28] His accusers would not have it any other way. In a perversion of a trial he was condemned and brutally executed, despite his being cleared of any political charge, as corrupt judges continued to assert against him.

The significance of this tragedy has to carry over into the wider concerns of CHAPTER TEN. It was as close as Sufism could come to the painful corollaries of the pronouns in religion, since theology and society, in their subtle inter-bonding, turn entirely on the role we give them and the personhoods they so deviously transact and ineluctably entangle.

VII

A review so concise does scant justice to the breadth of Islamic Sufism and the wealth of its literature in poetry and devotion. We have traced only the pronounal thread as the clue to all else. It remains here to turn back from what the Sufis, as loyal Muslims, made of their personhoods in response to divine unity and their "master Muhammad", whom they saw as the paragon of all their goals and intentions for the self.

The turn back is to the steady theme that followed from the Meccan scene, namely how original Islam appealed to, and laid total claim on, the individual response. Doubtless even from the outset, responding to *al-balagh* – "the message"[29] – meant the awareness of others likewise in the one initiation. But they remained relatively few and heavily "minoritised" by a hostile and prestigious majority.[30] Their adherence cut across kinship ties and called in question – as over usury – strongly rooted economic interests. They seemed like would-be subverters of the Meccan order – pagan-religious and civic-pagan. Being a *haram*, a sacred precinct, prospering – without generous natural resources – by dint of its local energies and its sacral status, Muhammad's "Allah" seemed to Mecca all too threatening.

The first Muslims in that Meccan setting became such only with a personal response. The thirteen years of their endurance, if not among the émigrés to Ethiopia,[31] took a toll on courage and staying-power. The ultimate emigration to Medina (at the time still Yathrib), the factors to be reviewed in CHAPTER SEVEN, inaugurated a collective that issued through several crises into a crucial escape from the burdens of minority experience.

The actual event, however, has long been seen in Islam as the ultimate test of courage. To be a Muslim leaving Mecca took even sterner will than enduring to be while still there. The change of locale was pivotal. Family ties were being exchanged for the faith-ones of exile. The journey, itself precarious, had the significance of a pilgrim choice. Its issue was hazardous, Yathrib no more than a potential haven. The politicization of Islam into the corporate thing it would become in Yathrib would not end the personal equation. It would monumentally transform the first Meccan shape of it.[32]

CHAPTER SEVEN

The Muslim Personal Pronoun Plural

I

In his famous Mathnawi Jalal al-Din Rumi sang:

> Adam's clay was kneaded in the limits of a trough
> Yet he was exalted above heaven and the stars.[1]

For practical purposes Adam needs something in between. Though other faiths have brought the tribute of emulation, Islam is distinctive in its explicit confidence in statehood as the key to the viability of a religion. It represents the most politically constituted of the faiths. Though the Qur'an has very little to say about statehood or forms of government, its strong Medinan rubric: "Obey Allah and obey the Apostle" took institutional form in the political Caliphate[2] and power became the partnering dimension of faith. While a politico-imperial "Christendom" developed out of a despised "Christianity" as a cult-in-community, the power theme in Islam stands at the heart of its founding history. It has its shape in the two "halves" of the Qur'an. The Scripture holds it as the original and defining narrative. It is *de fide* inside the messengership of Muhammad, as the post-Hijrah achievement conceived out of the pre-Hijrah experience.

The latter occupied the previous chapter. The former is the theme now. The preached Islam may have been "kneaded in the limits" of Mecca, which would remain the home of its essential message and the focus of its prayer, but the making of its world destiny came with its Medinan entry on established power which the Hijrah from the one city to the other sought and found. Then the plural pronoun "We Muslims" came fully into its own. So subtle a change ensued in the ethos of Islam that it is fair to ask whether the Hijrah, in being decisively a move into the future of Islam, was not also an equally radical move out of its past? Certainly immediately perceptible changes came about – all of them stemming from the logic latent in the Hijrah itself. Few in Islam would agree with that query, suspecting it either of ill-will or of a complete misunderstanding of the genius of the faith. Nevertheless, there are features of Islam now, to be explored later, which return large numbers of Muslims in diaspora to a Meccan situation, exempt happily from old Meccan perils and hardships, but essentially one with it in holding the faith once again as only a preached witness.

"Holding" – if a provocative word here – exactly fits the issue. It is assumed by Muslims who hold without demur to the Medinan dimensions, that the absence of these is an impoverishment lacking all that the post-Hijrah success attained. Otherwise, however, an Islam currently "Meccan" only, could be read as Islam in its truest, primal form. To deny this would be to call in question how it all began and, for thirteen defining years, continued.

II

The pronoun, singular or plural, is a right symbol of the developing contrast from the arrival in Yathrib of the *Muhajirun*, followed by Muhammad and Abu Bakr in their hazardous transit thither after the safe departure of the venturing group. As noted in CHAPTER SIX, the emigrants had taken a personal step in setting faith-allegiance against kinship ties, in forsaking one citizenship in dubious quest of another. It led readily, and for evident reasons, to a sharpened sense of community. Collective action had been sealed in their coming. They had accepted to share a corporate fate should it prove adverse. They were cast upon fellow believers in Yathrib, the *Ansar*, or "aiders", whose readiness to harbour them had made their Meccan exit possible. Faith-ties thus had a fresh corroboration across other local loyalties.

Moreover, those *Ansar*, as yet, were far from the whole muster of Yathribites, still less of the several surrounding, Jewish and other, tribes. If the old chroniclers are to be believed, Muhammad's advent had been sought because of discords in the city needing to be resolved and for which his help, or mediation, might be useful. With Yathrib so far from being unanimously open to his coming, the path ahead needed careful negotiation which, in turn, argued a strenuous discipline among and between his own. Their capacity to let faith sunder them from Mecca had now to bond them into a solidarity steeled by the emotions of exiles – familiar to history as these are and in less tentative situations than the Medinan scene.

Aggravating their predicament was the likely response of the Meccan Quraish to their departure. Still implacably hostile, they had let Muhammad elude their watch on him in their own territory. He could well prove a more elusive and formidable problem for their strategy once off the noose they had on him within the city and its environs. He would not now be returning, rejected and disheartened as, lately, he had arrived back in Mecca from a failed venture to Al-Ta'if in a bid for acceptance in a firm locale. The venture to Yathrib had stouter promise of ultimately availing as a base for the effective organization of Islam.

Moreover, the status of Mecca as a *haram* shrine ensured that the Hijrah could in no way be taken as a permanent abandonment. The *balagh* of those thirteen years meant to reclaim it for an original purity of *hanif*-style theism and its Abrahamic associations. Yathrib would be no abiding substitute, however vital its immediate succour for the cause.

Thus the Hijrah was likely, on every count, to prove no more than a hiatus in the confrontation. It also held an inner logic that the encounter could hardly stay merely verbal any longer but would pass to other factors. The Quraish anyway were now out of earshot and, having allowed the preacher to escape their city-watch on him, would need to have it reach after him in vigilance – if not in more. In no way could they think or say of his emigration some bland: "Good riddance." Muhammad at large could only be potentially a greater quandary for the Quraish than a Muhammad walled in Mecca.

He, for his part, could hardly fail in Yathrib to register what his presence there would require of him. It must necessitate skilful consolidation of the new locale, toughening the position of the *Ansar vis-à-vis* the factions at odds with the new arrivals. It is clear that, much later in the Medinan story, there were some defections of Meccans back to their city as well as new accessions to Medina by recruits implementing their Hijrah later. The treaty of Al-Hudaibiyyah in the year 6 AH provided, at that point, for the mutual return of these fugitives by either camp. The situation as to loyalties was evidently fluid even after the "signal victory" at Badr. From the outset, it demanded a strong "community" temper, in measure self-generating, by the sharing of a common faith in a hazardous time.

It became steadily more so as hostilities were joined, and the exigencies of war sharpened the opposing "causes". Mecca knew its trading caravans to be vulnerable, with Medina lying on the landward side of their route northward. Its merchants were accustomed to buying off marauding tribes by pledging a share in their commerce-yields. With the strong religious fervour of their message, the Muslims would not be susceptible to such temptation. Choice for the Hijrah was no prescript for a mercenary passivity, even without the tribal feuds and tensions among which the new faith moved.

When hostilities were joined and Badr as *Yaum al-Furqan* "the day of the criterion", marked Islam as successfully encountering the more prestigious Quraish, it felt itself massively confirmed in a valid destiny. By the same token, "neutrals" had to be either more circumspect in their evasive wiles or more exposed to Muslim pressures for alignment with Islam. The sundry Jewish tribes in the Medinan region were especially vulnerable in the post-Badr situation, suspect as actual, or alleged, allies of Mecca, and as proven less than religiously ready to acknowledge that anticipation of crediting by their traditions Muhammad had initially awaited at their hand.

The sequence of events in the post-Hijrah years is familiar enough from the *Sirah* of the Prophet – the several skirmishers, Uhud and "the Trench", confiscations and acts of vengeance against the Banu Qaynuqaʿa and the Banu Qurayzah, the Pact of Al-Hudaibiyyah, the Return Pilgrimage and the final capitulation of Mecca in 8 AH in a pattern of emerging victory, aided by Muhammad's marriages into acceding tribes and the insistent sanction of success. All supplied the context for a steady heightening of Muslim identity and the solidarity it both demanded and shaped. The inevitable belligerence of those years and the crowning sense of its entire legitimation set their abiding mark on the temper and the ethos of the faith – a mark it has perpetually retained.

The reader of the Qur'an passing from Meccan to Medinan Surahs is aware of a Hijrah almost as lively as the *muhajir* who knew it physically – and for comparable reasons. Any study senses the changing psychic scene, the transformed feel of the text in tune with the locale. To be sure, Surahs are sometimes composite and have to be studied astride the divide, in case it should be so. But Muslim exegetes have long been confident about how to date them all, as either pre- or post- the watershed. Islam assumes a more insistent collective identity. The distinction between "believers" and "unbelievers", between *muʾminun* and *kafirun*, *khashiʿun* and *khasirun* ("the pious" and "the losers") and other absolute antonyms, becomes strident and assertive. The exigencies of warfare require embattled devout to watch on guard while the others pray and then reverse the roles. Even vocabulary registers the Meccan/Medinan contrast when words acquire a developing if not an absolute contrast.

Thus *fitnah*, meaning broadly "a trial" or "what tests", means – in Mecca – the persecution the first Muslims incurred there in fit scorn for heeding an upstart preacher pitted against a strong civic régime. By and by, it comes to mean the test Muslims in Medina undergo when loathe to risk their limbs or orphan their children in the wars. Ultimately *fitnah* becomes the sedition against the crest-riding cause Muslims have to root out from the *mukhasirun*, "the losers", who conspired against the cause. They, too, in turn, were a further factor in the hardening of identity. For they had to be ruthlessly exposed – and the more vigilantly the more stealthy their machinations. No militant cause can expect to escape such malevolents "testing" their tenacity.

Another term that carries an evolving meaning – though perhaps more among jurists retroactively than in the actual *mise-en-scène* – is Jihad. *Jahidu fi sabil-Lahi*, "Strive in the path of God" is a Medinan summons in the martial context and is rarer in the Meccan Surahs. However, it traditionally signifies the faith-obedience *per se* and the moral obligations which accompany it, i.e. "the greater Jihad" of true devotion in the heart. That seems to be the meaning in 29.69: "We will surely guide to Our paths those who strive in Us", and possibly also, in the first Meccan terms, in 22.78 which, though ascribed to Medina, has been thought Meccan in part and refers to "the faith of your father Abraham" as those on whom "no hardship is laid". It bids them "Strive for God with the Jihad rightly due to Him". But, unmistakeably in the post-Hijrah scene, Jihad (whether "greater" or "lesser") implies the campaigns to be waged. The double sense of the word is eloquent enough of how far belief and conflict were fused into one "endeavour" after the Hijrah. The *balagh* was still the call to faith but the faith had moved into the summons to fight. The *fitnah* that had earlier been the thorn of a preacher and his disciples became the treasons of a "fifth column" lurking in his camp.

III

Keeping the analogy of some Qur'an-reader's Hijrah out of, and into, as replicating what the emigrants learned in real history, the transition from Mecca to Medina is evident also in the steadily growing definition of Islamic norms and rituals. The average reader senses having left one world and moved into another. There is now even stronger emphasis on the "unbelievers", "those who err and on whom (Allah's) anger rests". Those words, to be sure, come in Surah 96 – if long tradition is right – at the very outset of the Qur'an in Mecca. But its reference to the pagans, to Jews and Christians, becomes more pronounced and "separatist", in respect at least of the theists, early during the Medinan period. There is a new stridency in the denunciation.[3]

The supreme symbol of this sharpened Islamicity as an assertive identity in more than word only was the change of the *Qiblah*, or direction of prayer, from Jerusalem to Mecca, as recorded in Surah 2.149–50. It seems to have caused dismay to many Muslims in the second year of emigration, as an apparent forfeiture of the long significance of Jerusalem and its part in Muhammad's "Night Journey" to the "more distant sanctuary" there. Since "the face of God is everywhere" any *qiblah* might serve. Yet Jerusalem was becoming "more distant" in that Islam was now more in antipathy, communally less in expectation, *vis-à-vis* Jewry and things Judaic.

The new *Qiblah* indicated that Mecca, with its distinctive Abrahamic *islam*,[4] had been in no way forfeited by the Hijrah. The preached Islam was evolving into a definitive community with its own symbolic geography, territorially pivoted where its separate origin had been. The newly ordained Meccan pivot was destined to play a crucial part in the age-long solidarity of the one Islam as the focal point of its own "ecumene of prayer".[5] There was a pointed irony in that Mecca could not have become the *Qiblah* save by prior exit out of it. Jerusalem had served its purpose and fulfilled its role of serving a faith-inauguration that could now transcend it. The now defining Arab/Arabian *Qiblah* gave a new symbolic cohesion disembarrassed – if the term is apt – of an inter-association where debts would persist but only consistently with the new and signal independence.

Hard on the heels of that change came the directives in the Qur'an concerning the Ramadan Fast (in Surah 2.183–85). With its twenty-eight days of a lunar month and thus rotation round the calendar of the solar year and its distinctive discipline, it brought unique character to Islam's ritual, distinguishing it sharply from precedents of fasting elsewhere. It made the individual believer steadily more conscious of a distinct identity, in a discipline that brought the very life of the body's private self into the body corporate.

The development of the "daily prayer-rite", prior to the finalizing of the traditional five,[6] had the same private/public effect of conjoining in one the personal and the collective acts through the movement into prostration and the rhythmic sequence back to erectness. Muslims, this way, acquired their corporate insignia transacted in their own physique as the centuries-old hallmark by which they and theirs would be definitively known – all so different from the potential chaos of Hindu rituals and the sundry diversified devotions of major religions. To be sure, Islam would lack, and not explicitly seek,[7] the ethnic distinctiveness by which Jewry, even in dispersion, was traditionally constituted but in a wider racial potential its inner experience of inclusivism would be no less compelling.

Meanwhile the stress of conflict was steadily hardening the mood of confrontation and the resulting reciprocal rejection by Islam and of Islam in the sanctions of war. Had the believers been defeated they would have faced the demand that they aposticize. In that they succeeded, whether at Badr or later, their faith was confirmed. Either way, the stern vicissitudes conjoined the field of war with the soul of faith. The physical and the religious were one in the juncture and in the event. Belief was confirmed in resisting the armed "mischief" (*fasad*) – a term which brought together both "depravity" and its "infecting influence" demanding resistance. Fighting had its sanction from religion as crucial to religion's security. The necessity of the one stemmed from the inherent urgency of the other. Thus a martial Islam had no inhibition about how its necessary "fight" might affect its spiritual meaning. Hence the logic that saw the "fighting that carried death (*qatal*) with it" (as war must) as "lesser evil than *fitnah*" (Surah 2.191 and 217). That verdict, actively implemented while the necessity lasted, gave Muslims a heartening and reassuring freedom which conscience, in a contrasted pattern of inherently pacific faith (as might be indicated by the nature of God) could not have allowed itself.

Thus the process and its ultimate emergence into victory gave Islam its characteristic form of vindication – a vindication rooted in the physical shape of its empirical credentials. Islam always held that such physical shape, in *al-fawz al-mubin*,[8] was fully accordant with the first Meccan mission. Finding it so was the *élan vital* with which Islam breathed as the tide turned in favour of its Medinan form. But the price was sustained vigilance. There were still the "dissemblers", the actual or potential renegades in the camp, ready to default if events dictated. By the same token, when they dictated otherwise, there was the inevitable risk of "pretension positive", and vigilance stayed urgent around it. This was the case, notably, in Surah 49.14, when "arabs" came to Muhammad saying they had "believed" and he was directed to tell them: "Do not say: 'We have believed' say instead: 'We have become *muslims* (*aslamna*)', seeing that faith has not entered your hearts."

Hence the vital distinction between "true believers" and the "false", made all the more urgent by the fact that the martial success which confirmed "belief" might also corrupt some only to feign for prudential reasons. Hence again the steady insistence on "true believers" showing their integrity by "doing jihad with their wealth and their lives" (49.16) – a duty which served strongly to deepen further the bond that bound them to faith and effort alike.

This powerful Medinan nurture into solidarity was corroborated by the shape of Muslim martyrdom. The *shuhada'* who had died in battle gave Islam the sanction of their ultimate jihad and so intensified its claim on all whom their example called to emulation, while sharpening the sense of combat enmity towards the obdurate "miscreants". Faith was toughened in that the unbelief that would not be persuaded in Mecca now sustained itself in armed array, requiring to be answered and overcome in those harsher terms – the terms that, for both parties, changed and darkened the original stakes. By the eighth year after the Hijrah and by dint of the post-Hijrah experiences in their cumulative quality, Islam had been welded into a growing solidarity destined, by Mecca's capitulation, to issue, by virtue of its founding story, into the most confidently political of world religions. Hazards aplenty were in store in the wake of Muhammad's passing a bare two years later – the chequered emergence of the Caliphate, the Sunni–Shi'ah schism and the problematic of the Umayyad dynasty with its shift of the centre of gravity to Damascus. But, through these vicissitudes a conviction of faith and power had been affirmed and realized. The two cities – the Mecca of a preacher and the Medina of a ruler – had decisively written their joint saga into the ethos of the faith. Damascus might displace them, and after Damascus, Baghdad, Cairo, Istanbul, but never to take away the symbol of their twinned history in that seventh century.

Their twinning divided the Qur'an in time and place attribution of its Surahs. It shaped the *Sirah* of the Prophet. It contrived the dating of the calendar by having the Hijrah with its destiny of the one into the other, the other out of the one. It determined the character of Islam. Whatever may be history about the Letters of Muhammad to world-rulers in his early sixties, they symbolize the truth of an Islam "expectant" – eager for a hegemony territorially beyond the borders of the Hijaz of Arabia, where Hijrah had first taken it. There would be an "emigration" of its armies into the Fertile Crescent, and thence into Egypt, Africa, Persia and Sind and beyond, not now seeking hospitable sanctuary in which to shelter faith but territorial right by which to erect its throne. The first significance of Yathrib for a Meccan missionary would pass, via his Medinan sojourn, into a more than continental régime of faith and rule, twinned as ever by warrant of the two generating cities.

IV

Keeping firmly in view the deep Muslim personalism of the individual believer studied in CHAPTER SIX, thought now has to enquire, in the light of the foregoing, what collective Muslims mean in their Islam, *vis-à-vis* the vastness of human diversity at large. What do the Islamic "we", the Muslim "us" and "ours", in the corporate saying hold for those outside the saying with their own Buddhist, Jewish, Christian, Baha'i or other pronounal identities?

We can set aside in present context the divisions and schisms in Islamic story and pose what may initially seem too radical a surmise, namely: does the Hijrah, as fact into theory, make Islam subversive wherever societies and polities are non-Islamic? If so, at least in theory, what might co-existence require in contemporary terms? Does the Hijrah in retrospect mean a perpetuation of the adversarial posture which then first ensued?

It is true that even in Medinan Surahs there are passages that might arguably undergird some concept of human rights across all peoples, not to be excluded by any "territorial" banning of them on the part of a "ruling" *Shari'ah* no other religio-legal criteria may invade or supersede.[9] Thus Surah 49.13: "We have created you . . . nations and tribes in order that you may know each other." Mankind was not "made . . . a single community" (5.48 and 11.118 with 16.93 and 42.8). Perhaps then, with racial diversity, might go religio-cultural variety, if this could even extend to tolerance of differing rites and codes. Arguably that might be drawn from Surah 22.67: "For every community We have ordained a rite of worship for them to observe," with 22.34 adding ". . . that they may mention the name of Allah" over animals at slaughter, for food.

It would, however, be precarious case-making to argue that the Qur'an is ready to be "ecumenical" in that sense. The Hijrah certainly shows that it could not co-exist with Meccan paganism,[10] but then should Hijrah be understood as technically ruling out its co-existence anywhere with any alternative belief-rituals, unless these were fit to be tolerated in their content and submissive to an Islamic hegemony?

Such, of course, was the *dhimmi* status Islam was ready to accord to "non-idolaters", Jews, Christian and perhaps others. These "minorities", however, had to be politically innocuous, pledged to acknowledge Islamic sovereignty and "bound over" to privatize their religious existence.[11] There could be no question of their recruiting from among Muslims. Their tolerance was a freedom to remain what they had been born, Muslims too being under the same necessity in that any Muslim forsaking of Islam, even for *bona fide* reason of conscience, must be seen – and requited – as "treason".

This defining of any faith-query as "treacherous" and, as such, punishable by death stems directly from the Hijrah in its Medinan sequel.[12] In that context of armed conflict, with the vigilance against conspiracy and disaffection it entailed, it could hardly be otherwise. Exercise of private conscience was out of the question, could never have been other than political and military "desertion", duly punishable according to the harsh laws of warfare. Whether it ought to continue so in a totally contrasted order of things remains a deep issue for Islam, seeing that a faith an adherent is not utterly free to interrogate and leave becomes at once a spiritual prison and forfeits all claim to honest credence. Yet the "treason" notion in "apostasy" strongly persists in many quarters in Islam and – as in the ambiguity of Surah 49.14 – complicates the very meaning of "Islam" and "Muslim".

More perplexingly, does the structure both of mind and realm, to which the Hijrah pointed and which its sequel minted, mean that – since Muslims ought only to be ruled by Muslims – their faith is a *regio/religio* that must, wherever possible, disqualify all non-Islamic rule, religious or secular? In its confident form that was the fact of *Dar al-Islam*, "the régime of Islam", as opposed to the not-yet Islamized *Dar al-Harb*, "the realm of conflict", needing to be brought into the former by the effort of Jihad. Such was for long the classic scheme of things – the sure, imperative and assertive form of pronounal usage in Islam, the "we" and "us" of a religion with polity by right and polity exclusively religious by the norm of the Qur'an and the *Shari'ah*.

By the middle centuries some modifying need came into view, suggesting, perhaps, some *Dar al-Sulh*, an "order of armistice", where Jihad might be in sanguine or sullen abeyance, where diplomacy and commerce could proceed between Islam and, for example, European non-Islam.[13]

Theory might then be laid aside but could it be so congenially for the Islamic mind? Was it only a piece of pragmatism "for the time being"? It is noteworthy, inside the great schism of Islam, the Sunni and Shi'ah, how both parties assumed a partisan *Dar al-Islam* doctrine, requiring their due form of faith and polity. In their frequent minority and subject role, the Shi'ah developed their concept of *Taqiyyah*, intriguingly adapting to a Sunni *Dar al-Islam* situation. For *Taqiyyah* meant a *pro tem* "docility" in somewhat *dhimmi*-style (though as confident Muslims in their own eyes), with the vital difference that their "submission" to a régime they inwardly disavowed was only as and until they could successfully overthrow it. They were, so to speak, positive "dissemblers" in that they never recognized the régime in their hearts, while waiting for occasion of some "hijrah" out of it, not in exile but in revolt. In fealty they were positioning themselves for the possibility of achieving their own version of *Dar al-Islam*, as did the Fatimid Caliphate in Cairo and the Safavids in Iran. Thus the schism in Islam was not about the emulation of the Meccan Hijrah: it was about the identity of the right Medina they must reach. There were many lesser exponents of the (revised) rubric that Muslims should only be ruled by the right Muslims. That principle, asserted very early in Islam by the Khawarij, remained a fertile source or ground of insurrection and instability in Islamic societies.[14]

How right the calendar was to date "the years of the Hijrah" from that crucial transition. How expressive of Islam is the dictum that "after the Hijrah there was/is only Jihad". Yet what Jihad, as potentially or actually aligning "our faith" with "our world", via "our society", "our norms" "our effort", "our vision" and "our power"? All faiths have these ambitions implicit in their being faiths. Islam reached a distinctive programmatic to fulfil them in the categorical principle in its origin.[15]

Thus the destiny it gave itself[16] meant a purpose to be universal not only in carrying world-wide a theology with which it witnessed, but in governing world-wide by a divine law protected and upheld under the rule of a power-régime, the two inter-validated, the one by the other. Their unity is perhaps best captured in the term *Al-Ummah*, often translated – in a non-"national" sense – as "the Nation (of Islam)". It tells the comprehensiveness of Islam as being both faith institutionalized and institutionalized faith.

The word, which is readily pluralized into *ummam*, occurs more than fifty times in the Qur'an, often referring to different communities, tribes or peoples, fragmenting what had originally been "one humanity" (2.213 and 10.20). It is also used of "religious groups" (as of Noah 40.5, Abraham 16.120, Moses 7.159) where it is close to the term *millah*, later applied to the tolerated *dhimmis* with their religious identities in birth. Muslims, too (2.143), are an *ummah* (sing.) but with the adjective *wasatan*, or "in the middle". The sense is often taken to indicate "having the golden mean" of non-excess and moderation, disciplined but not ascetic, realist not romantic as to human nature.

While in 2.143 Islam is still "a nation" or "community" and the ethical meaning certainly holds, it may be allowed to take *ummatan wasatan* at least to symbolize "the faith-people" constituting the religion around which humankind is meant to centre. That would certainly fit the Muslim sense of having in possession the final revelation in the ultimate juncture of religious belief and political power, together resolving both for belief and practice the human enigma. "Truly religion as Allah would have it is Islam/*islam*" (3.19).[17] It is a conviction which powerfully underwrites the characteristic assurance of the Muslim *Ummah* in its relation to the world.

V

Yet this very unification, as the Hijrah presaged it and caliphal history forged it, of *Din* and *Dawlah*, in the *Ummah* of Islam as the one faith-dominion, leaves open the question of compatibility with the world-scene or with the human realism it saw as its great quality. Further, how far was it compatible with the unfettered sovereignty of Allah?

There are aspects here that must be deferred to CHAPTER ELEVEN. In present context of Islam's solidarity, as a profound collective experience across great human diversity, we need to ask exactly how the ethos we have examined, via the Hijrah, belongs with common humanity and how it befits the sovereignty of God. Let the sovereignty come first for exposition though the two "interests" interlock.

It would be one thing, as first in Mecca, to proclaim by witness that God has granted the final revelation and directly recruited witness to it – primarily His "messenger" and duly his responsive hearers. Will it not be quite another to hold that He has endowed that "word of truth" with a power-régime deputed and authorized to sustain it and require it universally in the world? Faith-witness could duly claim a universal writ. With the power-sanction of political force it could not do so. For thus its witness would cease to be witness. Legitimate power on its behafl would transform it into imposition. It would thus be flouting the actual quality of witness as being invitation. Further it would be arrogating the sovereignty of God by annexing it to its own truth system. Let "the Spirit of truth" be understood to preside over a faith's reception in the human whole. It will then be innocent of constraint other than a free will to faith.

God cannot well be assumed to operate through an institution politically in place to effectuate His will, unless this instrument finds a conscience self-critical enough to leave room for divine participation, not if it understands and wields its power as self-sufficing in *Ummah*, *Shari'ah* and *Dawlah* terms. For then it usurps divine prerogative.

Are there not, somehow, things that must be "left to Allah", however disconcertingly for the dogmatic and collective mind? If so, will they not be more suited to divine correction in the pre-Hijrah, rather than in the post-Hijrah terms? To be too confidently entrusted to a power-complex is to have faith the more prey than otherwise to the chronic pretention or ambition of religions.

In an illuminating study of the Hijrah, Zakaria Bashier asks why there were no *munafiqun*, no hypocritical "dissemblers", in the Meccan period.[18] It was because, Islam being weak and opposed, "there was no need for hypocrisy", whereas, in Medina "to be a Muslim was to ride the winning horse". He further wonders

> about the wisdom of restraining the Muslims from fighting in self-defence throughout the Meccan period . . . Perhaps it was that Islam needed a period of time in which to establish itself peacefully and on the merit of its own intrinsic spiritual and moral strength, without the further support of military force.[19]

Bashier finds the Hijrah and its Medinan sequel dramatically changing that order of things but does not then ask about "intrinsic merit". Passive resistance in Mecca had merely been the best policy where confrontation – witness apart – had been impracticable. Further, Islam, unlike any other religion, lays down clear and unambiguous claim to government. It must follow that the divine sovereignty will be politically committed to a kind of proxy for its writ, constituted by the power-agency of Islam. This apparent unison between what Allah wills and that Islam rules seems confirmed when the same writer adds:

> Non-Muslim societies will never accept, nor enable, a truly conscious Muslim – a Muslim who is fully aware of his identity as Muslim – to realise the ideals of Islam.

It is a "false hope" to be exposed as "fantasy" that "a full Muslim (could) be accepted in a non-Muslim society".[20] He is here in line with the view that requires any such "stranded" Muslim to emigrate back into a *Dar al-Islam*, faith-wise and state-wise.

Happily this reading is far from unanimous among Muslims today yet it conveys the heavy identification of the sovereignty Allah means to exert with the role of Islamic power. On other premises this must seem a usurpation of it if not also an idolatry.[21]

The work cited goes on to make a very Zionist-type case for which there is no power without a state and no state without a territory on which to base it, no territory without force to defend it, no adequate force without state and land to gird it. All these in sequence the Hijrah afforded Muhammad and Islam. While the first Pledge of ʿAqabah sought only that Yathrib be taught the faith, the second undertook a physical defence of it. The sequence between the two Pledges captures the whole logic that invites witness into power.[22] Does Islamic statehood in these terms truly leave room for "letting God be God"?

The other concern has to do with the human realism that asks whether Islam responds fittingly to the way humans are and whether its *Dar al-Islam* "governance" provides the apt context for which human nature calls. The theme which plays a significant part in the communal quality of Islam turns on the double sense of *fitrah*, notably in Surah 30.30. *Fitrat-Allah* reads as "the nature on which Allah "natured" (or "fashioned") humankind, using the verb *fatara* which is cognate to the noun. It has been understood to mean a "natural" fusion between human nature and the faith of Islam. In the context Muhammad is enjoined to "set his face towards religion as a *hanif* " with the rest in apposition. Islam, culminating what those *hunafa*ʾ anticipated, is "right" for humankind and humans are "ripe" for Islam.

There is, to be sure, a case arguable from human nature that humans stand in need of authority in guidance and régime in life, of an intelligible interpretation of the world with a discipline to match the clues it offers. The Qurʾan itself asks pointedly: "Does man think that he is left on the loose?" (75.36). But is the view too sanguine that sees our humanness congenially religious in Muslim terms and those terms suited to our nature in the structured form Islam ordains?

What humans need, and religions need to afford them, has been endlessly debated. The offered websites either way are tangled as we saw in CHAPTER THREE. *In situ*, pre-Hijrah Mecca seemed to demonstrate that human nature stood in need of what Medina provided by régime and power. Yet, in that provision, crypto-Muslims too readily appeared, "their designs aided by the fact that it is very easy to become a Muslim".[23] Sincerity, being "honest before God in religion", is not simple to come by, as the Qurʾan repeatedly stresses in the plea for *ikhlas* and vigilance against self-deceit. There was a mosque of "dissension" (*al-ghurur*) burnt down by Muhammad's orders in Medina in the year of Tabuk (9.107–8). History, Muslim and all other, is eloquent enough that there is no way of politicizing humankind into goodness, vital as "governance" must be, while "governance" itself finds no exemption from the bane of subterfuge and insincerity. The amenability of human nature to religious tutelage is a knotty issue whatever the auspices presiding to achieve it.

Furthermore, the power sanction prompts renegades to emulate it. Around the fourth year of the Hijrah, after the indecisive engagement of Uhud, a segment of people in Medina, perhaps led by ʿAbdallah ibn Ubayy who resented the *Ansar*, thought to starve out the immigrants by boycott, adding: "Those who have the muscle (are the stronger) will drive out the weaker" (Surah 63.7–8). Muhammad's advent to Yathrib having been negotiated only with some of its inhabitants, even his honourable tenure there could perhaps be reversed by the power means to which he had adapted their city. Human nature seems prone to find political power proper to wield in its own hands than to concede its exercise by others. Endless debates around that paradox still engage all belief-systems. They belong elsewhere among "Faiths Pronoun-Users Now".

There is a deeper question still as to realism about human nature as an asset – or the lack of it a debit – for religions. It aligns closely with the Mecca/Medina sequence. Bluntly, it asks: "Ought not religion to stay witnessing in whatever its Mecca sets for it?" Must it not be only and always an activity of persuasion by dint of its mental and moral content alone? The instincts of Islam will veto the idea. For was not the fruit of the Hijrah in the eventual capitulation of Meccan paganism the very zenith of success? Doubt and untruth were banished from their stubborn bastion and the true light shone. Paganism was vanquished. Realists need have no doubt where their realism should take them.

The claim needs respect. Yet there is the inner issue as to the nature of the interplay between authority and conviction, between the "what" and the "why" of faith-allegiance. Sincere and intelligent faith can only well be reciprocal to a truth that has sought acceptance in terms duly deferential to those qualities. The authority that deserves to be trusted has to deserve the trust it expects. If it is to merit a worthily religious submission to its meanings it needs to merit what it seeks by submitting them in worthily religious form, free of all sanction save the witness they bring. This will not be the case if its claims are such as connive with human fear, or opportunism, or gullibility, or prudence, or perverse ambition.

There are accents in the Qurʾan that are clearly alert to this. "There is no (need for) compulsion in religion" because "the right has been clearly distinguished from the false" (2.256). There were two occasions (4.82 and 47.24)[24] when Muhammad plainly sensed the "hard-going" of the way of preaching witness. "Do they not reflect on the Qurʾan or is it that there are locks upon their hearts?" The realism to know it so in the task of persuasion is only counterpart to the realism that knows humankind – out of an innate faculty of selfhood – finds truth most surely in a patient gentleness.[25] If "truth makes free" it can hardly do so out of some bondage of its own.

Even so, it seems fair to say that those who, as in post-Hijrah Islam, are reassured in finding truth compatible with a power-structure enjoining it, also find a strong sense of community generated by that partnership. *Din* and *Dawlah* underwrite an *Ummah* that is at once a religious system of creed with code and a body politic dispensing law and ritual. A truth system that is freely open to interrogation, as being also dependent on persuasion, may have a looser cohesion. The contrasted pattern of religio-political order will be more liable to generate comparably absolutist sects.

The carving out of Pakistan and Bangladesh (first West and East Pakistan) from the sub-continent of India at mid-twentieth century was a salient example of "Hijri" Islam, a costly assertion of the will to Islamic statehood as the only right expression of Muslim identity, rather than participation in a multi-communal India. A "Hijrah" was made, though for many in panic and despair, not from the sort of situation experienced by the first Muslims in Mecca, but from the prospect of permanent minority status among dominant Hindus, albeit – then – offering a "secular" order for a co-existence of religious diversity.[26] The two Muslim States withdrawing from that concept may have been pragmatic in doubting its viability but they were also giving eloquent expression to what the original Hijrah exemplified, namely that the destiny of Islam stood in the quest for power. They were pleading the principle that "after the Hijrah there is only Jihad": or, rather, renewed Hijrah was the form Jihad would have to take.

In practical terms, for the Muslim League and its leader, Muhammad Ali Jinnah, the policy for Pakistan proved a massive evocation of communal fervour. Through all its birth-tragedy and long anguish about its Islamicity, Pakistan has signified how deeply Hijrah, power and iden-tity-awareness belong together across the long centuries.

VI

There is a large irony, however, to be briefly noted here and belonging more immediately to CHAPTER ELEVEN. It has to do with the fact that perhaps an entire quarter of the world's Muslims today find themselves in a Hijrah of dispersion, not in quest of power that could be made Islamic, but in exit out of one that was, or – in the case of Muslims in present-day India – in consent to remain where it could never be had. Muslims in Europe and the West have no feasible anticipations of creating Pakistans. With Indian Muslims they are in a Meccan situation (hopefully without its dire vulnerability) but with no "pledge of 'Aqabah", sought or given, that might admit of their emulating Muhammad, in sequel to their migration, as insistent state-builders.

All is a strangely un-Islamic kind of transition and does something quite revolutionary to the feel of Muslims saying "We" and "us" and "our", as crucial pronouns of all discourse.[27] What is revolutionary may oddly be also salutary. For it means that – back symbolically in Mecca – Muslim community awareness, no longer sustained by statehood, has to locate itself in the ever availing ritual of *Salat*, and Ramadan and Hajj, while accommodating to the norms of citizenships which, though seeming to jeopardize all that Islam "ought to be", require it to become a different Islam.

What, then, is a "European Muslim", "a British Muslim", "an American Muslim", or by any other denominator of what is now a far-flung dispersion? It is not that Muslims have now come into some *dhimmi* condition. Though citizenship is open to participation they have to respond both in thought and practice to minority situations affording them no classic Medina.[28] The Muslim pronoun plural for them is the "we" of rite and culture, of mosque and *shahadah*, of occasions they will not, in the old way, regulate and control, but may freely and creatively discover, thrown back in the process on the resources a new *Ijtihad* can identify and a new *taqwa* redeem.

CHAPTER EIGHT

The "We" and the "I" in the New Testament

I

Near the opening of Shakespeare's *Macbeth* there is an exchange between the King Duncan and the two returning campaigners in the field. Could we lift it quite out of the play's martial – and sinister – setting and read the two men as one, it would well fit the pronounal situation in the New Testament. Duncan's greeting ran:

"I have begun to plant thee, and will labour
To make thee full of growing . . ."

The garden analogy seems somewhat odd but he continues:

". . . Let me enfold thee and hold thee to my heart . . ."

and Banquo's answer comes:

"There, if I grow, the harvest is thine own."[1]

If Shakespeare's imagery was not here at its usual perfection, soul-culture, thus doubly pledged, exactly suits the Christian discipleship of the Gospels and the Letters of the evangelists and the apostles, in fealty to their Lord.

They are a literature full of the personal pronoun – the "me" and "mine" of Jesus in the Fourth Gospel, the "I will follow thee" of the naïve recruit, the "my Lord and my God" of the maturing Thomas. The early spread of Christianity, we may fairly say, was a progress across human frontiers and morally into new dimensions of personhood. It practised both the travelling arts of hospitality and the pastoral arts of nurture out of pagan bewilderments into disciplined belief and life.

On both counts it needed to be epistolary, making a habit of the pronoun that greeted, saluted and embraced the new neighbourhood of society in Christ. Its deepest "letter-treatise", that of Paul to Romans, concludes its ripe theology with a pressing list of names, where a flow of "and also's" seems unwilling to break off because omission would be unseemly.[2] The pronouns "thee" and "thou", "we" and "ours", possessive, persistent and always relational, were the strings of its music. Even the obscurest of its Letters, that of 3 John, bids its recipient – in place as a local host and leader – concerning his transiting guests: "You must speed them on their journey worthily of God".[3] It seems clear enough that the growth of office and then hierarchy in the Church's ministry was owed, in part, to this practice of guest-receiving and farewelling across the Mediterranean world. For, in a climate of spying and persecution, the valid membership needed to be verified by "letters credent" and who should issue and check these if not some recognized "president" of local worth and status? The word "commend" became so familiar a usage as to be applied to what God had done in Christ, as where His love might be verified in a world given to much suspicion against its possibility. So closely were doctrine and practice intertwined.

II

It is with this plural unity to which the very textual shape of the New Testament witnesses, as memoirs about Jesus communally required and Letters shepherding their diversity as inside an apostolic unity, that we must begin – the impressive "we-ness" of the Scripture. It had to happen. How could that rigorous exceptionality of an ethnic peoplehood persist beyond the recognition of its admirable historic mission? "You shall speed it on its destiny worthily of God", as 3 John 6 might have phrased it. For "worthily of God" was the right criterion, recommended in CHAPTER THREE as apt to apply to those intrinsic decisions by which a faith might test itself.

How could it be "worthy of YAHWEH" that so blessed a vocation-in-covenant could remain forever the exclusive prerogative of one identity, a single race, an erstwhile tribe of nomadic families? Might it for ever exclusify the mandate to "bless all nations" and argue that these "all" would need to accept their "benediction" in terms that made them never eligible for some like vocation to which, while in no way rescinding the pioneer one, they could never aspire? Were they to remain forever the passive recipients of a largesse unilaterally monopolized? Was there to be no way by which they too could "bring their glory and honour" into the divine employ?

The liveliest in Hebraic prophethood itself had sensed there was an urgent need to de-monopolize and de-ethnicize the heritage of Israel and contemplate servanthoods to God parallel – if only partially – to their own. "My salvation to the ends of the earth", was the sense of things for the Isaiah of 48:6, with his cry: "Listen, O isles', of which there were none in Israel land.

Yet that sense of the wideness of the human world, as we saw in CHAPTER FOUR, was always under the proviso that only via the Hebrew agency could the blessing come or the vision be served. There was always the double bind that the universal could never escape the necessity of the one particular, seeing that only the particular was warranted with the message. All must "seek unto the Jew".[4] One might observe that it remained the same with the Christian Church in that the Gospel it uniquely possessed was universally given and received only on its terms. The radically different factor, however, was that the indispensable agency was in no way itself an ethnic "race" but a people in whose "messenger status" all could participate in what thus became a conditionless integration where land and speech and tribe and culture were equally participant. Baptism, unlike circumcision, was not a bodily ritual transacted in the very flesh as a seal of "flesh participation". The Christian "word" was – as Jude 3 had it – "a vernacular salvation".[5] The inner secret of "people-hood in God" was surely, by its own inherent logic, destined to be a vernacular dignity open to all the dialects and diversities of humankind, thanks to an inclusive master-narrative that had incorporated each and all in a kind of "exodus" for "the bones" of all the Josephs of this world, for every Moses of a "native" vintage.[6]

The sense of this discernible destiny out of privacy with YAHWEH came convincingly to birth in the context of the ministry of Jesus of Nazareth and found its adulthood in the early Church as the direct consequence of what the Cross had signified both as to God and humankind.

Our first task in tracing the story of this "we-ness" in Christ has to go to his work and words in Galilee, to his parables and proverbs, the sayings and incidents of his itinerant teaching prior to their climax in Jerusalem. Of his emphatic Jewishness there was never any doubt. It is well that in the growing twentieth-century interest in Jesus the fact should have been stressed with proper, and learned, emphasis. With that welcome partnering of scholarship around the New Testament, and the correctives it has brought (for example, to perceptions of the Pharisees) thanks to Jewish scholars overcoming the reluctance many had earlier felt about a Jesus monopolized by Christians, much has been gained.

"Jewishness", however, is a very flexible denominator and that of Jesus had distinctive features which carried over into the nascent Christianity of its highly Jewish originals in the authorship of the New Testament. That feature, which was noted in CHAPTER ONE about the psalmist of the 139th, of an inclusive human quality, likewise characterized the sundry parables of Jesus. There was no point in asking about the sower with his seed or the wayward son and the grieving father, or the idle labourers in the market-place, whether these are Jews or "Gentiles". The women seeking a lost coin from her necklace could well be Palestinian/Canaanite.

The shepherd with the one lost from the hundred, like the others, is an inclusive figure.

Thanks to the Jewish ban on usury, there is something needing that context in the story of the "steward", skilfully handling a well-known bit of evasive tactic in the loan-lending of fictitious purchases.[7] But the canniness is universal. Where distinctions were significantly made, it was "the priest and levite" who "passed by on the other side", fearing ritual contamination or travel delay, and the Samaritan who had compassion. Otherwise, the characters in these stories behave as all humans do. There could be situations highly local, as when insurrectionist land-tenants sought to oust landlords from their absentee ownerships but the tactics, which all hearers then understood at once, were such as all humans can contrive. The fishing nets might be those of Galilee where Jesus was among fisher-folk, but the sorting of the catch had no inevitable Jewish label. Just as Abraham Heschel could ask "Who is Man?" and answer with a lyrical book, so Jesus could no less readily find the Jewish in the human and not confine the human to the Jewish.[8]

When, as in his "retreat" into "the coasts of Tyre and Sidon" and – encountering a "Syrophenician woman" – his Jewishness was promptly at issue, what the situation said to her instinctively was something she was invited or coaxed into recognizing as the only way in which it could be transcended. Then, in the outcome to her petition, transcended it was. Only so could the Jew/"Gentile" divide be – not ignored – but overcome. It was likewise in the Johannine story of the woman at the well, at the rendezvous with the disputed possession of "our father Jacob". Such was the nature of the situation, in either case, that it could only be unravelled from the Jewish side. Jewish self-possession had made it so down the long centuries, insofar as it inferiorized all other identities so that these felt embarrassed by its distinctive-ness. It can only be – if we may use the term – from within the "Semitism" that the non-Semitic can be "equalized" in its presence. Initiatives can well be ventured from both sides but the Jewish one has, by definition, the larger reach for magnanimity. Such magnanimity was at the heart of Jesus' teaching and practice.

It reached into a universal humanness in another realm – that of the renegade Jew, the so-called "publicans" with their Latinized names and their profiteering collusions with the Empire, "Sons of Abraham" still, birthwise but not otherwise, and needing to be reclaimed such by new-birthing into grace. There was much scandal to be incurred when Jesus invited himself to be Zaccheus' guest with a crowded street in earshot. "The friend of tax-gatherers and sinners" signalled what a different thing "Jewishness" might be.[9]

The "Matthew" of that Gospel is clearly minded to present Jesus as a new Moses, gathering together into one corpus his sayings as "the sermon on the mount", with twelve disciples called round him to symbolize "the tribes of Israel". The evangelist is carefully preserving, as his heritage, the vital sense of peoplehood but one now constituted beyond particular birth and clan – those disciples with their Greek-formed names present in the act of personal discipleship as the ground of their audition. And, like the parables, those Beatitudes stay for no criteria of race or clanship, being exclusively ethical descriptives. There is at once an enormous debt to a crucial Hebrew theme of "chosen people" yet, with it, a clear emancipation. There is even, in the "reviling and the persecuting" they are warned of, an echo of what the old "chosen-ness" too had undergone. The transformed continuity is evident as "a new testament".

To be sure, there was a necessary confinement of the Jesus ministry, brief in years and – for the most part – severely local in setting. As holding within itself a hard initiative, it could not fail to be caught in constant tension with the rigorism it challenged. There are evident signs of this in the Gospels. The newness did not make its way blissfully and unscathed. For entrenched establishment was being challenged. But "the lie of the land" is there for all to see and "the common people heard gladly", sensing their open participation in a liberating hope. Likewise, the scruples and "murmurings" of ruling authority came into sharp contention with it. For there were occasions enough over the ritual – as opposed to the compassionate – Sabbath; over a teaching that relied on inner credentials and did not cite scripted "sayings"; over readings of divine ways and how "forgiveness" might avail.

When, in reading the Gospels we now have, we have made all due allowance for their matrix in the bosom of the nascent Church, there are no legitimate misgivings that deprive us of a broad, reliable delineation of a teaching "Christhood".[10] Moreover, it remains the central informant even of those who are minded to jettison its witness altogether. Thus the ultimate situation as to the written New Testament entails, at one and the same time, a necessary commitment of faith and a sober satisfaction in such commitment. Those who have come to believe in the authenticity of its "new peoplehood" may find themselves well sustained by the Christ of Galilee.

III

But the pronoun "we" minted by that peoplehood owed itself supremely to the Cross and Passion of its Lord. Beyond the human inclusiveness of Jesus' teaching lay the world-incorporating meaning of his suffering Messiahship. It was in being thus "lifted up" that he "drew all to him", all, that is, not in the "magnetism" being somehow irresistible (that would violate the liberty of the soul) but in its being everywhere accessible, not withheld for any reason other than individual refusal.[11] That Johannine sense of things was, of course, sequential to the sort of event – in faith's eyes – the Cross of Jesus had been. Inasmuch as the Church itself came to be the Church that way, the reading rightly told it in those theological terms. Was it not that way with all the Christological formulae as to "the Son's sending", his "coming down from heaven", his being "the Lamb slain from before the foundation of the world?" All were contingent on the actuality in real time and place seen as requiring to be stated that way, by a stating that reached back into the entire hinterland of Hebrew theology as to creation, covenant, and Messianic hope.

Those phrases, feeling far into eternal provenance and realizing their fulfilment in a crucified Messiah, could not fail to interpret it onward and outward into the wide world. It was not of an order to be privatized in Israel as other conceivings of Messiah had been. The love it was seen to prove was of a "world" and about a "whoso-ever". Had Jesus been a private Messiah he might have led a chosen few into the wilderness to live so purely as to merit in a perfect Sabbath the intervention of "the son of man", or perhaps an apocalyptic deliverer rewarding their devotion. No "into all the world" could then have ensued.

Likewise had the awaited one chosen to be political and insurrectionist, making national liberation his destined task – a "salvation" faulted by its lack of depth and realism. As the disciples came to read their Master's mind, none of these could be "the cup his Father gave him". They had, indeed, been options presented to his ministry, whether as inner tests of will, or by things at issue with the "authorities", and even through the misconceptions of disciples. Jesus' reckoning with them in decisive rejection came to be, increasingly, the meaning of his "Sonship".[12] Only so was the Messiahship finalized in his Passion as being cumulatively present from the outset.

Thus the ultimate fulfilment of the hope of Israel would be realized in Jesus crucified as "light to lighten the nations". Luke captured the truth of it in his story of "the song of Simeon", celebrating "light to the nations" and "the glory of Israel" – in that order. "The glory" that would always abide came from the universal light, and dual theme of the "eyes seeing salvation" and discerning it as "prepared before the face of all peoples". The old man's song, by Luke's genius, served to herald the whole logic with which the early Church knew itself bent outwards to the world, needing a new "we" for its pronoun.

CHAPTER THREE tried to trace that logic in the event of why and how Jesus came to, and through, the Cross – the event which fused into another – the corroborative perception of its redemptive meaning. These two-in-one as fact and significance made the Church to have a Gospel and made the Gospel to take the Church. If we follow the "light" metaphor, it was as if there happened a kind of incandescence between the two events where a burning and a glowing meet as one. The *why* of the Cross had to do with how wrong the human world could be as represented in the will to it: the *how* was there in that "Father, forgive . . ." inclusive in the same world-wide way as the evil, too, had been. What was expressive in the one of the whole world's capacity for sin was representative in the other of the heart of God. A Messiah world-wide in those terms required to be taken world-wide by the community of recognition that knew it for what it was. And "the community of recognition of the Cross" is the surest definition of the Church and, accordingly, the meaning of the Resurrection.

It is important to realize that the commissions about "going into the world" in Mark and Matthew were being impulsively obeyed long before they were verbally formulated in those (cf. Matthew 28:19) Trinitarian terms – terms only doctrinally reached after the obedience had been under way some decades and only formulated thanks to the process itself. For it is clear that those shapes of confessional faith came only in the sequel of its self-interpretation. This plainly waited for and waited on the enterprise of telling the founding story. "He came down from heaven", "the only begotten in the bosom of the Father", "and the Word was God" – these and kindred language about the birth of a child and the mind and ministry of a man came only *after* birth, mind and ministry had historically occurred. For only so could they have come to be understood as eternally true in God. Christology was a sequel to experience in time and place as telling where these had found their source.[13]

IV

The growth of faith and Church together into this open-ness, this new people-making "we", was both spontaneous and difficult. There were massive obstacles to be overcome, scrupulous sources of reluctance and misgiving to be negotiated. There are also many hazards in tracing the story. For the documentation is tantalizingly silent on many points scholarship strains to penetrate. We need to try to listen to the silences. What is not in doubt is that the break-out from the old privacies YAHWEH's people believed He cherished happened and happened decisively in the Jewish apostolic quest for "the Gentiles" as those who would be no more such in the old sense of not being "the people of God". Whatever the silences hold beyond our sure hearing, whether of tensions between Jerusalem and the widening diaspora, or the pros and cons of continuing circumcision, the new "peoplehood" was born.

If we can rely on the author of the Acts of (some) Apostles it seems to have occurred in a spontaneous way with unknown disciples in Cyprus and elsewhere taking "Greeks and Gentiles" into the inclusiveness of Christ. Then there was the historic decision of the Council in Jerusalem that circumcision was not to be binding on non-Jews joining the fellowship. For the old "peoplehood" in YAHWEH this was no easy verdict. Cherished privilege seldom relinquishes its status without qualms and controversy. The pain of these is evident enough in the conflicts Saul/Paul had in his own inner being. For he resorts to a strange complex of arguments, both Midrashic and "Gentile" to warrant a decision that cost him dearly both in soul and society.[14]

The assured Pauline case was told in the Letter to the Ephesians (2.12–19) in assurance to those "who were in time past Gentiles in the flesh" – as Tyndale renders it:

> without Christ and reputed aliens from the commonwealth of Israel and fremde (strangers) from the testaments of promise . . . now in Christ Jesus ye which awhile ago were far off, are made nigh by the blood of Christ. For he is our peace who hath made of both one and hath broken down the wall in the middes that was a stop between us and has put away, through his flesh the wall of hatred . . . for to make of twain one new man in himself, so making peace; and to reconcile both in one body through his cross, and slew hatred thereby: and came and preached peace to you which were far off and to them that were nigh. For through him we both have access unto the Father. Now, therefore, ye are no more strangers and foreigners but citizens with the saints and of the household of God.

The accomplished unity of the new society could not be clearer, the incorporating "we" unequivocal. We have to say, in tune with Robert Frost:

> Something there is (grace) that doesn't love a wall,
> But sends the living ground-swell under it,
> And heaves the stubborn boulders quite away.[15]

In the different Petrine idiom of the First Letter of Peter it is much the same. Tyndale again:

> Ye as living stones are made a spiritual house and a holy priesthood for to offer spiritual sacrifice acceptable to God . . . ye are a chosen generation, a royal priesthood and a peculiar people that you should show the virtues of him who has called you out of darkness into his marvellous light, who in time past were not a people, yet are ye now the people of God, which were not under mercy but now are under mercy. (1 Peter 2:5 and 9–10)

He uses the very descriptives about a "holy nation and a royal priesthood" which were formerly the sole prerogative of Jewry. It is as if their being "in Christ" means that he, Christ, has become to them precisely what the old Temple had once been to its solitary nation. Revelation 5:10 has the same theme of an inclusive people "made (to be) unto God kings and priests", thus able and warranted to serve in terms of the "new covenant" the vocation of the old, now no longer ethnic. How dramatically in its several doxologies that same Revelation (almost tediously some might think) insists on piling up its synonyms: "Thou wast slain and hast redeemed us to God by thy blood out of every kindred and tongue and people and nation" (5:9) all "bringing their glory and honour" into that citizenry (21:24).

It is intriguing to note in the First Epistle of John – a letter with only one hundred and five verses – how its embracing "we" occurs no less than sixty-five times, with "us" in just half that telling frequency, even though part of the time its "John" is addressing as "ye" the same folk. The Letter is clearly blessedly aware of interior identity as a thing undoubted. "We have known and believed . . .", "we know we are in him . . .", "we know that the Son of God has come . . .". For both writer and reader, conviction has made community and community confirmed conviction. The personal pronoun plural was indispensable to the confession of the faith.

What is often overlooked in contemporary concerns around Jewish/Christian relations is that this crucial widening of "chosen people" destiny into "chosen peoples" was entirely the work of Jewish apostles. The entire text of the New Testament – albeit in Greek and not in Hebrew[16] – was the work of Jewish pens, with the sole exception of the Greek, Luke. It was not that tedious "Gentiles" invaded the privileged status out of curious envy – though there were large numbers of non-Jewish *proselutoi*[17] who yearned for inclusion in it or were attracted by its ethical monotheism. Far from being an invasive take-over or subversion, it was a generous extension, a hospitality inspired by the coming together of two related factors, namely the perception of Jesus as the crucified Messiah and, with it, the dawning sense of a vocation to share themselves as "chosen" with all who would realize, with them, the intertwining of these two realities.

It follows that the validity of the inclusion of the "Gentiles" in Christ proceeds not from some abrogation or forfeiture of essential Jewishness but from a positively Hebraic decision about its nature. To be sure, it was one which other Jews feared, suspected and finally rejected. In its decisive making, it had to do with a deep interrogation – as between these two readings – of the very nature of Jewishness, and not, as many would prefer to find it, a sorry surrender of all that Jewishness meant and was set to go on meaning.

Inevitably, this widening into "chosen peoples" entailed heavy social costs and temperamental pains – not least among them the abrogation of necessary circumcision for inclusion in this "new Jewry-in-Christ". That "mark in the flesh", hitherto so imperative, had long been a sharp deterrent for Greeks and Romans who had sensed the appeal of Hebrew religion but had baulked at a degrading violation of their body, "the badge of the tribe". When it could be seen as no longer any *sine qua non*, the access which its abeyance allowed into the desirable moral assets of Jewish religion was earnestly welcome to many as the spread of the Gospel attested.

Thus there ensued, not a taking-over by "Gentiles" but their "taking-into" by Jewish apostolic hospitality of mind and word. Faith alone would be the sufficient access into new "peoplehood" called to inherit and pursue the Abrahamic "mission" of the old "world-benediction" as both recipients and participating purveyors. For, while the Gospel was historically an opening-out of a Judaic benison to the world, it was essentially an inclusive human heritage happening that way.[18]

This reading of a Jewish verdict about its destiny, explicit in the very making of the New Testament, came only in the context of a sharp and aggravating dispute around it, stressed as it was by intensifying factors in the psyche and the locale. The Jewish thinking in its genesis seemed to other Jewish minds both aberrant and renegade. No Jew could ever read a mandate in his Jewishness to forego its exceptionality in the will of YAHWEH. In their minds the trust of the privilege could only, and for ever, be unilateral, a destiny never to be foreseen. Had not centuries of tribulation paid for its preservation? Was it not enshrined in the immutability of the Lord who had bestowed it on the fathers and their seed?

In the event, tragically by the turn of the first (common era) century the Christian Church came to seem to be a very "Gentile" thing. The reasons were accelerated by the Jewish Revolt of the sixties and the Fall of Jerusalem in 70. As noted in CHAPTER THREE, Jewry clung around Torah and synagogue and the Rabbis in the trauma of the loss of the Temple. Those reasons, however, also had some affinity with the crucifixion itself, inasmuch as the issues that had been raised by the authorities concerning Jesus extended also into the implications of "believing in his Name". Moreover, the Cross, for "official" Jewry, had been the supreme divine disavowal of Jesus as "Messiah". They had no mind, therefore, to approve or allow a community affirming it to have been the supreme divine insignia of Messiahship.

The New Testament document itself bears many marks, carries many echoes, of the resulting tensions. It is well that it should. For it could hardly honestly be the document of that decisive "opening-out" of heritage Judaic and not be also evidence to its tribulations. Modern scholarship could wish that the data were far more complete and traceable, around – for example – the ethos of the Letter of James and the entire *mise-en-scène* of what the historic Council in Jerusalem in Acts tells with such brevity. The personality of Paul is, of course, the sharpest locus of the stakes involved. He labours strenuously both in Romans and Galatians to vindicate his confidence that in becoming a Christian apostle he remains a loyal Jew and that the irrevocable covenant with his people abides in perpetuity inside its "Christian" fulfilment. That confidence has its sharply latent perplexities we had better face in the setting of a final CHAPTER ELEVEN.

His experience, three times related in The Book of Acts, certainly captures the heart of the matter, namely the contentiously Messianic identity of Jesus crucified. It was this he was "pursuing" in anger en route to Damascus – the butt of his persecuting zeal. The vision and the voice on the road – from their celestial origin – seemed to belong with Saul's intent to disown the Christian travesty concerning who and how "the Christ" should be. But when the voice said: "I am Jesus" Saul's whole world was shattered. *Where* the voice came from certainly denoted YAHWEH's "Messiah", but *whom* it identified upheld the entire Christian theme. The "pricks" metaphor suggests that his very zeal had been kindled by a fear that that theme might be true. For zeal is often excited in such paradox of convictions being undermined before they finally collapse. Those who fear to be dissuaded the more vehemently persuade themselves. According to the historian of the journey the "Gentile" mission was born in that encounter. It was to be the supreme biographical text of the entire New Testament "newness-in-openness". It was hardly strange that the struggle about the one should resolve so far around the other.

Yet, in its distinctive ethos, the Fourth Gospel is no less profound a witness to the things at stake. Its authorship is very carefully crafted to interpret the Jesus whose ministry underlay the Christology in which his ultimate meaning was being comprehended, yet a meaning already latent in the immediacies of Galilee and Jerusalem. In the evangelist's mind it was a meaning which could only be told in its final terms but those terms, nevertheless, set in the context from which they had emerged, i.e. the steady round of itinerary in word and deed.

Thus the reader needs to appreciate this John's design. He moves, in part, by a series of interviews contrived to illuminate and even transact the things at stake inside the scenes and episodes which the Synoptic Gospels handle in more directly narrative ways and with a degree of authorial in-reading less weighted than John's. Among the most pointed of John's interview scenes is that of the conversation with Nicodemus in Chapter 3. It brings into play, with "a ruler of the Jews", the personal dimensions of the radical initiative we have reviewed. It was no small comment – insult even – to inform such a one: "You must be born anew." For had not Jewish birth and lineage ensured "belonging to God"? The point the evangelist had made in 1:12 about birth into "the Kingdom" was "not of blood or paternity" but open to all by faith alone in the "becoming of the children of God". So Paul had already assured his Galatians (3:26–29). Nicodemus was being educated into the same meaning.

Little wonder that his perplexity, too, brought out the implications. It was not a matter of "undoing" original birth. For only there could the "newness" occur. Grace would recruit the man Nicodemus had always been, and would remain, but in the new idiom of the open Christ. John's logic in his Chapter 3 makes the very case apostolic action had already practised.

The story of the Samaritan woman makes the same point. The conversation between her and Jesus is full of subtle allusions and clearly owes much to the writer's conscious "drift" in the trust he has in the Jesus he is telling. A "foreigner", even a woman, becomes a receptive emissary to her own people who find her fully credible. Thus mission on the part of all and sundry is learned (by us) as being implicit in this "Saviour of the world". It is no longer a prerogative – as it was for the great Hebrew prophets[19] – of those "to the manner born".

Likewise in Chapter 9 this "John" presents us with a scenario reminiscent both of events in Galilee and attitudes in the early Church. There is dispute about the identity and the credentials of Jesus but now there are cryptic folk around, fence-sitting between the options, evading questions, "not wanting to be put out of the synagogue". The erstwhile Bartimaeus of Luke's narrative is used to illuminate the tense situation of the first Church in its diaspora. We readers are learning both the tensions and the cost of faith around this Jesus as this Christ, the two being presented in one in the bi-focal perspective of the Fourth evangelist. His point is supremely made in the cast he gives to the narrating of the Passion.

V

There are two final points to any honest study of the pronoun "we" in the New Testament – faith and text alike – before we move to the pronouns "I" and "me". The one is the strong concern the new faith had for the continuity of its debt to its Hebrew birthing. The other must be the temptations to which all insistent "we-ness" is prone, the liability to narrow into sharp sect-mentality. Both features of "we-ness" are evident inside the New Testament as a scripture. The second was tragically accentuated outside it in ensuing years.

Given the powerful emotions and tensions explicit in the story, it is remarkable how abidingly deferential, how instinctively grateful, the early Church was to and for its Hebrew roots, how solicitous for the gentle persuasion and careful cultivation of the traditional Hebrew mind. The pains it took to justify and commend the logic by which it re-assured the dubious that "Gentile" inclusion was no cavalier surrender of Jewish morals, no forfeiture of Judaic probity. There is a dark and dire element of calumny in the notion that the New Testament is a virulent seed-bed of anti-Semitism. In the light of evidences we must examine it never was so.

The most notable field of them is the Letter to the Hebrews. With an anonymous authorship and an uncertain destination, its very title exceptional,[20] it constitutes a deeply theological effort to present what, in Luke 24:27, is captured in the phrase: "Christ in all the Scriptures". It is clearly a powerful venture in careful persuasion of Judaic Christians into constancy in face of adverse pressures or of enquiring synagogue members hesitant about Christhoods. In a quite distinctive way it argues for "the Messianic Jesus" proved such in the steady, actual vicissitudes of his day-to-day ministry – a portrayal caught in the play on words in 5:8: *emathen epathen*, "He learned in that he suffered". By arguments that ring oddly in modern ears, the author is at pains to meet Jewish scruples, argue on Jewish lines and move Jewish loyalties towards what he sees as their due destination in the authentic Christhood of "this Jesus".[21]

His readers could find themselves still discipled to Moses if only in terms of the contrast drawn from him to define the role of Jesus. They could appreciate the whole priestly system of their erstwhile Temple[22] by its issue – as the writer sees it – into "the high-priesthood" of the crucified and ascended Christ, "ever living to make intercession". The Letter is exemplary in the art of "commendation" whereby where people have spiritually belonged and dwelt can be found to yield the very reasons why they should consent to "develop" beyond it into a larger soul-abode for which it was ultimately meant. Whether effectual or not in that concern, the solicitude in the case-making leaves us now in no doubt about the author's deference to, and earnestness for, the mind-set of his readers. He, therefore, bequeaths a salutary lesson for contemporary religious pluralism in the art of a communication that mediates, honest alike with past and future faith.

Distinctive as the Letter to the Hebrews will always remain, it serves to highlight what perhaps may be called the steady "Semitism" of the entire New Testament, the Scripture of communities in diaspora that cherished Hebraic psalmody, instinctively sought out and cited Biblical precedents, shaped its own "Jesus narratives" around proof-texts from psalm and prophet, and believed its new "Gentile" recruitments in sense and soul proper to the heritage that had embraced them. To be sure, possessiveness of things Hebraic could only seem perverse and provocative to those who repudiated the "Gentile" inclusion and vetoed its ground in any

Messiah crucified. For them, there could be nothing appropriate, still less conciliatory, in what to them – far from being right borrowings – could only be deplored and denounced as wanton thievings.

The blame for the bitterness of that controversy might – as very part of it – be laid angrily at the door of the initiative that made Jewish/"Gentile" Christians the new people they were. However, given that the controversy was explicit in the entire situation, the onus could equally well lie with those rejecting the logic that brought it to pass. The bitterness of that alternative locus of reproach has persisted through many centuries. Its long and tragic incidence in no way incriminates the creative initiative that was the making of the New Testament faith and text. For these proved, as far as that initiative allowed, their entire devotion to origins still dearly present in the newness they had embraced. There was a continuing "we" of the Hebraic in the wider, bolder "we" of the New Testament Church in the sense of a destiny not forfeited but fufilled, not abandoned but attained.

If we say "wider and bolder" must we not say "riskier"? If so, the word points to another area of keen solicitude for things Judaic inside the New Testament. It has to do with the "risk" of "Gentile" inclusion. What of those aspects of paganism that Jewry instinctively abhorred – idolatry, licensciousness, profanity? Were all these to be admissible – with these "Gentiles" – into the divine sanctuary? What of the moral antiseptic needed against Graeo-Roman obscenity? Was not the ethical law closely bound up with the ritual law, godliness with Sabbath, cleanliness with piety? Might abeyance of ritual-duty import negligence of discipline on all sides?

Such fears, readily registered by Jewish apostles in Christ, were carefully laid to rest by the lively moral disciplines of the New Testament Epistles where nurture in due behaviour turns squarely on doctrinal faith. "Forasmuch as . . ." "therefore present yourselves . . ." were the twin formulae. The old law would not be foregone: it would be subsumed into the new pastoral care of the Church in heir to the ethics of Jesus carefully preserved in the Gospels. Such could be the social re-assurance available to Jewish fears, lest the new openness humanly should imply some new compromise divinely.

Moreover, conceptually as well as actually, the ritual law (which Jewry itself forfeited in large measure in 70 CE) could be seen as the "pedagogue" conveying all believers to "the law of Christ".[23] Paul's argument was that the "end" (i.e. "goal" or "purpose") of the law was fulfilled in grace, whereby the "command" was transformed into a "love" that sustained what the law intended but achieved it by a different route – free of the old incubus of "merit", pride and self-esteem. Thus the resulting "we" of incorporation was no sanguine tolerance of incompatibles, no random human chaos, but a genuine peoplehood, radically wider but no less authentic than its original in "divine possession".

VI

What then, in New Testament context, of the snares and pitfalls of religious "we-ness"? Certainly the text betrays their presence. For no faith is immune from their laying in wait.

Two related characteristics throughout religious history identify the sectarian way. They are an intense interior cohesion and a strong self-differentiation from others. They demand a stern form of allegiance and practice of will to rigorous criteria of truth safely kept within them. These qualities, whether we see them as worthy or deplorable, are in some sense inseparable from the nature of religion itself, purporting to handle what is transcendent and absolute. Yet is it not the most hallowed of trusts – the care for ultimacy – that also suggests modesty, humility, even reticence, so that what might otherwise make for bigotry and obscurantism makes way for gentleness and sober witness?

The New Testament text is open about its own involvement in the hazards of a sectarian instinct. The sharpness of the issues joined between Judeo-cum-"Gentile" Christians and the strong partisans of the synagogue is evident enough in the Fourth Gospel. Sects tend to generate a temper responsive to their own, both inside the larger loyalty that would contain them and *vis-à-vis* rival faith systems. Powerful psychic factors intervene among the strictly doctrinal stakes and these – as in the Gospels – can be loaded with disputed history. Pauline and Petrine and Johannine directives to the churches are robust concerning things, moral or credal, held detrimental to honest faith, yet are also ready with such restraints as: "Count him not as an enemy" or "Receive him as thyself", since all are encompassed by human frailty.

The limits of mental tolerance are of course drawn by tolerance itself, inasmuch as it cannot endorse intolerance and many issues are finely poised. Heresy, not least when soundly identified as such, has to be allowed to administer its potential and salutary scrutiny of what orthodoxy holds, lest it stay no longer orthodox. The apostolate, as far as we can know it in the New Testament, needed – and found – a disciplinary authority over against at least two sharply "sectarian" elements, the "gnostic" and the wilfully pretentious. The Letter to the Colossians concerns itself with the former. The second-generation writings in 2 Peter and Jude with the latter. Neither mince their language in castigating excesses both moral and doctrinal.

The situation, on all counts – inter-Jewish, gnostic or esoteric enthusiast, or neo-pagan – was aggravated sharply in the second and ensuing centuries. For its part, the documentary New Testament presents its "we" and "us" and "our" pronouns in no way immune from stresses of dispute and the susceptibility of "frail, earthen vessels" to sect-spawning temptation because of the shape of the very "treasure" they contain. But there is no doubting the splendid new inclusion of "the nations" to which its apostles and folk believed themselves called because of "Messiah Jesus". It was, for them, a destiny which, out of a cherished privacy, surely awaited and required their translation of it into universal terms. "Our fellowship is with the Father and with His Son Jesus Christ" was learning how it must follow that "You also may have fellowship with us" – follow, that is, as the divine logic and the human embrace.

VII

The plural "we" can only be a multitude of "I"s and "ours" a personal "mine". It has often been noted that the Christian faith cannot well be confessed without the singular pronoun. So it was in Paul's: "The Son of God loved me." So it was with Thomas in the cry: "My Lord and my God." This strong accent on private personhood in the New Testament pronoun scene is the simple corollary of the de-ethnicizing of peoplehood to God. If the community of faith has to be "gathered" rather than entered by birth, and if the onus of access is freely laid on each, then an individual response is crucial. So many personal interviews occur in the Gospels, from the call of sundry disciples, Zaccheus and Bartimaeus, fishermen and publican, a woman at the well, two volunteers and an invitee at the close of Luke 9 and a Nicodemus, the enquirer in the dark. It was always a matter of "soul by soul" and freely, since there was no press-gang in the Kingdom of Heaven.

The pattern is the same in the parables of the Kingdom. They concern a shepherd and the one sheep to be retrieved, the housewife urgent about the one lost coin, while the wandering son has to resolve to "arise and go" home after a bitter encounter with the truth of himself. Where groups of husbandmen or casual labourers in the market-place are involved the initiatives they take are their own. The self-option belongs with the "whoso-ever will" of the invitation.

Emphatic as this individuation is in the Gospels there were notable precedents in the old order before the sense of corporate peoplehood emerged in the experience of exodus. Abraham, to whom Paul appealed as having a pre-Mosaic relation with God, became a paragon of individual obedience in forsaking his family at the call of a personal fulfilment. Jacob, "wrestling with the angel", became by the bestowal of a new name a symbol of a personhood drawn into a radical encounter with its own guile and yearning. He, as well as any, could serve for measure of inescapable selfhood as a dire arena of passion and pride.

Furthermore, the very confidence of Judaic incorporation in its proud Davidic, Solomonic form, with the due sanctions of land, kingship and contrived Temple, proved at length to be undermined by its own crimes and follies. In reproach of these, the great prophets, the Isaiahs, Micahs and Jeremiahs of Israel, were minded to interrogate the ability of things "national" and "chosen" to yield the fruits of justice and sanctity. When, in popular terms, there was nothing but "putrifying sores . . . like unto Gomorrah", those anguished minds turned to the theme of some "remnant", "a holy few" who might replace a fallen society they could not otherwise redeem. Or such a "remnant", as in the experience of Jeremiah in his native Anathoth, might be reduced even to the single individual keeping lonely faith with YAHWEH, his hand – apparently – alone on the plough.

In this way, as for Jeremiah and Ezekiel, the very covenant itself might be thought of necessity to pass from the "nation" to the individual. That radical re-conception was, in some measure, corroborated by the physical trauma of exile, the forfeiture of land and ritual, and the necessity to summon inner resources of fidelity in private terms. To be sure, there was also an urgent intensification of communal identity in response to exilic distresses, if only to sustain "land-love" and hope. Yet even so, such doggedness demanded personal resolve and individual tenacity. For despair, in the end, becomes a very private turmoil.

The Christian tradition of personal discipleship drew gratefully on this spiritual dimension in the exilic times of Jewry as it found voice in psalmody and story, where the very hope of return to the land required the scrutiny of personal worth. "Who is he that shall ascend to the hill of the Lord?" could well pass from Hebrew lips in Babylon on to those of the individual Christian in Corinth or Philippi anticipating a Eucharist in some house-church of those cities. The devout selfhood of such psalmists in Jewry, as studied in CHAPTER FIVE, proved to be both school and precedent for the Christian believer, also in a sort of "exile" and much travelled in a hostile or contemptuous world. Such too could well cry, in their new idiom in Christ: "O God Thou art my God . . . my expectation is from Thee."

In that very dispersion, precisely in being innocent of land-necessity and ethnic membership, individual Christians of New Testament vintage were cast upon their own resources. They were, as we have seen, a much travelled society, depending on hospitality and thus evocative of personal nexus and privately reciprocal expectation. While the inarticulate presence of "strangers" can well accentuate personal loneliness, a "stranger" who is already a faith-participant can be a factor in an enlivened person-hood both ways, once contact has been made. Certainly the pressures of adversity, suspicion and prejudice to which many were subject in the birthpangs of new community in Christ made for a resolute quality of personal character and a lively individuality.

The Letters in the New Testament bear ample witness to this testing shape of things, with their directives and appeals. Nor – as 1 Corinthians attests – was there any escape from fractious human frailties and perver-sities within their communities. By the very nature of their faith-enterprise they were prey to inside spoilers as well as external ill-doers. Their encounter with Roman hauteur and persistent paganism, with the ever-open issues of Jewish legacies, required of them, as the Epistles clearly show, a sturdiness of will and patience of mind.

Beyond these aspects bearing on the personal equation from immediate antecedents in the teaching of Jesus and from examples, patriarchal and exilic, it would be fair to take a New Testament Christian personalism further back still into the Biblical doctrine of human creaturehood. It had not been tutored in the sort of philosophy examined in CHAPTER TWO, the mind-set of Asian distrust of a human significance. Instead, it was heir to the conviction of a divinely intended world, where a human "dominion" was patently in hand – a mandate to be and answerable in turn to divine judgement. It was left in no doubt as to the serious meaning of existence, neither malign nor accidental but an authentic endowment for which the body, the organ of all else, was instrument and home.[24]

There can only be a personalism of the most attenuated kind, if the body is excluded from positive significance or disparaged as some "prison" from which the essential self must yearn for "escape". Hence the radical emphasis throughout, in the Biblical world, on "flesh and blood", the physicality through which all spiritualities proceed – the comprehension which was to find its supreme affirmation in Christian sacramentalism – to which the New Testament itself has the ultimate clue in the mystery of the Incarnation.

It was this sense of the creaturely body's "hallowing" "in the image of God" that sustained personhood, by no means paradoxically, in that other New Testament awareness of the perverse vulgarities to which the body might be prone, when not safeguarded by a lively self-restraint and a steady "sense of the holy" for which it was the wondrous realm. There might be courage and dignity in a Buddhist-style asceticism based on the body as a "temptress": the same virtues were differently evoked by esteeming it "the temple of the Holy Spirit". Was it not in these terms that the pastoral education at work in the New Testament Letters sought to shape the "magnanimity" and *sophrosune* it expected from Christian personhood, against all the odds of time and place?[25]

VIII

With all the foregoing factors in play, we have, however, to take the "I" and the "me" of Christian personhood back firmly into "the love of Christ", as truly leaving the disciple with "no other option" but its constraining claim.[26] It was as if each should take stock of the real world in the light of "Messiah Jesus crucified" and know for what they were meant. Or, in the words of a contemporary pre-ordination poem:

> Read the world and yield thy heart,
> My glad call obeying.
> Serve Me with thy utmost art,
> Brooking no delaying.
> Mine the ordering, wounded hands
> And the thorns that crowned Me.
> Evermore My passion stands
> Energising round thee.

It was in such terms that response to Christ was always personally made and made in terms of ministry in His meaning. The lingering Judaic idea of a potentially "collective" Messiah, rather than a looked-for individual one, could then have its fulfilment in the Church where all could partake in "messianic" response to the human world, but only in the meaning and power of the great "pioneer" in Jesus the Christ.[27]

This was the theme of the *imitatio* as we learn it in the Letters of Paul and 1 Peter – not only, or even mainly, asking on moral concerns: "What would Jesus do?" and appealing to his spoken words, but letting the principle of redemptive love in his Cross and Passion control and inspire the policy of the heart in all situations. "Let this mind be in you which was also in Christ," Paul told his Philippians (2:5): "Arm yourselves likewise with the same mind," wrote Peter (1.4:1). Thus the central events of the faith claimed their personal reproduction in the believing and belonging self as the guiding spirit of behaviour.

It was thus that there quickly developed what some, perhaps confusingly, have described as a "Christ mysticism", in the *confessio*: "I have been crucified with Christ, nevertheless I live, yet not I, but Christ lives in me" (Galatians 2:20). Seeing that this reading of one's selfhood could not obtain in co-tenancy of the will by aggressive, indulgent or anarchic lifestyle, Paul and others came to read in Jesus' an actuality that could translate into a personal "dying" in respect of that errant option and, only so, a "new living" in the entire self. Hence, for example in Romans, the liberating writ: "Reckons yourselves dead to sin but alive to God," or: "Mortify your members . . . rise to newness of life." Faith in the central event of Messiahship, and so of Christianity, could translate into the central moral and inward event by which the self, so willing, could inwardly "die" to its unworthy expressions and "live" for a "Christ-worthy" hallowing of its whole potential on those terms.

It is in this way, quite contrastedly, that the Christian faith proposes to deal with the heart problem of Buddhist faith, noted in CHAPTER TWO. The self that might otherwise be "selfish" obviates that ever present option, not by striving to escape or atrophy selfhood altogether (impossible anyway),[28] but by consecrating selfhood in a servanthood for Christ that emphatically employs our selfhood to the utmost but does so in terms that have simultaneously subdued its selfishness and – by this soul-posture – must do so steadily day in and day out. Thus the self is given back into its own honest custody on grounds that effectively hold it to a radical dispossession in its belonging now to Christ as Lord.

Paul effectively formulated this operative perception of "the self in Christ" in 2 Corinthians 4:5, where the sequence has to do with what is preached" but fits exactly what is lived. It runs: ". . . not ourselves but Christ Jesus as Lord *and* ourselves . . . your servants for Jesus' sake." The servanthood validates the abiding ego which – as a locus of love, energy, will and action – could alone be its ready means, its indispensable condition.

This being the ruling pattern for the pronouns "I" and "me" it follows – to return in conclusion to the plural "we" and "us" of New Testament apostolate and authority – that these, being individually subject to the same personal vocation, were set for an uncompulsive quality of heart. Authority had to do with what was imperative because of Christ but it was not imperious. The pens behind the Letters admonish, advise, warn, beseech and commend, but they do not bludgeon or dominate. Peter, for all his stature from accompanying the Lord with a dark treason in his story, ranks himself among fellow elders[29] (1.5:1), while Paul, with his impressive warrant to "boast", is always throwing himself on the affection of his readers and "fellow-servanting" with the fractious Colossians and the impulsive Galatians. His large, almost proprietary, role in the organization of "the Gentile" offertory for the mother city, Jerusalem, works with the entire spontaneity of dispersed and private contributors. It was thus an event significant of a bonded collective learning to say "we" as the language of a scattering of simple "me"s.[30]

CHAPTER NINE

Two Great Sexes Animate the World

———

I

So says the archangel Raphael, according to John Milton in Paradise Lost, where he is tutoring a questioning Adam newly confronting the meaning of existence. Could Milton have been echoing John Donne's The Extasie:

> Love, with another so
> Interanimates two souls . . .
> Our bodies . . . did us to us . . . convey.[1]

"Two great sexes" indeed – but why the "two" and the "great" since, outside the obvious duality, there are no others to add nor to compete?

> Humanity! truly we have created you male and female and made you to be nations and tribes in order that you may know each other. (Surah 49.13)

> Male and female created He them. (Genesis 1:27)

So two Semitic Scriptures. Whether religions have creation origins or begin from a sort of clueless "here we are" in egohood vested in bodies, all faiths concede the "interanimation" of human sexuality.

What other verbs the two poets might have added inside their "animate", "Two great sexes" populate the world and, so doing, perpetuate its story. "Two great sexes" navigate this world, negotiating all its destinies in their perennial fertility. "Two great sexes" dominate the world for through them flow the thrusting desires of culture, the teeming emotions of the arts. And whether in the temple architecture of India, or the license of ancient Rome, or the obsessions of our contemporary "sexism", "two great sexes" captivate or titillate the world.

Other verbs around the "two great sexes" might suggest themselves, "consecrate" most tellingly of all. The pronouns "I" and "thou" relating to male and female in sexual terms carry religious meaning no trivialization can exclude. What they transact in intimacy has ever been a fertile source of religious imagery. It is the crucial testing ground of moral conscience and the social order as faith-systems are set to interpret and to guide them.

The "I" and "thou", as "male and female", are always singular in the twinning of duality, as the Christian marriage Liturgy insists, always "this man and this woman".[2] The poet, Pushkin, might boast that he could love a different woman every succeeding night without any waste of shame, but – if and as he did so – the transaction was always one to one. "Males and females" abound in multitudinous array but in every act of genital love that Scriptural precept of "male and female" is known in inalienable privacy. If, as Milan Kundera thinks, "in eroticism we seek the image of our own significance", an "I" only finds it in a "thou".[3] That truth requires to inform all related themes in sexuality.

> Total they mix . . . conveyance need
> as flesh to mix with flesh or soul with soul.[4]

"Conveyance" may be a crude or even sordid word about coitus but it has us know that we can never be "solipsists", seeing that sexual desire is always an exchange. We can only be "integers". This will be so even though contrived only "for the time being," when we blatantly dissipate what we "conveyed", in repudiating all liability for its total, flesh-borne, soul-engaging reality.

Love in sexuality and sexuality in love prove to be the most prolific users of our human pronouns. With "thou" and "I" we bind and wound, we test and tease, we pledge and plead, in the inter-possessiveness of our hearts and bodies. Around these "I's" and "thou's" come the third parties, the triangular situations, the plural societies that share the texts of the human drama.

As and when the religious faiths bring, out of the infinite, their other pronouns – if they do – how well do "Thou" and "He" and "She" or "Who" intend their people to converse? And what should we think of "gender" in transcendence? This chapter is hard pressed to know, but that pronouns are the core of the perplexities is not in doubt.

II

It may be well to begin in India, not only because Hinduism is the oldest of the great religions but because Hindu temple architecture luxuriates in phallic imagery. What has been called "the phallic consciousness" is where – however crude or brutal it may seem to modesty – sexuality has the initiating symbol. Its primacy had always to be answered by the equally requisite reality of the womb and all that serves it in its unobtrusive gentleness and latent will, while the phallus tells its significance in proud erection.

Was it then the implicit ground of the Biblical myth of creation, which made the male the place of origin of the female, via the borrowed rib? There are Hindu myths that imagine some unitary original, later divided into the two sexes, while a Persian mythology tells of a creative woman who generated males, a progeny of sons who then fear for their survival, lest she who alone gave them being by a power they lacked, could equally well destroy them in their helplessness.

All myths aside, the phallus could be seen as playing the supreme sexual role. In erection it seems the very assertion of manhood, responsive to be sure, but arrogant on its delicate base. It so readily spoke to Hindu minds of all natural fertility. Shiva was "the Lord of the phallus", the linga calling for the vulva or yoni, the "ring", of which Shakespeare had his Graziano make bawdy play in *The Merchant of Venice* about "Nerissa's ring". Shiva's spouse, Parvati, would be endlessly initiated into the potency of Shiva's organ. Krishna, too, could make himself tirelessly erect among the cowherds, having stolen their clothes and invited them to come, naked, to reclaim them, providing each girl with a semblance of himself, engendering myths about nine hundred thousand copulations.

Such sexual hyperbole apart, the male sequence of phallic emergence out of expectancy into assertion tells a physical experience only properly understood inside the wholeness of the selfhood whence it springs and towards which it instinctively moves. It is ridiculous, ludicrous and grossly pretentious otherwise, its assertive gesture destined to futility. Known for the relationality it so signally anticipates, it is the achieving of male-ness, a mysterious source of life, an original creator. Thus it is symbolically much more than the mere penis on which Freud's theory of female envy fastened. It is, rather, the initiator of physical intercourse, activator of the womb and mysteriously "pleasuring" the indispensable partnership that engages two – otherwise inviolate – personhoods.

Given the emotions from which it derives and the meanings its very posture tells as to bodily destiny, it has to be more than only the body's gesture. Whatever may, or may not, have been intended in the Hindu mind by its lavish exhibition in Indian art, it can only truly be the partner in a conjunction by which two parties inter-define themselves. The male can only have originality in the sexual act because the female owns the reciprocal dimension which gives either the creativity which, differently, is the monopoly of the other. It is strange how limited in recent years the word "intercourse" has become, as now denoting only physical coitus whereas of yore it could tell many sorts of society, personal and intellectual.

This inherent interdependence has to be the ultimate source of the true evaluation of sexuality, the Christian ideology of which comes later here, aware – as it needs to be – of how far it has been in default. For all faiths, the due ordering of humanity's "two great sexes" has to make its inherent physical feature sustain and argue its total role in selfhood, in selfhood not partialized by lust or power or commerce or other denials of the wholeness of the selfhoods it indwells. It is not to be assigned to some "lower self, below the waist," where "all the dark gods lurk" as if only some "upper part" were the region of light and sanity. Dire alternatives do indeed attend upon it. They are only to be mastered in a self, male and female alike, discipled to love in its capacity to be the supreme fulfilment of selfhoods in reverent awe, wondering to own themselves so mysteriously endowed.

The issue around the phallus as a conspicuous symbol of Hindu art and architecture turns on how it is discerned. There waits on it the strange paradox that, while it may visualize for admirers the pulsating force of aggressive lust, it can also evoke a kind of ascetic revulsion that carries a contrary stimulus to its negation. Either way, it remains the sign of fertility in every realm of existence in line with the readiness of the Qur'an, in Surah 2.223, to liken "women" to *harth*, or "tilth," "the field" the ploughman makes fertile.

Yet does male imagination need the ubiquitous temple symbol either way? Things visual, it is often assumed, are where sexual desire is kindled or moved to respond, so that the reaction that turns away is the less likely. It remains a question for the Hindu mind and spirit – capable as much in Hinduism has been of the cult of abstinence. What of having aggressive maleness visually presented if, either way, it perverts the situation, whether towards the lascivious or the abnegatory? For both disserve the final truth of the selves-in-sex.

There is a similar paradox against the praise – or reproach – of "puritanism" in the West ever since the term came into use.[5] Is it a sort of bogey, or a gibe, directed against what must be deplored as inhibiting, or as binding what should be free? Or is it an alertness about what has to be worth its freedom? In the latter event, it is crucial to the sexual fulfilment – vitiated, otherwise, by lust flouting its real nature no less than by the withdrawn-ness that fears what that nature is. Using "puritan", like assessing phallic symbol, can never avail rightly unless we ask what it purports to admonish. Liberty, indulgence, abnegation are all ambiguous terms until we seek, in and beyond them, the ultimate truth in which sexuality engages selfhood.

Whatever Hindus in the sub-continent mean by the plethora of the phallus in their art and temples, the symbol is rife in African paganism and in sundry cultic forms among the oddly-named "Indians" in the western hemisphere. Yet no imagination lacks it anywhere. For it may be visualized where-ever the mind wills – in phallus-like stone pillars, in a flute, a cigar, a pen, or even by monks with fingers round misericords of chapel stalls while the liturgies linger. Nature too produces it in rock formations or endless botanical features if we will so to read them. But let not a censoring conscience merely reproach such prurient ideas in the name of a refining sensitivity anxious to exclude them. Though doubtless unworthily indulged, such minding of the male phallus has to call itself back to the truth, namely that its demanding, appealing entity, asserted from penis gentility, is set to seek and anticipate what can only be in a completion outside the selfhood it brings. It has no monopoly of its reality: it equips for what it intends and what it intends is mutuality.

The gender it represents is always more than the sexuality it transacts – a vital truth often now forgotten in lustful preoccupation with its symbol-quality. There is always the question that novelists come to, however deviously, between the usual parties – "Is it me you want or IT?" Sadly, all too often, the novelists' answer stays sordidly "IT". But, truth to tell, "IT" cannot be had without the other "me" affording it. Everything then turns on how the two inalienable "me's" bring their self-hoods to according it. There are endless encounters where "IT" is had only in excluding the authentic "thou" whose "me" is never met or known. The true wanting of the "IT" has to be the real wanting of two "me's" in the fulness of their complementing genders – which brings us to the nature and the mystery of marriage.

"Interstices between the inter-sections" was Samuel Johnson's defini-tion of "a net." How apt it might also fit the casual, profligate world of "the IT" that fails ever worthily to say "thou" and "me" or only says it to partialize the gender role in the sex-expression! What webs and tangles then eventuate – psychic, social, and spiritual, quarrelsome, passionate, wistful, wasteful and ardently destructive – the world of pronouns, rela-tive, interrogative, possessive and gender-chaotic.

III

Might it be legitimate to align the Genesis 1 account with Plato's myth in the *Symposium* of a primordial, bi-sexual being? That narrative – by a consensus of scholars – is held to be some four centuries later than Genesis 2, which derives woman from the rib of the male Adam.[6] But the Hebrew term *adam*, before it became a personal name, simply meant a "being," a "creature," a generic word – "a human". Did not the Jewish Kabbalah imagine each soul "androgynous" in its original state? "Male and female created He them" – given the mandate to "be fruitful" – certainly implied an equal co-creativity and, in respect of offspring, a pro-creativity, bespeaking an entire equivalence. "In Our image and after Our likeness" would surely need to be read as implying some unitary being, as seems to be confirmed in Genesis 5:1–2 when He "called *their* name Adam . . . when *they* were created", as both male and female. That name "human" is given by God, whereas it is "man" who later names other creatures. To be sure, gender is ever present and the generic term *adam* promptly becomes a personal name of the male. It would, therefore, be too bold to argue some Biblical bi-sexual identity as neither "male nor female", seeing that gender belongs to their creating. It is not, however, over-bold to read, in the singularity of *adam* in the Genesis 1 narrative, a clear caveat on the "helpmeet" imagery of the earlier Genesis 2 story. While "helpmeet" has lovely nuances and belongs even with YAHWEH himself, it has been used to inferiorize the woman in long, unthinking tradition. It may imply some subordinate role, more dispensable than the central male role.[7] Those implications are excluded in the Genesis 1 account, where "male and female" come about simultaneously in the non-gender "man". They are two equals, equally autonomous. Even so, Genesis 2 has so far shaped theologies that it remains difficult to assert against it the differing perception rooted in the precedence of Genesis 1, where there is a clear and equal co-humanness both prior to, and defining, the emergence of consciously distinguished genderings. "Male and female" as interchangeably "human" is at odds with long traditional perception of our sexuality. It deserves to inform and discipline all our exploration of its meaning. "Two great sexes" will not then be in the ratio of sun to moon, *pace* Raphael and his pupil, Milton.

Exploration promptly arrives at the concept and the institution of marriage, which, however diverse the precepts and the practice, seems to be acknowledged in most religious systems. Since, in the crudest terms, the phallus belongs only to males and only females have wombs, nexus between them dictates a complementarity society must somehow institutionalize. To be sure, nexus may be entirely casual or "recreational", but child-birth being a sequel to pregnancy and pregnancy a sequel to intercourse, the sexual union – we must acknowledge – is "pregnant" with more than offspring. Vital interests are present and will not be denied – identity, paternity, inheritance, property, kinship liability, family nurture and relationship. Pregnancy begins in an instant of conception but persists through a cycle of months and ends in a long dependence, where the womb that bears and the paternity that initiates have created an ongoing inter-liability told in the very features of the child. Life-inaugural bears indelibly the lines of its gendering. It is these, in the very entail of fertility in the flux of time and in the web of society, that necessitate the formal, legal and familial structure that, in sundry forms and manners, marriage affords. What transpires in private coitus belongs in a social order that requires its public reckoning. When, in that telling phrase, Genesis 4:1 records that "Adam knew his wife", it was a "knowing" – for all in the perennial sequence – that demanded a social "knowledge" embracing the several public factors around the past and future of the child.

The inherent issue around the thrust of sexuality and the ordering of marriage is how to relate an impulse which is more than procreation to a situation which must also enshrine it. This will necessarily be so, even if the procreative element is deliberately elided, merely risked, or consciously allowed. Given the far reach of western attitudes of "casual sex" via the ubiquity of films, videos, web-sites and virtual images, all cultures and the faiths that indwell them are in similar measure entailed in this pattern, irrespective of the norms they have traditionally underwritten.

Sexual love is by its nature commitment to community – the intimate "community" within the act and, thereby, the larger community out of which the intimacy stemmed and into which it duly reaches. Yet, at the same time, that sexual unitiveness insistently asserts its privacy and its immediacy. The destiny, by any fully human criterion, is willingly and gladly to recognize and achieve the harmony of both dimensions, so that marriage fully attains the one and readily fulfills the other.

The impulse has been well described by the early Islamic writer Ibn Qutayba:

> The song of love touches men's souls and takes over their hearts, God having put it in the constitution of His creatures to love dalliance and the society of women, in such wise that we find very few but are attracted thereto by some tie or have some share therein, whether lawful or unpermitted.[8]

"Whether lawful or unpermitted" – but what is to make a "song in the soul" "lawful" and what "unpermitted", if "dalliance" be a divine implanting? And what of women having in their hearts a desire for "the society of men"?

If there is a "natural" impulse which none the less needs "permitting" and so "bridling", these, in turn, must be argued from "nature" – the nature that concedes its own need of discipline as integral to its expression. If the concept and the practice of marriage are to enshrine this it must so read the impulse as to recognize the discipline and so regulate the discipline as to achieve the impulse duly. This must mean the avoidance of two contrasted errors. The one is to see marriage as essentially a restraining monitor, the other is to disparage it as a conspiracy against the liberty of love. When the first error is corrected the second will be properly refuted and disowned. The entire issue between them entails some wrestling with the whole concept of what is "natural". It is wise to take stock of attitudes which, either way, make a travesty of the inter-nexus of love and marriage.

The idea of marriage as confining or constraining the sexuality between male and female has arisen in counsels of human despair, fear of the risk of parenting, or some mood of Swiftian horror in contemplation of the futility of human depravity.[9] In an odd sort of way, it could also emerge from a sentiment about nature in general as "cold", negligent of human feeling and finally indifferent to value. Thus the French novelist, Albert Camus, included women in the natural order of "sea, sand and stars", where love-making could be no more than a momentary intimacy – or seduction – entirely irrelevant, and part of no intelligible scheme of things. The ideal of marriage, therefore, could only be underwriting an illusion about a significance it could never afford.[10]

More deeply, however, negative assessments of marriage are drawn from Asian ideas of ascetic self-discipline or the restraining of the deceptiveness of love in the context of transience and the frustration it must bring into all human hopes. Or the law of *karma* may be predetermining the entail of one's present sexuality in ways beyond all personal wistfulness of desire, so inhibiting the free engagement with the sexual urge. In face of all such inhibiting ideologies – or lack of positive ones – marriage declines into a biological necessity for the perpetuation of the species undertaken with less than enthusiasm. Pressures of poverty and degradation may conspire to the same result, if they are not themselves a stimulus to the only human solace that remains.[11]

But the most significant factor in the view of marriage as "restraint" has been drawn from Christian doctrines that made it "a remedy against sin". Primed by Plato's perception of the physical "body" as a "prison" the pure soul must escape, and by their reading of Paul, Christian Fathers, like Augustine, conceded the propriety and necessity of marriage for the biological task of birthing generations but restricted it to that functional significance. Sexual expression within a sacramental bond of personal unison they ignored or disavowed. Sex itself was seen as an evil only excused by the marriage bond and within that bond, abstention was better than copulation.

They reasoned, from the way of male erection, that response was not under rational control. Genitalia in males operated only at the behest of lust.[12] How those western Fathers had their mind confirmed by the Hindu phallic symbol! Thus the wayward male sexual urge put men under the power of women – a situation only restrained by the pledge of marriage with its due Christian curb on all but procreation. It was male frailty and proneness to passion that made women alluring. Thus Augustine and his kind read the "helpmeet" terms, not as a mutually fulfilling gift in person-hoods reciprocally realized, but a partnering for birth alone. Otherwise, concupiscence "waited at the door". For Jerome also marriage – child-bringing apart – was no better than fornication. It called for the chastity of continence. Only an infant was alibi for sex-impulse and – hopefully – "the birth of virgins". For then, as he said, "he gathered roses from the thorn" of matrimony.[13] The incidence of intercourse, on this view, was heavily restricted by "banned days" in the yearly calendar and sexuality was held incompatible with prayer. If the pressures of impulse had to be reluctantly admitted, the concept of sex as "duty" found currency, in that a partner's refusal might turn lust elsewhere. Married sexual access was liable to be seen as a debt owed rather than a mystery realized.

These were western Christian readings. The Byzantine world of eastern Orthodoxy had room for the exchange of meanings beyond the taint of lust and read a theological mystery in which the parties "crowned" each other, rather than a legal contract. Priestly blessing solemnized what was made authentic by partaking in the Eucharist. When breakdowns occurred only the legal contract concerned the civil power, so that faith in indissolubility could ride with actual divorce.[14]

Happily not constrained by Augustine and Aquinas, the eastern mind could transcend crippling suspicion of our human sexuality and invoke the sacramental dimension which western Christianity, outside Roman Order, has notably recovered in the twentieth century.[15] It has been, however, a recovery which has had to wrestle with an accumulating disparagement of marriage in the popular mind, western – and insofar as westernism runs – world-wide. This disparagement, depersonalizing the sexual mystery, sees marriage as trespassing on the liberty of love. If ancient Fathers argued that eroticism was "irrational", so let it be. Why should over subtle reason interfere? "For God's sake let us love" as John Donne once cried.[16] To sift this conspiracy theory means deferring discussion of what is "natural", but involves the course of thought in a very different theory of "restraint" from that of Augustine.

IV

Augustine wanted marriage to imprison concupiscence by confining sexuality to procreation. Current thinking suspects or arraigns it as imprisoning what can only well be free. This mind-set has no room for any paradox of "captive liberty". It sees no logic in the sexual perception which, in nakedness of soul, holds partners intimate life-long and trusts another being with the gift of the inmost self. Instead it cries: Banish such thought of any life-long journey into exploration, a progressive act of mutuality constraining all times and seasons to its gentle ends. All such is fantasy. Must not passion only "die into marriage"? Eros is a "kindling truth", but only to diversity, to flux, to chance and change. The state of "being married" only deadens and defeats the ardour that may once have launched it on its way. Why not relieve tension and heighten excitement, toying here and there, as impulse indicates and times admit? Promiscuity can merely say: "That's nice" and, adding, ask your name.

By contrast, marriage seems a dead end. The poet Shelley thought that love died when put under constraint and that passions could brook no government by law.[17] Engels, rebelling against the Victorian perception of marriage, castigated monogamy as a brand of slavery.[18] For all such minds, there was something hypocritically condescending in the sentiment of matrimony, disdaining – as it were – the dignity of women in a sort of obsequious veneration. Thomas Hardy, for example, could only have upbraided Jeremy Taylor's *The Mysteriousness of Marriage.*

> The dominion of a man over his wife is none other than as the soul rules over the body, for which he takes a mighty care and uses with a delicate tenderness. The man's authority is love . . . it is nowhere enjoined that he should exact obedience of her.[19]

Not exact, perhaps, but still expect? And what of a reciprocal "authority" of wifely love?

In his poem "the Conformers", Hardy argued that being married diminished passion. "Stolen trysts of heretofore, We . . . shall know no more, when we abide alone, in frigid tone of household speech."[20] Hardy's *Jude the Obscure* was a thinly veiled attack on marital "respectability" and the alleged duplicity of vows, and what he saw as the tyranny of conventionality. The heroine was presented, ambiguously, as reserving her selfhood from irrevocable commitment. Wedding vows, if not somehow warped in measures of self-hatred, would explicitly limit the proper freedoms of both parties either to belong or to withhold belonging. Nothing sexual should be thus committed to any "thee only" rubric. Refraining this way, Sue only breaks Jude's heart and, in a Hardean paradox, lights on the very crux of how commitment fulfills.[21]

D. H. Lawrence wrestled notoriously with kindred issues and has one of his characters say: "To isolate oneself with one person is only to secure oneself in one's illusions."[22] In his essay on Nathaniel Hawthorne, Lawrence wrote: "Woman is a strange and rather terrible phenomenon to man."[23] Indeed, but all misgivings about the venture marriage makes have to yield to the truth of its acceptance as "to be achieved". No social structure guarantees its own efficacy, least of all where motives can be so mingled, so readily tumultuous, so deeply risk-prone. Marriage is being shaped all the time in the shaping of the selves, whom in turn their venture must progressively define and constitute. It must have us accept the social, temporal selves we are. Inter-availability, whether in love-making, birthing and parenthood – through and beyond all these – has to be a steady, interactive practice of tenderness, ever ardent for its meaning, ever watchful for its frailties. The vow that binds tells only in the love that stays but love stays more surely for its vowedness. "I and thou" are at once "doing" and "being" pronouns.

"Each be other's comfort kind, deep, deeper than divined."[24]

Through all the foregoing there runs the question as to what is "natural". Let appeal to "nature" resolve all sexual issues. "Nature", however, is so far the ward of culture and, being culturally bound, can only give equivocal answers. Thomas Aquinas and much Roman Catholic theology with him argued from what, by his logic, he perceived as the "natural" *telos* in the physical organs of "the two great sexes".[25] Through much of modern western tradition, and through Islamic social history, roles have been assigned to women as "meant" for childbirth and motherhood and in a sort of "debt" relationship to men within the married state. Despite physical co-creativity and mental pro-creativity therein, and despite shared personhoods in the created order, this stereotype has been the norm, and the bane, of a too far polarized sexuality through long centuries of Islam.

Deferring the theme inside Islam, it is useful to review the "naturalness" of sexuality, however construed, in the context of nineteenth- and twentieth-century feminism in strenuous effort to challenge and redeem the readings of it. There could hardly be a better exemplar of that feminist task than the novelist George Eliot, writing under a male pseudonym while mastering an art in which mere women were not supposed to engage. Her studies in human characters sought the rehabilitation of women, the querying of male assumptions, all the more judiciously for her skilful subtlety.

While her contemporary, Charles Dickens, was effectively celebrating the virtues of home and extolling female home-makers, to the annoyance of thinkers like John Stuart Mill, George Eliot was expressing the pent-up social privations of women, either marrying for escape from "governessing" or into a destiny of "social life which seemed nothing but a labyrinth of petty cares, a walled-in maze of small paths which led nowhere",[26] in a society where women were not supposed to use their minds or take initiatives but merely to be "the angel in the home", the facilitators of male satisfactions. Elizabeth Barrett Browning had made the point in *Aurora Leigh*:

We sew, sew, prick our fingers, dull our sight,
Producing what? a pair of slippers, Sir . . .[27]

– sequestered, mode-bound and tied to male expectations. Was not the surname usage derived from "Sire"? What might lead to feminine independence was withheld by social norms. Marriage was the right destiny told within its due parameters as convention had them. George Eliot had defied them by her liaison with George Henry Lewes, through whose initiative her genius found its way into publication.

Yet powerful symbol as she was of the protracted and much harassed quest for womanly independence, there was a significant rider in her advocacy. There was, to be sure, a cruel fallacy in the so-called "intention of nature" about the female role in subservience, yet – precisely because it was a fallacy and a snare – there was a nature-truth that must, at all costs, be rescued from neglect or suppression. The very urgency of feminism could over-reach itself and distort what, soberly, it would always need. That nature-truth was how femininity possessed "an art that was itself nature, an art which could mend nature".[28] Qualities of gentleness, the tenderness of motherhood, the patience exacted by the claims of infancy – all these, indeed, were nature.

Their precious reality was not to be forfeit to the exigencies of campaigning against the case drawn from them by male self-interest. Rather, their deep reality in humankind should inspire their translation, appropriately, through both "the two great sexes". While their immediate incidence in womb and breast must be for ever female, their quality could find spiritual reproduction of a male order. Correspondingly, women, as their exemplars and first practitioners, should be liberated from invalid limitation of the relevance of femininity and be set to carry it into active roles from which – too long – convention had debarred them. "De-sexualized" in that way, against old and crippling norms, the emotional range of women and men alike could reach towards a common benediction of both grace and relevance. The child-bearing that for ever marks women off from men would no longer do so in the old socially demarcating terms in which men too long assumed a mastery. Instead it would transpire in a more equal and compassionate setting.

The practical problems attendant on this vision are, of course, legion and difficult of solution in the complexities of economics and the bias of long tradition. At least, the "appeal to nature" has moved away from prejudicial interests and closer to the counsels of divine Sophia.

V

There is a similar movement of hope in the Muslim sexual scene, though facing more stubborn hurdles and moving by a different chronology. Islam, by a culture enshrined in *Shari'ah*, has a long tradition of male supremacy via a perspective of womanhood as, essentially, nature's sphere of child-bearing and of male control. The traditional male management of female living-space and social nexus, the habit of veiling and the ordering of marriage as a legal contract and of a male initiating of divorce, have all contributed to a patriarchal, masculine scene through the Islamic centuries.

Even so, Islam's contemporary feminism has a sheet-anchor in the Qur'an itself. Surah 30.21 reads:

> One of His sign is that He has created partners in marriage to be yours, from your own selves, so that, dwelling with them, you might find rest, and He has ordained between you tenderness and compassion, wherein truly there are signs for thoughtful people.[29]

The key word *azwajan* incorporates both man and wife as "mates", implying the entire mutuality of the married state. The words *min ayatihi*, "from His signs", places marriage potentially among the "sacraments", in that it calls for attentive reverence as to an index of divine mercy. However, Muslim practice has always seen marriage as a legal contract between two parties, revocable with provisions for post-divorce care, and crucial for lawful sexual access. *Zina*, or sexuality outside such contracting is a sin and reprehensible.[30] Even *muta'*, or temporary marriage, has to be contractual. This legal context of marital relations is an important principle in Islam and signifies the significance of sexual access.

Nevertheless, social inferiorizing of women can be sustained from other Quranic passages and, though monogamy is coming to be the norm, with permission of marriages up to four and the ready possibility of recurrent marriages, the current quest for women's rights remains a heavy task.[31] While the achievement of selfhood can never be independent of gender, reaching for it in many Muslim spheres of life and custom is a strife against many odds.

Segregation largely stems from a Muslim perception of women as a hazard or temptation for men, from which male society outside the immediate family, needs to be shielded by a protection which will preclude women from exercising their charms to their own undoing. Thus the Islamic situation is in urgent need of that inner reciprocating of those "gender skills" of human nature as truly drawn from secular feminism or a Christian sacramentalism or the tradition of Judaism.

Any turning back of gender polarization and of male dominance in Islamic society seems very far to seek, despite the courage and tenacity of feminist writing. The almost ineluctable destiny of marriage and marriage not itself within female option, but family arranged and "forced", the pain of discarded wives, the "shame" avengings of sexual initiatives on the part of recalcitrant daughters, and the early age of marital coupling – all these frustrate the reforming impulse their enormities arouse. Those initiatives face an acute tactical dilemma whether to retrieve and maximize in their favour all they can from the Qur'an, or whether directly to plead secular grounds which have to write off the sacred text as affording only dubiously equivocal support or as being itself inimical and needing to be left aside. Special pleading makes for dubious advocacy.[32]

Despite the emphasis of 30.21 on the love present in marriage as "God's sign", the verse with its plural *azwaj* and the pronouns plural – not dual – finds the enjoined "love and tenderness" compatible with plural and/or sequential contracts. Thus the sacramental theme of a quality of mutual love never minded for rupture is only potential in the text and not mandatory. Quranic precepts are also acutely aware of what in the West has been called "the incessant jury of men's eyes". In *The Harem Within: Tales of a Moroccan Girlhood*, Fatima Mernissi tells of a growing youth having to be expelled from the harem, because "he had a man's stare". She describes the resilience of women-folk, "living according to the rhythm", but negotiating "the cosmic frontier" . . .

> two kinds of creatures walking on God's earth, the powerful on one side and the powerless on the other (men and women) . . . I asked Mina how I would know on which side I stood. Her answer was quick, short and very clear: "If you can't get out you're on the powerless side."

Meanwhile "one develops the muscles for happiness just like walking and breathing".[33]

Here in contemporary Islam is a field where inter-faith dialogue – so often marooned in merely indulgent intellectual debate – needs earnestly to wrestle for a theology of human sexuality duly "worthy of God"[34] and thereby duly emancipatory in the sexual scene both from the profligate and the tyrannical.

VI

No faith may well come to such a purposeful rendezvous except as witness to its understanding of humans under God and in honest modesty about the efficacy of its sexual ideology. Both witness and honesty confine the rest of this chapter to a summary of Christian sacramentalism, foregoing more inclusive review of religions and marriage, as the best hope of comprehending the human "I and thou" in what Thomas Hardy called "the strongest passion known to humanity".[35]

The traditional formula in Christian marriage: "Wilt thou take . . . ?" "I take thee . . ." is performative language, at once contractual and sacramental, followed at once by the personal names, as received in baptism. The so-called surname, or family name, is not used. In decisively transacting themselves, male and female do so within the faith as to an undiscriminating humanity, confessed before God in baptism where the names derived. The sex is identified only to entrust it – to "marry" it – into an equal personhood.

This truth requires us to recognize how long and how far the institution of marriage has flouted and defiled its meaning. The debit side of all structured things is only disavowed when their genuine "estate" is understood. There is no incrimination without an ideology. Co-equal stature inside a common humanity – such as the names affirm – makes them eager tokens of a sacramental "we".

It is well to begin with coupled bodies. For, thanks to the Incarnation, Christianity is quite deliberate in its "materialism". The body has its vital role. There is no spirituality which does not proceed from it and move with it. In this controlling perception, male/female intercourse becomes a hallowing mystery, one of partnering limbs and inter-serving organs belonging inherently with persons. As persons, and not mere shapes of flesh, their junction is a unison loaded with emotion in a possessiveness that intends itself. Its physical mutuality argues neither subordination nor dominance. For these would denigrate and desolate the heart of the transaction as something given and received in the integrity of a selfhood reciprocally unreserved. As such, it was never fit to be trivialized, fortuitously varied or callously diverted. Blight happens where persons bestow their passions wantonly, serially and haphazardly, being thereby diminished and impoverished, self-alienated from the fulness of themselves. Both parties are then cheapened in a treachery at the core of surrender.

It will doubtless be argued that such transitory nexus is entirely feasible and endlessly repeatable in the bosom of society. Fleetingness can readily attach to what is idly indulged but only by the banishment of gratitude, the exclusion of wonder in the deriding or dismissing of the sacramental mystery, in merely doing, having and desiring vacuous sex. There is more in mutual sexuality than the discharge, or the precluding of semen, more than the mechanics bodies perform, more than the thrill of an hour, more than experiment with experience, more than diversion in the bedroom. A "sign" of bonding has been exchanged in the body's terms, as more than a gesture of satisfaction that incurs no liability beyond its woeful partiality.

"Falling in love" is odd language when, in truth, we are rising into it "with supple joints and lively vigour led",[36] "where all honour done returns its own".[37] Such sacramental reading of our sexuality has to be set in a theology of nature for which "all that is is holy", handled by a will to find it so. Love in its intimacy is then one with the gratitude that discerns a willed creation everywhere and rejects all desecration. Nature's benisons have their point only in their due appreciation. For, as Montaigne observed, humanity is "wondrously corporeal", its two "master parts", body and soul, male and female, divinely "mated",[38] their "sweet and natural functions" God-meant. Thus known, the body is neither prison nor snare but "nature's minister from God."

The Christian faith in the Incarnation, "God in Christ" corroborates this theology of nature. It stands as a truth of our vocation in human-ness, in being the self-expression of the divine nature, giving us all a "priest-hood" in the body. Hence it follows that formal marriage can duly "solemnize" (as the archaic word has it) its meaning in a ritual of cele-bration, where society has a proper stake, needing no surreptitious privacy. Making it an occasion pledges its translation into achievement, a wedding thus creatively related to weddedness. "This holy estate"[39] is duly sacralized, conferring the dignity of "husband/wife", to be duly pioneered the better for having been openly avowed as the "quality" of being and becoming – a present simple set, as grammarians might say, for a present continuous. It is inviolate only in being cherished in those terms, at once volitional and irrefragable. The ring, apt symbol of these things, is given and received, the longed for "quality" being transacted and affirmed.

VII

"Be ye therefore well deceived" the cynic or the sceptic will say. Such romanticism cannot long endure, concealing the deadlock in the wedlock. Human nature cannot sustain such constancy nor underwrite such sure fidelity. Vows are illusory and pledges vain, but only if the troth – we reply – has not first determined with itself that they shall not be so. Intentions rightly undertaken have their abiding capacity within their competence and marry intention and competence in the one transaction staying by its own authority within. "Love's not time's fool". Does not the Liturgy speak of being "enterprised and taken in hand"?[40] Here is no "daring-do" as too often in the modern novel, where romances are supposed to be precipitate. Rather, a steady mutual discovery takes the intelligent emotions of marriage into a glad coherence of will in the sense of common goals and a unity of ideas about home, nurture and fulfilment. The status exchanged enables the achievement it seeks.

The arch in building has fitly been invoked to tell the meaning of marriage. By dint of its engineering the weight it has to sustain is incor-porated into the strength by which it does so. It is enabled by its own solidity. Its limbs have sought each other from their separate springs: the keystone holds their own destiny as one. Space is thus created and a world is held in place, sheltering its times and fruits. It is twinned in will to be one thing. Marriage, we might say with Charles Williams, is thus "more sacramental than any other occupation".[41] Each may truly say: "This – with you – enworthies me." So love belongs with lovers, comprehending what their bodies signify as mediators of the mind and servants of the will. Either is able to anticipate a steady inter-loyalty through the vicissitudes they cannot control, but their committedness will sustain, not faltering when it "alteration finds". Hazards have been anticipated in the very shape of the vows. It is not that moods, scruples, stresses, do not arise. It is that their incidence does not promptly issue into questioning the whole relationship. Instead, the original pledging reaches for a more perceptive patience to resolve them. Like diamonds, it has durability told in its very elements. Shelley gibed about "the longest journey, chained to a jealous foe", unaware that arches have no chains, unless for lanterns hanging.[42]

Inter-dependability in marriage as not for withdrawal or forfeiture is only what was inherently present when "first love" was discovered. That was no moment frozen into permanence by an arbitrary institution maintained by inertia. It lives by a momentum of intent for ever renewed by glad surprise. It is a thing of courage as well as delight. Love is a "commandment" in the Biblical world and becomes also a sacrament in the New Testament. It belongs with monotheistic faith since it banishes wayward notions of idolatry as practiced by the vow-breakers, and brings a singular devotion to the whole theme of unity.

Often is has proved that male treason inside marriage has spelled its undoing, so that those who deserted what marrying love had meant had – it must be assumed – never truly known it. A self-upholding power was always the secret in its kindling nature, the authentic quality in its first awakening. Thus treachery, either way, only happens when the sacramental situation is repudiated. The troth in marriage was never to some fantasy of human idolatry but to a flesh and bone person whose reality, reciprocal to the lover's own, means an honest, mutual realism and the reining-in of wandering and disordered passions in a firm preparedness for due self-giving. Promiscuity is a kind of paganism, in that erotic experience beyond mere physical sensations, holds soul-emotions that are finally religious and condemn the irreverence that prostitutes them. How can the consumation which gives in strong possessiveness argue a desertion that turns all into violation? Is there not death in the discard?[43] Neither party stayed in self-sufficiency in the meaning of their intercourse: should they revert to it in the sundering one – or two – sided repudiation tells? "Betrayal is always self-betrayal where love is concerned."[44] Given all that is sweetly explicit in the marriage of kindred minds and wills, the utter illogicality of desertion needs no other pleading than its own implicit contradiction. "For better or for worse" is not the language of an accountant's ledger, nor yet a doctor's temperature chart: it is how a constancy undertakes vicissitudes, how an arch upholds a world.

This sacrament of sexuality is a Christian *confessio* and can only claim to be authentic on Christian grounds. But what, then, of the validity of divorce? What of its ever more widespread incidence? What, further, of sexualities quite oblivious of any monitors, legal or religious, exempt from all register of bodies as "temples of the holy"?

The paradox is that we need the sanctity of marriage to underwrite the feasibility of divorce. This is not because we concede that human passions are essentially chaotic but because we do not. Negations do happen in the heart. When they do, it is not for anything inauthentic in the sacramental principle but because of its effective disavowal. That principle, never optional in its authority, is always violitional in its claim.

The quandary then is how to affirm the sacramental nature of human love while not enforcing it against the grain of its evident denial in the conduct of the parties, either or each. In every broken situation redemption has to be prior to rigorous enforcement of what, by dint of irreversible failure, would be arbitrary violation of hope for personhood. For personhood is that for whose inherent worth all sacraments exist.

The quest for such redemption can never well be negligent of its price in respect of the order it foregoes, lest witness to the hallowedness of any future union be imperilled. Hope would then be forfeit in the very liberty meant to sanction it. Vows once ruptured can only be retaken in pain and penitence since only by the paradox of grace can they be again authentic. Vital for society is the dependability of love and pledge, seeing that society is surer when marriage is cherished in the social order, with marital privacy and public well-being one hallowing.

The point of intimacy was well made by the novelist, Cesare Pavese.

> Casual love . . . always keeps certain mental reservations as a form of self-defence. Hence there is no such thing as a completely satisfying love-affair. To find it good one must surrender oneself to it unreservedly – in short – marriage.[45]

And marriage that owns itself such unreservedly. This is its significance in the public domain, inasmuch as private treacheries make public tragedy. Shakespeare knew this well as one of his recent biographers notes.

> To the conscience of educated Elizabethans . . . the death of a marriage was an integral, if not the crucial, part of the account of how England came to lose its soul.[46]

The reason, in part, was – and is – that there is abiding biological reality at work inside all cultures between parents and children. It is often urged that quarrelling adults spell no happiness to their offspring who would do better if they parted. That logic ignores the damage in the sense of treachery, the onus children carry from the enmity of their parents, the hard knock they take in psychic tension and emotional homelessness. The mysterious trust of family should halt the self-betrayal of parenthood.

But is the sacramental "we" of Christian marriage doomed into a minority culture, scarcely surviving in public shifts of wind or libertarian disdain? It would be faithless to fear that its charm is broken or its mystery dimmed. Realism can hold fear at bay while the task of defending and commending its glad sanity grows steadily more exacting. That sanity must find its gentle logic in the very given-, giving-, ness of love as known in limb and heart and will. Ever to have experienced sexual self-discovery is to have known an intimation of some freely-bonding, self-enthralling thing truly fitted to abide. To deny a troth-making sequel is to betray what gave it origin within.

Christian marriage, then, is rooted in human truth. It has "the justice of integrity". As with all else in human "dominion" it waits on a readiness of will. Its tokens are everywhere in our most honest self-awareness.

It would seem odd for lovers to tell each other: "You are not your own!" But that, in truth, is how it is. "Not your own" because – in your own knowing – you seek to be possessed. This being mutually the case, your self is re-possessed in the possessing of the other. Even a lively secular mind can take this in, as can all the sundry religious readings of human flesh and soul. To have it commended, formalized and – as far as may be – institutionalized in rite and ceremony, covenant and ring and symbol, spells no stale convention, no offending tyranny. Its blissful verifications are open to us all.

They do well to recruit all they may, from an apathy or a hostility that holds them in contempt or doubt. Their only final vindication lies in the personal autonomy that is our great endowment. By its leave and rule, the prompting and yearnings of the body need be no rudderless vessel but can pass into a captaincy able for their disciplined direction. Selfhood taken thus into its own full seriousness learns its supreme reward – the art of "rising into love".[47]

CHAPTER TEN

Our Dividual Being – The Irony of Mystical Union

I

The cathedral city of Lichfield in the English midlands had two famous native sons in the eighteenth century. The one, Dr. Samuel Johnson, was tutor to the other, the great tragedian, David Garrick. One clear truth emerged from the association of the man of letters with the player on the stage. It was the difference between Shakespeare as a text for a critic and Shakespeare as a script for an actor. Selfhood, too, has long been a theme for philosophy, a haven for psychology, a puzzle for religion. With and beyond these, it is a drama we must enact, a destiny to take in hand. Being the selves we are we can readily, in philosophy, make academic, and this may well be part of taking it in hand. Religion has to insist that "the text" of humanness can never be merely academic: it takes us "on stage" as a script whose meaning we present.

It was the native genius of the Buddha to begin with the burden of self-hood and – in a manner of speaking – to end without it, the self being liberated into the bliss of "non-being". It was an intelligent strategy, insofar as a complacent theism, beginning in a premature assurance with "God", might too zealously assume divine sanction. But the Buddha ran the risk of foreshortening a necessary perspective of things in time and space, long and far antecedent to the personal equation he felt impelled to take for starting point. Text and script together hold a drama to be comprehended in terms larger than the sense, total inwardly to each, of being in the cast. There theology comes home.

The central distinction, this way, between the Asian and the Semitic faiths, has been remitted from CHAPTERS TWO and THREE and was implicit in all the foregoing. It needs now to be taken further in study, via all their mystical traditions, of the issue of selfhood as inalienable and the hope, or goal, of self-absentness in absorption into "the One".[1]

Hence the deliberate chapter title, and the spelling of "dividual". "Individual" is an odd word. As a negative with "in" (as in "indecisive" or "indecent") it has us all, severally specific, members of a series but, as such, memorably "dividual", each being eminently "separable" from every other in the very nature of our identity. Indeed, "identity" itself is ambiguous, meaning our human membership and our member "loneliness" as the "I" partakes in all. "Socrates is human", but "this human is Socrates". An "individuum" is "one of a species when alone". In that sense we live within "dividual being", in not being other than the one we are, sharing that of which we are separately a sample, i.e. humankind.

This, as more than quibble about words, captures the very heart of our problem in selfhood. Each is the occasion of what can only be experienced in my "isolation" where "I" must personally transact my private instance of a humanity that is common to all. There is no text about life that is not script for a self – a self thus "dividual".

II

The fascination of the quest for mystical union has been perennial in the history of religions. The exploration of it in poetry and mythology, in the bye-ways of biography, is a major reward of religious studies. That it should be so stems from the profound irony of the self-escape of the inescapable self. Or perhaps, in deference to what is held by initiates about mystical experience, we should speak of "paradox" not "irony", the paradox involved if we want to ask the theorists of Buddhism what "it" is that "enters Nirvana", "enters" being an active verb requiring a "doer" who, nevertheless, "ceases to be" in the very doing of the act.

That doubtless is to over-simplify and needs a more subtle form of words.[2] Yet – even if crudely – it sets the matter plainly: "Can selfhood abrogate itself?" Yes! it might be said – by suicide. But suicide is the most dire statement by the self, a statement – self-made – about a self-unwantedness, that might justify itself in terms used by Fyodor Dostoevsky in the mouth of his "underground man":

> I have only, after all in my life, carried to an extreme what you have not dared to carry half-way.[3]

The actor, in such a fearful script, remains intensely present as a self, in enacting his own demise from selfhood.

Mystical quest for absorption into the unitive state is far other than the suicidal deed and promises somehow a "realization" which selfhood in the empirical world will never attain. However flawed the analogy, at least it serves to underline how every doing of a self is self-done. We live inside a subjectivity which leaves us still the ego-subjects of all our would-be self-transcending deeds and yearnings.

It is there where all religions start, in that the very ardour to yield up the self belongs where the self is, and where it is in a pronounal situation with inalienable "I"s and "me"s and "mine"s in the network of the "dividual" thing every self finds itself to be, coveting what William Wordsworth called "unchartered freedom" – a thing that only "tires".[4] As pampered children, we are "spoiled for choice" and our "choices spoil".[5] So the Buddha taught via the master-narrative studied in CHAPTER THREE. *Anicca*, as his Dharma termed it, setting all things in a distracting flux, fated always by transience, can never yield the satisfaction they only seem to promise. Wisdom must awaken to the illusory spell their appeal weaves around us.

We might even invoke the Hebrew psalmist's prayer: "O Lord, unite my heart . . ."[6] For there is then a dual situation, an "I" and "Thou", which a Buddhist seeker must transcend because it still ministers to the illusion of a "dividual" significance. The immediate clue for all is how to read the impulses of "desire" and what to do with them.

Their distracting, frustrating, potentially deceptive power is evident enough in all experience. In a poem on prayer, C. S. Lewis, cried: "Lord, dissolve my parliament . . ." For he seemed to himself as a cluster of "quarreling selves" that could not "bear an equal voice". "For I am Legion." God must discern between "the multiple factions which my state has seen, or will see".[7] George Herbert warned himself that "all worldly thoughts are but thieves met together." Asking elsewhere: "O what a thing is a man?" he can only say: "He is some twenty several men at least each several hour."[8]

Thus life invites, if it does not betray, us into a restless inconstancy, fuelled by desires it will not reward, and mortal time, anyway, will curtail or atrophy. Hence, the logic runs, the necessity to recognize the inherent futility of "desire", the *tanha* or "lusting drive", that has us asserting our possessive pronouns, demanding what is "ours" and severally clinging to what is "mine". Let them pass into an abeyance and evacuate themselves so that we cease to be cheated into expectancies reality can only dissipate. It will be our wisdom to anticipate the ultimate veto life and time will lay on youth and fame and wealth and power, on place, possessions and prestige.

This reading of the blight of transience, lying like a fate upon selfhoods, is the theme of *dukkha*, the "pain" of "impermanence" which has its bleakest formulation in Theravada Buddhist thinking. It has less darkly sombre, but still warning, tones in some Muslim Sufism and elsewhere across the spectrum of a perenially human religious mood. For the most part its case reads time as quantity and, in its urgency not to be undone, often fails to reckon with time as a quality.[9] Need we doubt the beauty of the rose because it faded or the splendour of the Parthenon because it was despoiled by time? The bare "duration" that languishes away may have been the maturation of some abiding thing. The measures of years and lives are more than the dates they spanned, so that the care of "transience" can be more than a realism for its flux.

Are the pronouns used to detach the self from history in this way not, in fact, detaching history from themselves? The point of departure is highly personal, busied with the self in its private dilemma of mortality. To be participatory in society and taking *social* stock of what the times are doing, inventing, transacting, corrupting or transforming, would be to sense a vocation to significance that could disarm suspicions of futility born of private fears, and enlist a new "desiring" after *public* good. Current history has always been a realm for courage, if also for the modesty of hope. There are happily aspects of religious mysticism, to which we must come, that seek its private techniques, not for their own inner sake alone, but to return more able from them to the business of the living world.[10]

Where, by the perceived implications of *anicca*, *dukkha* and the snares of *tanha*, the self is persuaded of the task, somehow, to forego its self-hood, to abate – as it were – being one, it requires the "discipline" – for Buddhists – of the Eightfold Path and, in Islamic Sufism, of the *Tariqah*, "the Way", with its "Stages" and "Stations" to be passed by "the seeker" to become "the wayfarer" and "the attainer". Through all its variants among the mystics of faith, "the Path" or "Way" brought the disciple to a "mentor", or guide, ministering as a "refiner" of his "silver" and a participant in his nurture. In the great "Orders" of Islamic mysticism these, if not the celebrated "founders" themselves, were senior "initiates" in their tradition, furnished with the Liturgies of devotion the pioneers had bequeathed.

The "goal" of the discipline was the attainment – in the Buddhist case – of Nirvana, or "non-being" as *anatta*, the ultimate "not-self", where the being we are calling "dividual", distracted, attached to phenomena, anxious and assertive, is truly "unified", but not in the sense cited earlier from the psalmist as still a personhood, well focused and inwardly "whole", but as "lost into undividedness", all "identity" transcended. It is the human viability of the "Way" that we have to interrogate by exploring the "irony" it seems to conceal.

In the case of Islam, and some kindred other mysticism, Jewish and Christian and Hindu, it re-minted the theme of the "unity" of God so that it became "unison in God", where the pronounal "Thou art my God", or "there is none but Thou", being the language of "otherness", could no longer hold.[11] For the intellectual Muslim mystic came a re-reading of the classic term *Tawhid* which traditionally had meant the urgent truth that Allah is One, *Huwa-Llahu Ahad* (Surah 112.1), but was now understood to mean the reaching of "the unitive state" – a single "We" beyond all differentiation. *Tawhid* is a noun about action, making or holding God as One, but now "having it so" was not a cherished dogma to be on all hands asserted and enjoined but, instead, an experience to be sought and entered, where vigilant doctrine was superseded by attainment. The re-minting was a grievous vagary much to be denounced by the purists in their orthodoxy. Similar tensions and "spoilings" wait on all mysticism.

Doctrinal antipathies aside, what of the actual techniques for mystical attainment? Abating the self obviously means escaping from sense-experience, as far as may be, with its appetites and distractions. The immediate call is for a régime of ascetic self-denial, a letting of the fire of cupidity "go out". That analogy was much loved in the Buddhist Dharma. For a fire that is deprived of fuel will not survive as fire.[12] The kind of early Sufi asceticism in Islam exemplified by Hasan al-Basri (642–728) may well have drawn its patterns from Christian example, despite the ambivalence of the Qur'an about Christian monasticism. But the logic really needs no external tuition. Appetites indulged are appetites encouraged. A reverse process has to be installed.

It is here that the first irony appears if – in fact – a self under its own discipline is more readily liable to intensified self-consciousness. May not the very abstinence be self-regarding, self-commending, self-engrossing? Is the hermit more credibly self-absent than the activist? Do not both have merely different reasons for keener self awareness, just as striving to be deliberately humble ministers to more subtle pride? If, when, a determination springs to action in the will to disavow that sense of accruing merit in the abstinence or the pride, will not the effort suggest a further round of self-regard? May there not be, as it were, an infinite regression of perversity?

Perhaps not. But the danger is ever present and every watchfulness for it is liable to accentuate it. Nevertheless, the techniques of "self-noughting" took their rigorous way. Some of the aspects of Muslim piety were noted in CHAPTER SIX – the taking of *Ta'widh* or "refuge", and the repeated "invocations of the Name". More expert "wayfarers" practised more prolonged and sustained forms of rhythmic recitation accompanied by movements of the body, designed to bring on the state of *fana'* or loss of empirical awareness in a "passing away" of normal selfhood and entry upon the mystical "unitive state", where selfhood was no longer there.

While many Muslim poets of Sufism loved the metaphor of "intoxication" and wrote mysteriously of "the masters" as "tavern-keepers", Buddhism favoured the "oceanic" language, where the "drop" thrown into the ocean has lost its "dropness" in the vast immensity. On the latter, an important caution needs to be registered. In the Buddhist view, this "lostness" is not "extinction", for the sufficient reason that, as the Dharma teaches, there was nothing there to "extinguish". Much western commentary on Buddhism misses the point when it thinks of "annihilation".[13] Seeing that personhoood is, *ab initio*, an illusion under which we labour and which we must forego, there was in the self a "no-thing" the discipline of "the Path" is set to realize.[14] Thus Buddhist "abating of desire" does not merely intend a curbing asceticism: it disavows the body–self experience altogether. What, in illusion, has believed itself as "being" surrenders both the being and the believing together, so "entering" where neither obtain.

Though some extreme forms of Islamic Sufism have tended towards such "the-body-a-prison" concept, it may understand its own style of *fana᾽* as an experience from which the empirical self could well return, enlightened and quickened, to normalcy again. A man who has been intoxicated is temporally "out of himself", but his *fana᾽* in that sense meant no final disavowal of the body and, thus, no forfeiture of the sacramental principle for which the body, while potentially our snare and our undoing, remains also the local theme of all things spiritual.

Outsiders from the Buddhist Dharma and its disciplined "Path" might well acknowledge the attainment of Nirvana, in blissful "non-being", as a philosophy of death. Could it then, at the same time, be a prescript for life and its living? For life and its living presuppose the habitation of the body and the sacramental "ship" the body alone affords for the voyage of personal being, the organ of all our emotions through which the soul is known, the immediate sanctuary of all things spiritual. Moreover, the Buddha and "the lesser Buddhas", the Bodhisattvas, are held to have known "enlightenment" but to have willingly deferred entry upon Nirvana in order to draw illusioned humans into its meaning, out of pity for their absence from it in the imprisoning business of their selfhood.

Again, then, a sense of paradox recurs, in that life – in the time of it – has a vital Buddhist relevance to the mortal disillusioning concerning it of persons in the world. In measure, that might align the deep Buddhist compassion involved with the Christian sense of the personal body as the indispensable sacrament of all spiritual grace.[15] This hint of mutual truth is, of course, complicated by the context of successive existences to which Buddhism is committed in its comprehension, and practice, of the Eightfold Path, whereas the Semitic faiths understand the sacrament of personhood in singular entrustment. Either way, the mortal self seems crucial even to the enterprise of losing it. In its *de facto* role the body is inescapable. That fact deserves to be admitted into relevance for any faith about its housing an illusion and a deceit. The Christian understanding of "the resurrection of the body", despite heavy problematics, at least keeps faith with its *pre-mortem* significance in the nature of selfhood. Might mystical union contrive instead to escape the self's "incarnation in its flesh" only in order to dwell in it more wisely? Otherwise, to suspect and accuse the body of being party to a delusion would seem to cancel the role it still plays in correcting the delusion it fostered.

III

The element of irony goes further if we ponder the theme of "desire" on which so much turns for every religion. The self in the body is a very necessitous entity, so that "needs" are implicit in its very nature – food, shelter, water in the realm of daily living. Being thus inherently appetitive, it is evident that we are liable to clutch and grab at any or all of the items of existence, out of fear of lack of them, or nervous prudence in ensuring them, or ambition to outdo others in the possession of them. Acquisition fires ambition. Wealth, fame, reputation, associations, become assets we grow eager to ensure or loathe to forfeit. "Desire", in all its range and urgency, proves a theme of always latent, maybe urgent, crisis, and a central focus of the liabilities of self to self-undoing in the very marrow of existence.

The checks – without balances we may bring to this situation – will register the crisis but not resolve it. The Buddha discovered – and wisely taught – that there were limits to the counsels of austerity, snares in undue pressures to asceticism. His perceptions have been endlessly confirmed through all the centuries. Simone Weil was a telling twentieth-century devotee of all that reflective asceticism entails both of anguish and of hope. She held that God had given her existence that she might desire to lose it. She set herself to bring His will to pass.

Two things seem to emerge as evident from extreme austerity in the abating of "desire". The one is how far it legitimates "a right desiring" and the cherished Greek virtue of *sophrosune*, the watchful "moderation" which figures also among the virtues of the Eightfold Path. The other is that even the most extreme austerity, far from diminishing self- pre-occupation, only heightens it. The ego that was to be "effaced" was the more inwardly underlined. An observer wrote of Simone Weil:

> The way she mounted guard around her emptiness still showed a terrible pre-occupation with herself.[16]

If we cannot forego "desire" in being always necessitous by the very nature of our selfhood we have, surely, to concede its legitimacy, thus making more urgent the discernment that should control its range and monitor its methods, in order to curb its temptations. It will be deeply ironical – and, indeed, ruinous – to tell ourselves it is only finally handled by a theory of its meaning that disowns its every presence. In measure, Buddhist faith indirectly concedes this, in that the *Sangha* or community of monks only fully obeys the Path by debt to the "laity" who will replenish their "begging bowls" in gratitude that these serve to keep Dharma-truth open to the common mind by the example.

Whether for that non-monastic role in society, or for the sanity of those in their mystical quest of what their Paths/Ways pledge to them as goals, it would seem that we are forced back on to "desire" in right partnership with discipline. Irony is resolved if we do not have to suspect "desire" per se but only to respect its capacity to be always suspect. Then will be restored to us all the sacramental potentialities of the persons we avail to be and of the bodily fulfilments, the intellectual adventures, that invite us. There can be a warrant for ambition, duly edited, a place for celebration wisely taken, a mind for achievement aptly measured. Rightly alerted by intimations from the mystics, we may be restored to ourselves in our dividual identity and retrieve from suspicion the positives of existence.

It may be, in practice, that this is what the Buddhist discipline achieves by virtue of a philosophy which can allow its practice to over-ride its own analysis.[17] Seldom has the "desire to desire" it repudiates been more ardently told than by Thomas Traherne in his poem "Desire". He thanks God

> For giving me desire,
> An eager thirst, a burning ardent fire,
> A virgin infant flame.

He finds it the very "Love with which into the world I came . . . which in my soul did work and move and ever, ever me enflame." He dares even to call it a "heavenly avarice" which he could liken elsewhere to "something infinite which talked with my expectation and moved my desire".[18]

Traherne was, doubtless, unusually susceptible to the charm of a rural world and the ever fascinating panorama of moving scenes and turning seasons. But his quality of sensuous life, its thirst held in check by what he called "discernment", was in little danger of lurching into cupidity or of lapsing into a grudging perception of the world. A "nature-mysticism" it might be, but it was also a fulfilment of his selfhood hardly to be attained by reading illusion into that "something infinite" as for ever disqualified from "moving his desire". That plain conclusion only confirms the irony we are detecting in views of selfhood that greet its seriousness only to take its "I am-ness" as illusion to transcend.

IV

This onus inherent in selfhood for being a self, necessitous both physically and socially, and, therefore, liable for its desires, is what requires us to

study the distinction, earlier anticipated, between two egoisms. It is a difference often blurred. Having the two distinct bears strongly on the
mystical quest for "the unitive state", whether as Nirvana or *fana'* or mystical *Tawhid*, or counterparts elsewhere among the faiths.

It can be expressed in the question: Does being selfless mean being
unselfed? The ultimate Buddhist answer will be Yes, in that selfhoods will
only ever cease their self-seeking impulses by the "oceanic" absorption
into "the One". The answer of many mystics will also be Yes, for the time
being, while remaining in "the unitive state" from which in life they will
return. The logic, either way, will be that the natural man, if not mystically withdrawn, finally or presently, from selfhood, stays inherently
selfish.

Broadly the non-mystical, certainly the normal Christian, answer will
be No. A moral unselfishness is blessedly possible within every selfhood.
It is a selflessness, in moral terms, which, far from evacuating its human
condition, emphatically recruits and fulfills it and that, in the most
ennobling terms. It will be an unselfishness which – in the words quoted
from Islam in CHAPTER SIX – "leaving self behind did self inherit".[19] The
self "left behind" was the one that made everything self-relevant in gain,
ambition, scheming and conceit: "the self inherited" was the one vicarious and vulnerable "even to its own hindrance" in the will to compassion
and grace. To that quality, like the Franciscan in Saint Francis, selfhood
was indispensable.

Egoism, then, or egotism, are terms we must distinguish as meaning,
either what we are *qua* existing or what we are by moral choice inside
identity *qua* perversity of character self-fashioned. The same distinction
belongs to egocentricity, if that term is employed, namely the fact of our
constitution physically as persons on two feet with one face, and our
capacity to live only in and for ourselves.[20]

These dimensions of a pronounal world, the "I" and "me" of instinctive human usage, are obvious enough. Their importance is how sharply
they bear on what is at stake between religions and within the techniques
and practices of mysticism. Do we adjudge life as a vocation towards
"non-being" in the Buddhist mode? Are we being called – as the mystics
tell us – into a self-abeyance that ceases from selfhood? Is the goal a culmination in itself or a discipline from which we re-engage with all things
empirical? How, we might simply ask, is each "I" well possessed of "me",
how properly dispossessed and, then, what "I" remains or should remain?

Paradox though it may be in the light of the theory of the Dharma,
Buddhist ethics are in no way absent from the pain and bewilderment of
the human scene. Whatever may be the sequence of lives or the cycle of
returns, the Eightfold Path is thorough and realist in its prescripts for the
social order, in its call for right mindfulness and moral awareness. The

underlying thesis is watchful against any liability to trust existence so that the bare fact of it is potentially a sin, but nevertheless responds to its sufferings in compassion. Might not that compassion be a sounder clue from which to reach a reading of the whole? At all events, it is well to hold that, since with all other humans we are each necessitous, we are all each necessary in the economy of the here-and-now whether or not we aspire to reach the mystery of "non-being".

Those who aspire so in Buddhist terms are no longer within the here-and-now, unless they have deferred entry into their attained Nirvana. In Islamic Sufism is the long tradition for which mystical *fana'* did mean a practical "return" to engagement in the common world. In any event, those "arrivees" blessed their times with splendid poetry, hallowing the literatures of their time and place and enriching the long centuries. The *zawiyas*, or "corners" in which they assembled, often on Thursdays to precede the obligatory ritual *Salat* of Friday, provided the spiritual nurture, the kinship of soul, by which day-to-day artisans seasoned the stress or poverty of their mortal lot. Their devotions afforded solace and perspective by which to weather the vicissitudes of life. They served to intensify in deeply personal terms the yearnings sometimes left unsatisfied by the remoteness of theology or the terrifying reaches of Quranic warnings.

The Sufi Orders which gave both private liturgies and public structure to Islamic mysticism were often locally fulfilled in economic guilds of crafts and craftsmen in the suqs and markets, where interests coincided with discipline.[21] There was then no question of withdrawal from wider human concerns, while into these could pass the energies of soul withdrawal had released. Examples were noted in CHAPTER SIX.

The practice of *dhikr*, the "recollection" of the Names of God which was central to their piety and which recruited the postures of the body and the harnessing of the voice, could also serve to embrace society at large in the relevance of what was personally recalled. The sense, that Sufism made more acute, of deeds in mortal life being "forwarded" into eternal account, made its devotees livelier in social conscience and induced more scrupulous behaviour. It was at least a monitor against indifference and truculence. Thus Ahmad al-Tijani:

> I am Thy servant, O God, from the time Thou didst set me in this vale of soul-making, of thought and experience, that Thou mightest observe what I sent forward into the world of immortality and decision.[22]

Insofar as the Sufi was "practising the presence of God" in *dhikr*, the mind-set silently rebuked those whom the Qur'an described as "concealed indeed from men, but not from God" where, as the Christian Collect has it, "all hearts are open" (Surah 4.108). There was thus in Sufi practice an antiseptic against those – as the Qur'an said – "in whose hearts there is a sickness".[23] To "betray the self" as these did was a condition which prompted the Sufi mind to hope of a healing penitence on the part of all such – a posture in contrast from the frequent condemnations reiterated in the Qur'an. Given the broad veto on "intercession", there could only be prayer that these "sick in soul" would bring themselves to their own healing prayer. At least Sufis found a keen perception of the reach – and mystery – of human sin and wrong. "A man must know," they said "that he is wrapping his net around himself."

Thanks to the Sufis there could always be a healthy alertness about the pitfalls and the vagaries of the "I" every one dividually knew in the very feel of the pronoun on the lips.

> If there had not been love, there would not have been any existence. Had it not been for pure love's sake, should there have been any reason for the creation of the heavens?[24]

Hence the significance – and the crisis – of every selfhood.

> Go, sweep out the chamber of your heart,
> Make it ready to be the dwelling place of the beloved.
> When you depart out he will enter in,
> In you, void of yourself, will he display his beauty.[25]

"Void of yourself" could refer – as we have seen – either to the ego-centric situation or ego-centric assertion. Al-Shabastari doubtless meant the former but at least notice was served on the menace of the latter.

Among the keenest concerns for inner probity of will and heart was that told searchingly by the great Abu Hamid al-Ghazali in his celebrated *Al-Munqidh min al-Dalal*, or "The Deliverer from Going Astray". He examined the inner motives in his career ambitions and resolved to forsake his academic role and, as a wayfarer, take the Sufi path towards wholeness. His rich gift of intellectual lore and his personal devotion equipped him to help reconcile the tensions between custodians of doctrine and the practitioners of *fana'*.

> Caught in a veritable thicket of attachments . . . I saw for certain that I was on the brink of a crumbling bank of sand . . . Perceiving my impotence and having lost my power of choice I sought refuge with God most high as one who is driven to Him.[26]

That personal story through physical breakdown, long travail and ultimate finding has remained among the finest Muslim narratives of the wrestling of an "I" with a "me". By this and his other writings, Al-Ghazali could be saluted as "the Augustine of Islam", for his probing mind and soul experience in fruitful commerce, either with the other.

His legacy serves to underwrite how so much of the social and moral relevance of Sufi discipleship came from the educative influence of its storied wealth and of its numerous shaikhs, pirs and revered local *murshids*. One such in Algeria was Shaikh Abu-l-ʿAbbas al-ʿAlawi (1869–1935) whose audience

> you would find sitting in front of him – hundreds, nay thousands, with heads bowed, as if birds were hovering round them, hearts full of awe and eyes wet with tears, in silent understanding of what they heard him say.[27]

The influence could be both towards a deeper inner piety and thoughts disconcerting to traditional minds. Thus in a story of the famous Shams al-Din al-Tabrizi:

> One day a person met him in the market-place and exclaimed: "There is no god but God: Shams al-Din is the apostle of God." On hearing him the people raised a furore and sought to kill him. Shams intervened and led the man away saying: "My good friend, my name is Muhammad. You should have shouted 'Muhammad is the apostle of God.' The rabble will not take gold that is not coined!"[28]

In this lively way the practice of Sufism held lightly to established dogma and ritual, in a readiness even to find fasting and pilgrimage fulfilled in the inwardness of the soul's own sanctuaries.

Its wisdom taught that all believers needed the mentors its patterns provided, since no person could be the touchstone of his or her own devotional fidelities. The guidance of higher soul-wisdom in the trust of *murshids* and "saints" was vital for right awareness of the "stages" passed and the "states" by which they were proven in the testings of the *Tariqah*. It was not book or speech from which, in truth, the knowledge came but from the infection of communion and the "emptying" of the self-sufficient heart. There were "heresies" of soul lurking in the self, requiring to be purged by "right illumination".

> He is no dervish true, That meanly begs for bread,
> But raises up anew, The living from the dead.[29]

The seeking self comes to be the thing towards which its bent moves. For "the soul and the heart assume the qualities of the Beloved by the attraction of wish and desire.[30]

So it was that the disciplines of the long Sufi tradition served to evoke and refine a warm and fertile spirituality throughout the cities and villages of Islam and in the several languages from Morocco to Malaysia in which it found its voice and scattered the stories of its saints and sages. So doing it underlined the irony wherby selfhood, in the very art of self-escape, ministered deeply to the life of everyday religion and the formation of personality in the lowly life of markets and of precincts to the mosques where scholars often found them suspect.

The wisdom we have reviewed thus briefly had other exponents who prized their secrets and reserved their mysteries in more private subtlety, as thus by Abu Sa'id Ibn Abu-l-Khair (967–1049).

> Said I: "To whom belongs Thy beauty?"
> He replied: "Since I alone exist in Me,
> Lover, Beloved and Love am I in one,
> Beauty and mirror and the eyes that see . . .
> Affirm God's being and deny thine own.
> This is the meaning of 'No God but He.'" . . .
>
> When me at length Thy love's embrace shall claim,
> To glance at paradise I'ld deem it shame,
> While to a Thee-less Heaven were I called,
> Such heaven and hell to me would seem the same.[31]

For such "the sea will be the sea whatever the drop's philosophy".

For such mystic intoxication was no longer just an ardour of love between an "I" and "Thou": it was an identification where duality was lost.

> The Spirit is mingled in my spirit even as wine is mingled with pure water.
> Lo! Thou art I.
> I am He whom I love and He whom I love is I.
> We are two souls dwelling in one body.
> If thou seest me thou seest Him,
> And if thou seest Him, thou seest us both.[32]

Others spoke of being "drowned in a sea of unification", personal identity abolished in the ocean of unity.

Given the assurance of the Islamic doctrine of *Tawhid*, it is the more remarkable that the Muslim community in its wide dispersion, was, nevertheless, able to integrate philosophies that so radically transformed its central thesis and stood in such contrast to the nature of Quranic ethics as regulating a "performative religion".[33] It also called in question the insistence of its Scripture on Muhammad's status as, strictly, Allah's "messenger", with a commission to preach and, by warrant of the Hijrah, to establish "a state of faith". These offered no obvious invitation to private quest for soul-abandonment into a "We-ness", where no guidance for plain and submissive obedience could have been suited or required.

It might be claimed that, in some way, the Prophet himself had undergone mystic experience in *sharh al-sadr* and the *Mi'raj*, but surely only in the utter exceptionality of his status as the apostle, and not for emulation

by the faithful, whose calling was to highly practical duties comprised in
Din and *Dawlah*.[34]

Yet it was part of the wide cultural geography of Islam that it could
prove susceptible to influences of thought and factors of society to which
venturing spirits could betake themselves, whatever the strains on loyalty
to the sure determinants of their religion. Judaism and Christianity also,
from differing angles, demonstrated a comparable readiness for risks with
orthodoxy. Concerned as we are with pronouns in religions, we need not
pursue further these examples of how, in some elusive sense, they might
be left behind altogether, or how – indefinably – they might be merged
into some all-inclusive "We". It remains to see how selfhoods must
somehow return from the "ocean" of their "lostness as selves" and re-
possess identity, either quickened by what was authentic in absenting
from it, or wiser by their disillusion in the venture.

V

If the "must" seems too harsh and the alternative too cynical, there are
evidences against thinking so in the sources themselves. It is intriguing
how, so often, poems about "We" are still prone to the language of
duality. An unknown poet sings:

> This mystic union, From self has separated me.
> Now witness concentration's mystery. Of two made one.

And adds:

> In union divine, With Him Him only do I see.
> I dwell alone, and that felicity, No more is mine.[35]

While Al-Junaid writes a little plaintively:

> In secret from the world apart
> My tongue has talked with my Adored,
> So, in a manner, we United are and One . . .'[36]

"In a manner" brings a wistful note into the confidence and he is the
dualist who adds, with his very personal pronoun: "I feel Thee touch my
inmost ground."

Do we not conclude that the "I" or our dividual being is truly
inescapable and that the very will somehow to elude it or elide it necessarily fails? For its very identity, is not a ready immersion in the world the
evident requisite, so that, due involvement apart, there is no taking selfhood into God? Further, we have to ask whether our human immersion

in the world is not the indispensable context and arena of our "entering into God"?[37] Perhaps also there is that truth in the other direction, namely that God's transcendent reality manifests itself in and to our responding engagement with His creation, bodies as we are. If so, then what the mystical "unitive state" seeks after will, indeed, be an inter-society but grounded in the divine "derivatives" (may we call them?) of creation and grace.

These are the areas of thought we must finally pursue, taking the divine dimension us-ward first. There has long been an instinct in some theology to predicate a transcendent Reality that was beyond all knowing and, therefore, all "unitiving" with us humans. Jewish Kabbalists gave it the name of *En Sof*, "the Infinite". Never encountered, *En Sof* had, nevertheless mediated "entire otherness" in emanations. It was with these religious history had to deal, whether in Old Testament story or elsewhere. Religious experience of every sort related with these disclosures, however received and interpreted, which were only *from* and not *about* the Infinite, of whom we could never say: "In Him we live and have our being."

If we supposed that mysticism was trying to "know the Unknowable" by "unknowing the self" it would – on this showing – be vainly engaged. For the Infinite was not accessible in the absolute sense. Initiates could never, in this context, be saying "We" in any but illusory terms. Two corollaries follow, namely that their hope must fall back on a theology of nature and grace and they, for their part, must return to their pronounal selves as the right realm of authentic mutuality between themselves and God, where – in duly circumspect humility – a loving "We" might be known.

There is a lively hint of this in the great Hafiz of Shiraz.

> There was a man that loved God well.
> In every motion of his mind God dwelt.
> And yet he could not tell that God was in him, being blind.
> Wherefore – as if afar – he stood and cried:
> "Have mercy, O my God."[38]

The unitive state was there but in an unawareness only dispelled when the sense of sin brought him to cry for grace. The association with the New Testament parable is clear. Perhaps it was something akin that made so many practising mystics anxious lest there was a hidden selfishness in their very desire for divine "union", that something needing their repentance was present in their aspiration. The saint and poetess Rabi'ah is famous in this sentiment.

> Two ways I love Thee: selfishly and next as worthy of Thee.
> 'Tis selfish love when I do naught

Save think on Thee with every thought.
'Tis purest love when Thou dost raise
The veil to my adoring gaze . . .[39]

She wants to avoid all self-seeking in the very act of the self's utmost seeking, and she is ever using the language of duality.

How right the Buddha was in the compassion that brought his "illumination" back into the social realm which the outward quest in Dharma had him leave behind. Perhaps, then, where we must return to "invest" the visionary encounter is where we do well to belong and with which we should ever re-commence. For it is in the moil of things that pronouns have their currency. Having them aspire to use a "Thou" for God most surely means our using it for fellow-humans. To think so is in harmony with theistic faiths in their confidence as to the created order and the realm of grace. Should we aspire to know God as "Thou" while we neglect what we are bold to call "His", namely "the works of His hands", the "gifts of His grace"?

Shaikh ʿAbdullah Ansari of Herat (1005–1090) was among the most urgent of aspirants to "the unitive state", bent on losing all sense of duality, as one for whom the fascination of the world was "like a mirage". To encounter the world was to despise it. He wrote:

> Urged by desire I wandered in the streets of good and Evil. I gained nothing except feeding the fire of desire.[40]

Nowhere could the ambiguity of "desire" be more starkly put. He might have exchanged the nausea of satiety for a destiny to ministry. The artist, Vincent Van Gogh, was familiar with the human detritus of the streets and could see "life as a trap of sorrow from which he longed to escape", but in terms of what, elsewhere, he told when he wrote:

> The crucifixion had brought darkness over all the land but only after it did so was a world of love possible.[41]

In those terms, to "escape to God" is to be given again to the very features of human experience which, age-long, have moved the mystics of the faiths to merge their selfhoods wholly in the transcendent, whether they do so by a philosophy of Theravada Buddhist "transitory suffering", or from a cult of soul-privacy athirst for God as the sublime answer to its loneliness. The experience that rewards them does not essentially "unself" them. For they remain immersed in their aspiration. It may in measure – we might say – re-self them for inter-human society "in the knowledge and love" of the God who is "God with us", and will not be "had" as Lord except in the company of His human creaturehoods.

This truth of things lies unsuspected – and full of irony – in the now popular language that talks of "leaving God for God".[42] It may hold validly if it means forsaking unworthy ideas of God, the God of complacent or dogmatic minds, where doing so would clearly fit Islamic warning about *shirk*.[43] It cannot hold if it thinks to reach the God of mystic and transcendent "Oneness" by forsaking, whether in anguish or high dudgeon, the world of His creation and the intercommunity of humankind. For it is in these realms that divinity belongs and humanly divine discovery is made.

It has long been a puzzle to many outside the Dharma tradition of mind how all things could ever have originated as inherently a trap and a snare, a prison for humankind. If we conclude that life is essentially inimical to all we hold dear as its primal values, do we not posit some calculating malice that contradicts all that could ever be worship-worthy? Could not the sickness, sorrow and solitariness that dominate what is read as *dukkha* to be escaped, be rather read as a scene that kindles and invites a vicarious compassion in response? The Dharma in fact teaches us to attain this vicarious compassion. Why not then on a conviction that it discloses the root of things, rather than strive for a behaviour it has pronounced to be against the logic of the situation that most cries out for it?

To think this way returns us to the doctrine of creation as comprising an originating beneficence, sadly and falsely maligned by the contrary thesis that will not have it so. Either way, our minds and hearts are faced with an option about our pronounal world. Since neither the implied malice nor the evident beneficence[44] are provable, as if brought into some test-tube, why not opt for that reading of the transcendent which both requires and evokes an active transcending on our part of all that is doom-laden or casual, indifferent or despairing, in our esteeming of the world?

> It was finely said of Jesus of Nazareth that he lived life as a continuous celebration and wanted to be remembered as a man with a cup in his hand.[45]

It was a cup that came to be filled with bitter things of this transitory and sin-prone human scene but it belonged also in the hand of God, being what a "Father gave".

CHAPTER ELEVEN

Faiths' Pronoun-Users Now

I

The "web-site" analogy for religions with their pronouns has one final point. It has to do with their non-finality. Web-sites need "webmasters" who keep them abreast of developments and to whom enquiries and comments may be directed. "This web-site is maintained by X on behalf of . . ." runs the common formula.

It has always been an issue for religious faiths – who will keep them up to date and maintain them in contemporary fettle? They may be constant but their constancy changes. Emphases vary and details undergo muta-tion. Even the most rigorous conservers have to concede that to live is to outlive. In any event the major faiths resemble continents rather than shires and have been required to admit diversity in order to maintain iden-tity or, otherwise, to let fragmentation contradict inclusion. Then new identities have been formed out of them in the way that Sikhism devel-oped from within Islam or Lutheran Christianity repudiated that of Catholic Rome sufficiently to warrant a new "enchurching" separate and free. Thence, in turn, came countering changes in the former entity, itself so far from its own New Testament original and destined further to adapt again the explicit terms of its authority. It is only the more bewildering for neutral observers to learn that all such changings, however radical they seem, are allegedly developing what was ever latent for their native wisdom in the ancient heritage.

There was a strong Islamic tradition that every century would satisfy the need for a *mujaddid*, a "renewer". Perhaps the great Abu Hamid al-Ghazali was such a one (died 505 AH) while Mirza Ghulam Ahmad aspired to fill the role at the turn of Islam's twelfth century, only to launch an Islamic "heresy". "Renewers" posthumously hailed as such may have fulfilled the task: others, self-appointed, only darkened it except for their splintering followers. "Heresies" know themselves as true versions.

Examples are numerous as with "Oral Torahs" alongside the first written one or a church affirming itself as being *semper reformanda* – "perpetually reforming" – as a duty. The destiny lies in the paradox of a contemporary abidingness for which all aspire, so that constancy itself is a time of trial.

This crucial issue of always having identity alert to its own definition, as being under the scrutiny of changing times, leads inevitably into the nature of religious authority and to the organs by which it is exercised. There is the intellectual task of due custodianship of Scriptures and of doctrine and ethics, and there is the relation those organs have to the realm of political power. Saying "we" and "us" cannot escape meaning "ours" as "these", and "those" must necessarily be the texts, the concepts, the instruments through which that "we-ness" is possessed and signified.

The urgent need of those insistent pronouns now is to distinguish firmly their religious use from their tribal, ethnic, racial or national currency. For many religions this is a supremely difficult task, to almost all highly uncongenial – so far and so long have the two sources and sanctions of identity been conjoined. However, it grows ever more clear that, in terms of a twenty-first century, there must needs develop a sense of religious claims and constraints in the socio-moral order as ready to acknowledge the global shape of human well-being and surrender the intent to legislate and dominate unilaterally inside the political nationhoods they have traditionally characterized. There are concepts of human rights across all nations that demand recognition and implementation through all national borders, with a writ mandated to require them – a writ not to be thwarted by warnings that what obtains within our borders is only the business of our rule and the arena of our *Shari'ah*. In the quest for a global ethic for a global ecology, the claims of a basic humanism deserve to override – and not to be over-ridden by – the exclusives of territorial religion.

This is to say that "being human" has priority over "being Muslim", or "being Hindu", or "being Christian", or "being Buddhist", with these denoting adjectives rigorously held to what they can contribute in the defining – and attaining – of "humanity" and not exclusifying to themselves what that task entails, while searching to serve it to the utmost of their lights and energies.

And not only so across national borders, but inside them. There are many countries where citizens comprise two, three or more religious identities – whether or not also racially distinct. It will be happier and truer if their one citizenship is genuinely cognizant of their religious diversity. Thus, for example, being "Egyptian" or "being Nigerian" or being "Sri Lankan" – like "being human" – should not read as "being only Muslim" or "being only Buddhist". Even where minorities are more numerically negligible in respect of national ethos, or even almost non-existent, the single human factor deserves to prevail against the kind of religious exclusivity, whether of law or culture, that virtually disallows a common human-ness or annexes to itself what the human meaning is.

184

The case or the logic for this reading of religions as ready to be inter-human derives from the nature of religion itself. It is not some "secular" counsel drawn from disavowal of their insanities and bigotries. Such counsels resemble a ship's helmsman presiding at his wheel unaware that the boat will only answer to the helm when it is afloat. For a helm is meant for navigation and navigation means negotiation with the ocean in its vastness beyond some hugged shore of our own familiars. To be content to be "without religion" is to have foregone wonder, awe, mystery and the wretchedness and glory of "unaccommodated man". Mere secularity has "ta'en too little care of that!"[1] For the core of *religio* is an awe about awe itself, a recognition of what, in its very quality, requires to be above our calculatings and our surmisings, our ethicizing and our devisings, as pondered in CHAPTER THREE – a state of being responsive to what "has decided us", so that we are its willing subjects.[2]

It is true that this state of response to what is inviolate truth can tend to fanaticism or obscurantism, if it is refusing to be accountable about its intrinsic claims. That is its temptation – a temptation to which all authority is liable, in the passion to be "absolute" for what is "absolute held to be". It is here the other impulse making all "religious" has to come into play, namely the humility proper to a right discipleship, as having nothing but what it has "received" from beyond all merit or contrivance. Things ultimate only in relative possession is the hallmark of "religion" in a due integrity. In this sense the multiple reproach a contemporary secularity has for religions is really asking them to be more fully "religious", not in renouncing the transcendent but in letting it more truly transcend, with their structures, rituals and teachings at best only serving and reporting what is more ultimate than they.

II

In this necessity of the religious mind, the nexus with state power and national interest is the likeliest counter-factor. For it is precisely the political dimension that complicates or corrupts the religious will to integrity. Apart, as we have seen, from accentuating the vested interests of land and power, of prestige and passion, it mixes the motives with which truth is held and prejudices the criteria by which it purports to exist.

The national elements of people identity are often blamed for their ferocity on the abetting agency of religious tenets and passions – and with much justice. However, there is equal justice in the accusation the other way round, in that religious faith is frequently suborned to the aims of political strife or national assertion. Only in reserving a lively critique of, and resistance to, this entanglement can religious faith affirm the "good faith" of its faith-holding. This must be so for reasons wider and fuller than those implicit in the secular deploring of the enmities they harbour and the disdain that cries: "A plague on all their houses."

Yet can religious faith ever have disinterest for the realm of power, even if it must ever suspect the interest of power-mongers in religious faith? Can either be seriously indifferent to each other, religion innocent of politics, statehood indifferent to faith? The latter, as argued earlier, has a duty to be "neutral" (subject to the common good and order) about the faith-identity of citizens so that the civic rights of minorities are not impaired. But can it be oblivious about the religious springs of judgement, of vocation or reproach, from which its policy must flow, the convictions by which its sovereignty is guided?

Secularism will interject that religion has no monopoly of these – a rejoinder that must be conceded, if we can assume that it holds these firmly, which is to mean that it holds them "religiously".[3] While – as we must delay to ponder – the writ of the secular mind may run readily in the West, there remain many territories world-wide where the conjunction of state and religion, of political power and given faith, is still dominant, not seldom adamant in its tenacity, and quite unwilling to concede a genuine tolerance of societal diversity, guarded – if not cherished – by political equality and spiritual liberty. Power for faith and faith for power are strongly entrenched and fortified by long sanction, held to be not only religiously proper but religiously imperative.

It was all there, we might say, in Judaic origins, with the absolute fusion of people, land and armed strength, the triad assumed fundamental to each element within it.[4] As noted in CHAPTER FOUR, the indecision within Zionism as to its religious meaning via secular attainment has made it problematic for Israelis either to dissociate its religion, in whatever terms, from the State's existence, or to conceive itself a religious polity. For, either way, the definition of Jewishness itself is at stake. The "sacred" reference in its Constitution was the ambiguous term "the Rock of Israel".[5] Inside its juridical borders it grants civic rights to its otherwise disadvantaged Arab, i.e. non-Jewish, citizens, but the Orthodox religious expression of Judaism has exclusive control of vital aspects of society and law and enjoys conspicuous monetary favours by dint of how the suffrage and party systems work in Israel.

The Zionist State must therefore be seen as *sui generis* in any comparative assessing of the nexus between religion and politics, between faith and power within national states. Religion there, in its Orthodox form, both takes and covets crucial advantage from the fact of statehood, while Judaism in its other, liberal, forms only gains from statehood occasion to serve it as if it were unambiguously secular, namely by moral integrity and in the satisfaction the State affords as a symbol of Jewishness.

Islam is the most forthright example of an unequivocal tradition of faith–power nexus. It is one which Muslims find it very difficult even to reconsider, let alone to forego. For its legitimacy is built into the very fabric both of the *Sirah* of Muhammad and the sequence of the Qur'an. Both passed from Mecca to Medina, in the Hijrah, or willed venture out of "preaching faith only" into empowerment of rule and arms, out of the sole office of witness into a destiny for state and régime. The seal of the legitimacy was held to be evident in the success with which it was crowned, the "manifest victory" it gained.

The Caliphate sustained both the pattern and the confident assurance of its validity. Through the Islamic centuries it has been variously emulated and assumed. Muslim nation-states read themselves as its perpetutation even though they fragment the inclusive *Dar al-Islam* or *Ummah*, "the nation", for which some zealots still yearn.

Thus, in conspicuous example, Pakistan demanded and achieved its Islamic separatism inside the sub-continent, despite the appalling cost in massacre, privation, upheaval and human tragedy. The emphatic case was that in majority Muslim areas, in so far as these could be consolidated, Islamic statehood was a *sine qua non* of "being Muslim", seeing that essentially "only Muslims should rule Muslims" and that "Islam never meant its Muslims to be minorities outside its *Dar*". Its *Dar* was the reality of its inseparable *Din wa Dawlah*, "religion and rule".

The logic of Pakistan was impeccable by Islamic reasons but otherwise acutely fallible. For – by geophysical necesity – it left millions of Muslims in a truncated India permanently fated to the unIslamic doom of minority status, "de-Pakistanised" – as it were – for evermore. If these millions persisted in Islam[6] it could only be in respect of *Din*, the religious norms of Islam – mosques, fasts, pilgrimages, alms, ethics, sermons, Qur'an recital, personal status law and that all important *taqwa*, the piety by which, beyond all statehood, the Muslim is defined. Were not these the sufficient Islam? That, shorn of statehood, they were not, we have seen in CHAPTER SEVEN. It might be that Indian Muslims, left to that religious destiny, could vindicate that, stateless Islamically, they were not orphans but that, co-existing with Hindus and others, they could be validly Muslim and Indian[7]. Either way, Islam would prove an ongoing actuality alike under the necessity, and the non-necessity, of what Pakistan expressed.

That loaded story of partition in 1947 had deep consequences for India proper (as the term had to be thereafter). Making Pakistan implicitly invited India to create "Hindustan", virtually to require that to be "Indian" one must be "Hindu". The secular polity of Jawaharlal Nehru and the Congress Party resisted the temptation firmly, in pursuit of a multi-lingual, multi-ethnic Indianism, despite the legacies of partition and the uneasy adjacence of Pakistan.[8] There have been recent signs that an unhappy equation of "Indian" and "Hindu" is gaining ground and that secular statehood may not endure in India. Whatever its future juridically, there are always emotional and societal factors that tell against it and against which, in turn, a resolute secularity of constitutional law and concept is the first and surest defence.

Instancing this twentieth-century saga from the sub-continent is only to reinforce the case against religions that say "us" and "ours" faith-wise while withholding the pronouns from any genuine "you" and "we" state-wise, thus inferiorizing the civic other and exclusifying the religious identity, to have it dominate the power realm. Islam would seem to be historically the faith for which a co-existence culturally, and – in this limited sense – secularly, proves the most uncongenial venture, both in concept and in fact, despite the urgency with which this present century awaits and needs it.

Can it ever happen in *Dar al-Islam*? It never will, unless an Islamic case be made for it. Does such a case exist?[9] If we return to the Hijrah we can arguably find it there, Islam being a "tale of the two cities", but only of the second on behalf of what the first knew. There can be no denying the complete priority of the Meccan phase, the *balagh*, the religious witness the Prophet had to bring. The quest for power in the Hijrah to Medina was no lust for mere brigandage. It enshrined the implementation – by then Arab lights – of the meanings Mecca had heard. The *Shahadah* itself does not proclaim Muhammad as Allah's "generalissimo", only as His *Rasul*, the one with the *Risalah*. It is to Mecca that Muslims make the ritual pilgrimage. It is Mecca that every mosque world-wide meticulously fronts by dint of its niche and *qiblah*.

The Medinan dimension of power and statecraft, however, is ineradicably rooted in the text of the Qur'an. Must it not, therefore, for ever dictate a political Islam? Hardly, if Islam is to be, as it affirms, a "final" faith and if it means to participate irenically in a global twenty-first century. For "finality" means that it is abreast of times in their changing and their changing is now into the necessity of a global will to inter-human compatibility, where the religious "we" and "us" and "ours" cease to be conceptually imperial and instead participate with what they truly illuminate by their wisdom, not what they covetously tyrannise by their ambition.

It is the obvious disparity between the 7th century in Islam's Arabia and Islam's 15th (21st) century in an ecumenical scene that requires us to argue – and argue Islamically – that what could be justified then by the *ad hoc* situation it once confronted, will not be so now in the global scene.[10] To think the one applicable to the other would be to consign Islam to a museum, an anachronism in a world where it no longer belonged.

That cannot be, in that "Allah is not overtaken".[11] Moreover, Islam provides for "consensus" around a developing "finality". It has the concepts of *Ijma'* and the "enterprise", mental and social, by which this is attained. It is, therefore, capable of an interior progressiveness of mind and will, a responsiveness to the demands of continuity, a capacity to overcome the "hideboundness" it calls *taqlid*.[12]

Furthermore, there is the Quranic notion of *naskh* or "abrogation", whereby – given disparities inside the texts of the Qur'an – one meaning might abrogate another. To be sure, the legists circumscribed the exercise of this potential. Ultimately, *naskh* apart, all exegesis hinges on the will of readership.[13] There is the possibility that "abrogation" can happen not, as normally by the later over-ruling the earlier, but in reverse of that, whereby Meccan "spirituality" takes its totally right priority over Medinan state-reliance.

What, further, realistically sustains that case is the patent fact that large segments of Muslim humanity, as noted in CHAPTER SEVEN, are in situations that are virtually Meccan where *Din* minus *Dawlah* is their permanent condition – Meccan, that is, without the persecution and with some share in *Dawlah* by dint of secular-style suffrage. If Islam, with all its formidable devotion to the political arm, can in that measure "de-politicize" its genius, the principle of a political secularity will have had its salient success. For no other faith-system has been so tenaciously reluctant for it, or unpersuaded of its grounds.

III

Rightly understood and sanely argued, the plea for neutral statehood means no abeyance of religious meaning, no disallowing of the religious witness or its due – if readily consonant – participation in politics. On the contrary, its witness, its guardianship of values, its measures of integrity will be both the more urgently needed and the more honestly brought. Faith itself will be the more on its mettle by belonging in an open forum, more honest in being not uniquely advantaged in the exchanges of citizenship.

For this limited sense of a "secular" state means, no more and no less, a genuine neutrality around the faith of the private citizen, consistent with his/her being a duly peaceable one, or exercising protest in ways that are not inherently subversive but only corrective of the political order to which allegiance is acknowledged due. This must exclude the hidden but intentionally disruptive attitudes noted in CHAPTER SEVEN.

Of course it may be argued that state neutrality this limited way may mean a complete indifference to the things of faith. It may also be that being ready for diversity means reading all as enveloped into indifference with religion made to retreat into some private realm where it may best do no harm and be fondly or foolishly indulged, over against a world that has no political or moral room for its wisdom.

These dire conclusions need in no way obtain. Rather the vital private liability for religious conviction the better braces and equips it for the fulfilment of a public relevance that is by no means relinquished. The end of advantaging one religious structure can better enjoy, or at least allow, the sobered contribution of all and make each the livelier custodian of its mind and heritage. There is a "secular" which actually ministers to the "spiritual" only by being such. Such has always been the case, whether in giving pause to faith-arrogance or sifting religious conviction.

Moreover, history will in measure ensure that a certain primacy persists where a faith has long informed a national identity. For pasts are not abruptly undone. Literature, poetry, the arts and architecture are the long perpetuators of communal heritage and, with them, of the faiths that have shaped and inspired them. Immigrant minorities do not immediately overturn a national inheritance. A reluctance to assimilate can be no conspiracy to usurpation in any realistic terms, least of all so when there is a breathing freely such as the secular principle, as here argued, ensures. Even some residual form of "establishment" may still survive – and survive significantly – so long as the effective *de facto* diversity is in place.[14] Even as an anomaly it can witness to the principle. Since it is not "privileged" any longer (if it ever was) to be "anti-" other faiths, it serves to make them all aware of their own faith-nature. This pattern and posture will be the soundest answer to the advocates, cynical or conscientious, of an entire secularization – the throughgoing "disbelief in belief" it was earlier agreed to defer, though it has been dogging heels all the time.[15] Theirs is an option which has always been available in a created order awaiting, not imposing, a human *islam*, a reverent surrender to the religious readings of wonder, gratitude and liability. The reason suggested at Surah 2.256 around "there is no compulsion in religion" is that truth shines by its own light, needs nothing extrinsic to its witness to sustain the case. Such is the context of the freedom by which it properly lives.[16]

The term, *ikraha*, in that passage might, however, absorb a different and subtle sense. Though normally translated as "compulsion", the root verb denotes "to be repulsive", "to excite disgust", "to repel" or "provoke ill-will". This religions, as we have realized throughout, have endlessly done in arousing a nausea about them in the minds of their instinctive despisers. Their websites have mouthed raucous pronouns in unseemly claims and violent zeal, in accents of bigotry and mental tyranny, kindling a form of secularity which, like Gallio of old, "would have none of these things".[17]

190

The case has long been made and is presently congenial to many at least in the western world. It need not be rehearsed further. CHAPTERS TWO, THREE and TEN have struggled with what – in the last analysis – irreligion eludes, namely a reckoning with selfhood that resolves into an ultimate reverence: the mystery of the "me's" we personally are, the "we's" we humanly experience. If "to be" is "to be received" then awareness will always be religious and will forever require the critical interrogation of religions. If only in that role, the outright secularist will still be exploring the necessity of religion and sifting it for help. The pronouns "us" and "Thou" will always be circulating, and always with a religious destiny.

IV

Since their grammars remain plural, it remains to ask what their several "holdings hold", whether for each other in their co-existing difference or for a sceptical and distrustful earshot among the aloof and heedless. If, for them all, to live is to "let live", what distinctively do they live to tell and to mean, to tell for illumination and to mean for relevance in the world we co-inhabit in the current terms of that co-habitation? In measure, all religion, in its integrity, is a "prehension", a "grasping after" what life signifies.[18] It is a state of being "awed" as the first and last dimension of its summons to reverence and revolt, to kindling wonder and a burdening guilt. However captured in the forms of faith or told within the soul, it is what all faiths reach for, if they do not genuinely undergo by dint of an attenuation implicit in human frailty and sin.

The Buddhist and Hindu faiths hold a peculiarly Asian, deeply non-Semitic, suspicion of what they apprehend of the perceptible experience that kindles religious awareness of our human-ness. For their "I"s and "we's" history does not "mean" in any Semitic sense. For it lacks the "intention" of a "creation" as Semites have it. That stance it sees as deceiving the unwary, inviting them into an egoism it will not sustain, offering a false impression of significance we must learn to forego.

What might seem only a bleak form of disavowal of all that makes the religious pronouns ambitious elsewhere becomes in Buddhism and some Hinduism the psychic strategy of their pronounal realism. Using pronouns at all means accepting some identity and a negotiation with time and place. Asian faiths find no escape from politics. They live like all in the toils of economics. They sink wells, irrigate fields, tend pastures, build roads, run markets, drive herds but, through their birthing and their rearing, their trading and their dying, propose a sort of "as if unreal" philosophy, a "detachment" that admits the mechanics of mortality without assuming their sure reality. In paradox they abjure the pretension of human significance but find a crucial significance in the will to do so. They remind the rest of us that there is a kind of "I" from which every "me" needs to be delivered – delivered from false illusion, from the ever acquisitive self. Others have to ask whether that legitimate "foregoing of our selfhood" is morally due and duly moral only, or whether it has also to be somehow total as if reading our mortality as the inclusive truth about us.

Thus the Buddha's pained experience of sickness, decrepitude and death was read as disillusioning desire and constraining the "I" towards the acceptance of non-being in any sure pronounal way and onward to the pure "unison" of Nirvana. Always the question presses whether Nirvana is "an experience" and in what terms, if at all, it might correspond to "the Beatific Vision".[19]

Whenever we listen to Asia in this language – and many in the West register a strange fascination in the Buddhist faith – we are sobered by the contrast with a Biblical/Quranic confidence in the intendedness of things, in the meaning told – or borne – in human history, and in the relevance of truth concretely to time and place. Yet, seizing upon the agencies and powers of their worlds, these faiths have been liable to the worst excesses of religious assurance, so far from the detachment commended by the religious Asians. Their confidence as to a human significance entrusted to their aegis, whether of land and kind in Judaism, or of prophethood and power in Islam, or of Messiah realized in Jesus as God's Christ, has engendered a self-perception supremely "attached" to its own "prehensions".

The contemporary Zionist form of this "attachment" has deeply left ambivalent the meanings others should draw from ongoing Judaism. Zionism has a sadly divided mind about its own intentions, these – on the way and in the issue – still awaiting definition on the ground. Is it giving powered terms to an old exclusivism, while still offering to all the benign vision of its Sabbaths, its imagery of family hallowedness and the sublime ethicism in its prophets? Meanwhile, Zionism will never undo itself: how it finally fulfills itself leaves things blessedly Judaic in desperate suspense. It is a suspense which passes over into the diaspora also with its abiding anxiety around assimilation and the pressures of the "Gentile" scene. Judaism presents a rich and blessed significance for a universal reach of recognition but always on the condition of its only right proprietorship, a custody it must always retain as its own. Why for ever so?

The Islam we have explored above and in CHAPTERS SIX and SEVEN, with its Meccan/Medinan watershed, affords the world of other faiths and none a supreme example of the theme of power on a faith's behalf and a deep interrogation of its present perpetuation in the age-long form. Its founding experience of Hijrah into régime and of régime for faith's success needs re-reading in the context of composite nationhoods and the sense of universal human rights and dignities. For such revision of its familiar

self in history it has ample agenda in its Meccan message of divine sovereignty, an earth deputed into human trust and all, that for economics,
ecology, politics and society, flows from this divine magnanimity via this
human privilege. Islam can hold a worthy place in an inclusive ambition
for that *falah*, that "well-being", to which daily, quinto-diurnally, the
muezzin invites all humankind.[20]

It is a summons which the fully self-aware Christian must feel stays in
need of the dimension it lacks. For – as studied earlier – it relies on a sacred
ethicism, a moral education, a verbal directive revelation, and the structures these deploy, for attainment of human good. It suffices for it that
we are brought to know, dispensing with the saving role that Jesus as the
Christ fulfills in Christian faith. The point of this vital difference between
mosque and Gospel, explored in CHAPTER EIGHT, concerns the magnanimity of God in reach into humankind and the measure of our human
situation and these in their mutual significance. Where Islam holds to the
way of divine law, Christian faith resides in the way of divine redemption.

The latter's radical realism about the evident perversities to which are
prone both human nature and its structures in society has to be taken into
the reckoning of every sacred faith and into the ken of secular responses
to our human waywardness. With his "categorical imperative",
Immanuel Kant held that our reason might promptly concede the case he
made and admit the force of its logic to our behaving. Thus, for example,
deceit, lying and fraud are only feasible by being in defiance of the principle of honesty, since it is only on the assumption of honesty in dealing
that people can be deceived. Thus the liar and the cheat offend against the
order of things. We can thus derive the "categorical imperative" drawn
from the contradiction involved in universalizing the effect of our action
and realizing that it breaks the very principle of our action on which its
success relies, namely that all men should be honest. George Herbert had
written more than a century earlier an answer to Kant's confidence in
reason in a single line: "A cunning bosom sinne blows all away."[21]

The philosopher in heart knew that too, but wrote of "religion without
revelation". In truth, even if we make some imperative sacred – or hold it
made sacredly so by God in His Scripture – it will be no more immune
from, or protective against, "some bosom sinne". To know ourselves truly
and our society, our politics and our religions, is to know that there is no
ethical "imperative" categorical enough to be proof against the vagaries
of human wrong.

This, however, means no essential despair. It is only the cruciality of
the autonomy of selfhood given into our creaturehood in all Semitic
reading of the created order and, indeed, of all Buddhist prescript for that
autonomy by the Buddha's clue that our mortality is to the only relevant
truth about our human-ness. A non-despairing hope for our human story,

precisely because of its realism, holds to the remaking, the forgiving, power of love in its redemptive travail. It can only do so by detecting such power in redemptive action on the part of a love worthy to be known as divine. In so doing the Christian faith exists by warrant of the evidence of such love in God and of God as love, which it believes to be present in the Christ-event, in the Jesus story as the scene and setting, not only of a teaching ethic, but of an action of grace that holds for all repentancing a forgiving mending of our souls.

If such be realizing what the ancient word "salvation" could ever have meant, then it is where Christianity relates instinctively to all other faiths. It queries all sanguine views of human amenability to exhortation alone, finds them ever less credible now than in some pre-Shoah, pre-1914, pre-slave trade, world. Late, no less than ancient, history is too full of our capacity for deviance and defiance. By all means, we need and must needs revere organs of guidance, *Shari'ah*, education and law, but the ability of these to yield their intention through compliance, submission and docility stays partial and erratic. Mecca's piety may have been rescued in its pagan setting by Medina's prowess but contemporary human problems are a still more stern scenario, with reaches of evil and perils of technology that involve us all, under God, in terms that law alone can comprehend neither for measure nor for remedy. Yet the vocabulary faith needs, of awe and wonder concerning a "divine" resourceful enough for such measure and remedy, is already there in the language of Islam and its Qur'an.[22]

Christian faith, however, can only hold this theme of divine love in "God in Christ", as its central witness, with an equal realism about its own reproach in long history and present stress of mind. What theology presents, history has too often betrayed. Christendom, in concept and structure, stood so far from knowing and showing the Cross as index to divine grace. Yet, as told in CHAPTERS THREE and EIGHT, the corrective was always there in the first defining story. To read ourselves as registered in the representative wrongness of Christ's crucifixion and, at the same place, to have identified divine love in his "taking of it", is to be called not only by its likeness, but into it.

Its qualitative encounter of wrongs so evidently human, and of grace so definingly divine, was "once for all" in meaning and inclusiveness, but it was also a "now and ever" as the pattern of reconciling Messianic community. The temptations of religion supervened. Order, prestige, heritage, corporate pride took over but that Messianic clue to theology was secure in the being of God and entrusted – no more, no less – to a faith-society called to live in its meaning, whether with or despite the structures its story would require. The Christ-bearing, Christ-serving Church has its endless shames only where it has its abiding summons, the vocation precariously housed in the forms of rite and symbol, order and tradition, through which it moves. "Give us this day Messiah's bread and deliver us from evil" is the given burden of its prayer, with all its liturgies "the imperfect offices of prayer and praise".[23]

What then, finally, of the sceptical, the agnostic, the hesitant? And what of "others" in the wide, even clamorous, sounding of religious pronouns, their sundry "us" and "ours"? We may perhaps surmise that all are somehow, somewhat, "religious" if we merely widen the range of the word, whether in hope or cynicism. We can feel we have grounds. Religions have too often wanted to be special, enjoying to be different.

There is art too. D. H. Lawrence was sure one had to be deeply religious to be an artist, writing:

I am a passionately religious man and my novels must be written from the depth of my religious experience.[24]

Or Dylan Thomas out of his Welsh Chapel nurture:

With all their crudities, doubts and confusions these (poems) are written for the love of Man and in praise of God, and I'd be a damn fool if they weren't.[25]

There are inklings of religious awe in unexpected places and the expected places had better attend to them. If we are thinking of the sacred, it is well to cast the net widely. We must be always alert for "someone surprising himself to be more serious".[26]

We may find only paradox in Nirvana yet appreciate the thought that wanted to attain it. Truths that doctrine holds, if their acceptance is to be truly religious, can only wait for recognition. They *become* truths only when faith has made them so by warrant of the virtue they possess, "compelling the recognition they preceded".[27] Faith always had this double quality as both a corpus of meaning told and how it tells in allegiance to it.

Conversely then, given sincerity, doubt also can have this double shape. In withholding a surrender to truth that will not compel, it will be cognizant, by the same token, of what truth waits to be for it. If truth is to guarantee our liberty, only out of liberty do we greet the truth. Institutional religion, then, must beware of being dismissive of those who hold off for honest reason. Nor may it well be rigorous in censure of those whose withdrawn-ness may give it longer thoughts. The underminings of religious language have made savage, if also naïve, inroads into the confidence that uses it.

Is there in all this the possibility of vicarious faith, of believing "on behalf of unbelief" or of disputatious "other" pronoun-users in their religious vernaculars of faith? The hope is real, if it is prudent and sober.

There are large agnosticisms that have no wish to be thus befriended. The arts – vocal, musical and poetical and dramatic – may be invoked to mediate but a personal *confessio* there needs to be. Instruments of meaning that are present in the arts have to belong with the final instrument that is the self alone – the self that must, however haltingly, be literate in heart and resolute in will, with pronouns in *confessio*. Passion Music in churches may not displace the Passion of Christ within the soul. The Eucharist will be more demanding on the self if less enchanting on the ear alone. The legacies of architecture belong in the fabric of the soul.

We end on Christian ground. On no other can Christians relate. Where other web-sites confessional find their web-masters now is theirs to say – who we are is by what is ours.

> The way of the Lord in the womb of the lowly,
> In the greeting of the Spirit for the patience and the travail.
>
> The way of the Lord in the flesh, in the word and the deed
> The oil and the wine in the wound and the pence at the inn,
>
> The bread and the breaking, the cup and the taking,
> The journey to birth and the wonder of angels.
>
> The pathway to death and the scars in the hands and the feet,
> In the mystery of the readiness of God
>
> For the Cross of the world.

Notes

Introduction

1 Robert Browning, *Poetical Works*, Oxford, 1949, p. 671.

2 *Ibid.*, p. 241.

3 Walt Whitman, *Complete Writings*, New York, 1902, Vol. 2, p. 230. On "The Spider".

4 T. S. Eliot: *The Family Reunion*, London, 1939, in: *Complete Poems and Plays of T. S. Eliot*, London, 1969, p. 350.

5 As, for example, by J. H. Newman in *A Grammar of Assent*, and Browning's "A Grammarian's Funeral", who "left play for work and grappled with the world", "mastering learning's crabbed text". Languages with their grammars and syntax may be images for faiths and their credos – all speaking about "truth" but by differing rules to govern it.

6 Dylan Thomas, *Collected Letters*, ed. Paul Ferris, London, 1985, p. 39.

7 As in Surah 5.18 where "Jews" (and Christians) are reproached for holding themselves "God's beloved ones". (The verse does not distinguish the differing grounds of the ethnic and the salvific for the conviction). Elsewhere also in the Medinan period the Qurʾan is sharply hostile to the self-image of Jewry. While it is clear that there is a strong "Arabism" around Islam and the Qurʾan, Muslims were never at a Sinai or passers through an exodus. The Qurʾan's "covenant" (7.172) is with the whole human cosmos. On Arabicity in Islam, see Ismaʿil al-Faruqi, *Al-ʿUrubah and Religion*, Amsterdam, 1962.

8 *Dawlah* – the state, and *Din* – the faith and its practice, the twin referents of Islamic society, the dimension of Medina and the dimension of Mecca on either side the Hijrah or "migration" between the two cities.

9 Surahs 6.164, 17.15, 39.7 and 53.38. See further CHAPTER SIX.

10 "Religion with Allah, is *islam* (or Islam)." (3.19) Cf. also 3.85, 5.3, 6.125, 39.22 and 61.7.

11 The "individual" is an *individuum*. The "in" is not a locative: it is a negative, as in "insolvent". This means that our being is within a "me" that cannot be other than an "I". It is, therefore, "dividual" in that each is "separated off" from every other in bodily form, and, as Pascal had it "we die alone", similarly living so. "Dividual" means "transactable", inherently participating.

12 Does not the hermitage which isolates the hermit only deepen the reality of the identity that is being – somehow – foregone? It may diminish occasions of acquisitiveness while intensifying self-preoccupation.

13   The problem is perhaps identified by a careful note, in Chapter 10, of the ambiguity of the words "egoism" or "egotism". They *may* tell of ethical "egocentricity" in greed, disdain, snobbery and personal cupidity but must then be ever distinguished from the physical "egocentricity" which has each of us inescapably "housed" in the persona we are. The utmost (moral) self-lessness can only be attained inside a selfhood which it will ever need, never eliminate and always employ.

CHAPTER ONE   The House of My Pilgrimage

1   *The Oxford English Dictionary.*
2   James Montgomery (1771–1854) was a journalist in Sheffield, a passionate advocate of the abolition of slavery and a prolific hymnologist – some four hundred in all. His published hymnal was a major factor in the popularity of choir and congregation singing in Victorian England. The "sip of water" allusion is to Emily Dickinson's poem: "Thirst" – "when we die, a little water supplicate of fingers going by". *Collected Poems*, ed. M. L. Todd and T. W. Higginson, New York, 1982, liii, p. 215.
3   "Epiphanies" at tent-door among the patriarchs; "the tent He spread in the midst" (Psalm 78:60) whether in exodus wanderings or Shilohs in the land; and for the Isaiah of 40:22 the canopy of the heavens as "a tent to dwell in". The imagery is inherited in the Christology of the New Testament, as in John 1:14: "He tabernacled among us" and the sense of fleeting years in 2 Peter 1:13.
4   It is intriguing that he writes "if", not "when", for the *parousia*, or "re-appearing of Christ" (which would obviate dying for those still alive), was yet in apostolic view. What is most remarkable about the early Church is that its faith survived that deep disconcerting of its hopes. Faiths have often to rethink the terms in which they understand themselves.
5   The citations are from the version in The Book of Common Prayer, favoured here for its closeness to the English of its day, so worthy of the poetic original – given its elucidation more prosaically by aid of other recent versions.
6   Quoted from Max Muller, *Sacred Books of the East*, London, from 1875, Vol. xlii, pp. 88–9.
7   It is noteworthy how the Muslim Qur'an also makes awed reference to the womb-story of every personal "genesis", through the cycle from conception to birth.
8   Dag Hammarskjöld quoting Linnaeus in "The Linnaeus Tradition and Our Time". See Wilber Foote, ed., *The Servant of Peace: A Selection of Speeches & Statements*, London, 1962, p. 155.
9   G. K. Chesterton, *Collected Poems*, London, 1933, "By the Babe Unborn", pp. 318–20.
10   Louis MacNeice, *Selected Poems*, London, 1988, ed. Michael Longley, "Prayer before Birth", p. 93.
11   Called *Centuries*, as being in paragraphs numbering to a hundred, they were written in the third quarter of the seventeenth century but only "discovered"

and published in the twentieth. Thomas Traherne (1637–74) was Rector of Credenhill, near Hereford. "Salutation" comes in his *Centuries, Poems and Thanksgivings*, ed. H. M. Margoliouth, Oxford, 1958, Vol. ii, pp. 4–6, and see: *Centuries*, I, 29.

12 See K. W. Salter, *Thomas Traherne*, London, 1964, p. 83, because "God is the object and God is the way of enjoying", *Centuries*, V, i.

13 See note 11, vol. ii, p. 39, "The Approach", and Vol. 2, p. 155 "Amendement".

14 See Erica Wagner: *Ariel's Gift; Ted Hughes, Sylvia Plath and the Story of "Birthday Letters"*, London, 2000, p. 139.

15 Charlotte Mew (1869–1928), *Collected Poems*, London, 1953, "Here Lies a Prisoner", p. 67.

16 By the transfer of adjectives so characteristic of the Hebrew tradition. On the case for reading Psalm 139 as a ritual hymn of political "kingship", see S. J. L. Croft: *The Identity of the Individual in the Psalms*, Sheffield, 1987, stressing, e.g., "I shall count them my enemies".

17 James Joyce, *Portrait of the Artist as a Young Man*, London, 1968, p. 257. In his case he was wanting to escape from God. "We have had too much of God in Ireland. Away with God!"

18 Karl Popper, for example, wants to question old-style empiricism had via Francis Bacon and John Locke and opt for non-inductive "expectations" which are somehow inborn in us and not, like the scientific method, always provisional.

19 So thought the great twentieth-century medievalist C. G. Coulton. *Of The Vision concerning Piers Plowman* (mid-fourteenth century). There are several critical editions of his three versions.

20 William Wordsworth, *Poetical Works*, ed. T. Hutchinson, 1905, "To Enterprise", line 97, p. 216.

21 John Donne, *The Poems*, ed. H. J. C. Grierson, Oxford, 1933, "The Extasie", p. 47. "Us to us" may well be a pair of lovers abed, but no less extends to all human inter-dealings.

22 Verse 18 – the original is unclear. One version has: ". . . to finish I must be eternal", in which case his "reckoning" with themes of experience must "arrive" at their being inexhaustible. Either way, the crux is the living awareness of which the body and its senses are the means.

23 As elsewhere quotations from Martin Buber, *I and Thou*, 2nd edn, English trans. Ronald Gregor Smith, New York, 1953, p. 65.

24 The word "only" is crucial. Buber readily recognizes that there numerous situations where people are rightly "means" to each other and in capacities where utterly "personal" dimensions would impede or prevent the function fulfilled, as in medicine, education and the economic order. See p. 132.

25 *Ibid.*, p. 75.

26 *Ibid.*, p. 76.

27 Applied to Jerusalem at the consecration of the Temple in Solomon's Prayer, 1 Kings 8:29 (cf. 9:3 and Deuteronomy 12:11), for the Temple was "where" one encountered YAHWEH in the meaning of "Who He was" made cognizable as at a "rendezvous". Hence "thither the tribes go up" to "the Name of

the Lord". What is there geographically is also present historically in "the mighty acts of the Lord" whereby His meaning to them and theirs to Him took "event-shape". Cf. Isaiah 56:5.

28 Martin Buber, *Moses*, London, 1946, pp. 46–53. The famous formula, if read as a teasing enigma, could never have served to hearten a slave-people summoned to one of the most exacting adventures, namely exchanging the Nile's benison for the hazards of the desert. They are given to understand that only in the "going" can there be the "knowing" of the God of exodus.

29 Surah 17.110–111. Allah "has", possesses the Names by which He is to be addressed (prayer) but by which He is not described (theology). That distinction in the sense of the word "call" (i.e. "name in address" and "name in character") was long a taxing theme for the classical Muslim thinkers. See CHAPTER SIX.

30 Buber, *I and Thou*, pp. 50 and 61.

31 Emily Dickinson, *Collected Poems*, ed. M. L. Todd and T. W. Higginson, New York, 1982 edn, no. 1225.

CHAPTER TWO   The Personal Interrogative – Arjuna and the Gita

1 William Morris, *Political Writings*, ed. A. L. Morton, New York, 1973, pp. 150–3. Morris (1834–96) proved a lively advocate and contriver of beauty in design and of a socialism that demanded for all and sundry occasions and qualities of art-in-life. He would have found "desireless action" a total contradiction of his being human.

2 Many are the translations of the Bhagavad Gita. Among them, usefully, that of Franklin Edgerton, Cambridge, Mass., 1972. See also *The Vedic Experience*, ed. Raymond Pannikar, Mary Rogers et al., Berkeley, 1977.

3 John Milton, *Paradise Lost*, Book xi, lines 675–80, 693–94 and 697.

4 It is an open question whether the Krishna who accosts Arjuna is fully "deity" or as an *avatara*, though the sequel in the Gita suggests the former.

5 In the sense that it sees no creating, presiding purpose in history and moves from the human phenomenon as a burden to be escaped by the discipline it commends. However, there may be some "divine" element in the attainment of "non-being", seeing that this Nirvana is not rightly thought of as "extinction". See CHAPTER THREE.

6 See Martin Buber, *Two Types of Faith*, trans. N. P. Goldhawk, London, 1951, where he discriminates between Christians required "to believe in . . ." whereas Jewry practices "trusting in". The former means that Christians have to opt, by this faith, to become such, whereas Jews by birth are "already there".

7 So the Bharatiya Janata Party currently insists as being the age-long truth of things in the sub-continent. Thus the "secular state" concept of Pandit Nehru and the Congress Party after partition was the more remarkable as a contrasted reading of the meaning of "Indianism". However, the other sentiment was no small part of Gandhi's long hostility to Christian mission, despite the admiration he had for the ethics of Jesus.

8   This reading of *tat tvam asi* is adopted by Wilfred Cantwell Smith in his *The Faith of Other Men*, New York, 1962, pp. 23–36, I tried in *With God in Human Trust*, Brighton and Portland, 1999, to develop, in a framework of Christian theism, the similar theme of a "mastery to which we are subject", as called to belong within that which transcends us, and do so obediently, as the true "liberation" into a "mastery" of ours. But would Hindus want us to conclude, too readily, that this was what they meant us to understand by 'atman equals *Brahman?*

9   Robert Browning, *Poetical Works*, Oxford, 1905, "Abt Vogler", St. xi, p. 480.

10 See further below. Cf. the remark of Nietszche. "In order that love may be possible God must be a person". *The Antichrist*, trans. A. M. Ludovici, Edinburgh, 1911, Sect. 24, p. 153.

11 The title of his celebrated study noted in CHAPTER ONE, trans. R. Gregor Smith, New York, 1958. See also, Maurice S. Friedman, *Martin Buber: The Life of Dialogue*, New York, 1955.

12 The crucial passage in Exodus 3 can hardly be read as a philosophical enigma, or "I am that I am" as a sort of riddle. The context is deeply "existential". At "the burning bush" Moses has relayed to YAHWEH the query he knows his beaten-down people will put to him when he goes and announces to them that they are summoned to escape from Egypt by the God who has appeared to him. They will ask: "What is His name", i.e. what proof have you? Where is the guarantee? Is "He" trustworthy? The divine answer, given to Moses to give to the enslaved people, is that He will be known as the God of exodus only in the exodus experience. "I will be there and will be what there I will be". The Hebrew must be read in this future, highly active sense. An enigma would never motivate the fearful. However, if we are minded, we could, perversely, align the words in some Hindu way.

13 A kind of "personalism" seems to emerge in Chapter xi of the Gita, but not as ever to allow a sacramental understanding of the body, or of creation as the arena of tributary human "dominion". See below.

14 An archaic terms, used in Oxford of a now abolished exam, but covering "due reply", or "sum to be paid" or "what is exchanged in academic debate". If there are "precepts" from Krishna that address the kind of conscience with which Arjuna begins then reality is "moral", and not of a quality as to over-awe him into a worship called to leave conscience behind.

15 Sebastian Moore, *The Inner Loneliness*, New York, 1982, pp. 23 and 40.

16 The more so if the ultimate bliss of knowing "the Imperishable Lord" is reciprocal to the wholeness of the human "knower". For "theism" – like the Christian theme of Christ's Incarnation – is always a truth as to man if ever being a truth as to God. Hindu "theism" would agree only on its own terms.

17 R. C. Zaehner, *Hindu and Muslim Mysticism*, London, 1960, p. 61.

18 *Ibid.*, pp. 57–63.

19 T. S. Eliot, *The Waste Land and Other Poems*, London, 1950, pp. 11, 29.

20 In *Swanson on Swanson*, New York, 1980, the famous actress, Gloria, married in all to six husbands, wrote of how, to save her career, she aborted a child in 1925 and lived with the guilt of it. Telling the tale in 1979 to a

Buddhist monk in Kyo San, Japan, he said: "We all choose our parents . . . no blame." She believed him and added: "In 1898 . . . I picked Joseph Swanson and Adelaide, his wife, to be mine." Of our origins such, sometimes, are the hazards.

21　See, for example, Peter Berger, *Invitation to Sociology*, London, 1963.

22　William Golding, *The Hot Gates*, London, 1965, p. 87.

23　That "future of the past" is a large part of what the much misconstrued theme of "original sin" has always meant. The problem "re-incarnations" have is that neither the analysis of, or responsibility for, the entail of previous "existences" are susceptible of conscious inspection. However, society soon gives us to know that it is no *tabula rasa* on which we are set.

24　Thomas Traherne, *Centuries, Poems and Thanksgivings*, ed. H. M. Margoliouth, Oxford, 1958, Vol. ii, pp. 4–6. See note 11 in CHAPTER ONE above.

25　Selfhood situations are such that nothing done is ever free of "motive", seeing that "vacancy of mind" does not exist. Nor can there be action ever coupled with absolute "disinterest". However, deeds can aim to be free of calculated self-interest, though even then they will not escape a certain (valid?) satisfaction that it was so.

26　"Imagine!" from John Lennon, *Apple PAG looo4*, July, 1971.

27　Rudyard Kipling, *Definitive Edition of His Verse*, London, 1943, "Song of the English", p. 170, and "Buddha at Kamakura", pp. 92–3.

28　See his, *The Wretched of the Earth*, trans. C. Farrington, New York, 1966. The case he made for a "necessary hate" (given that territorial imperialism had only succeeded by an accompanying pattern of mental "inferiorizing" of all things native) was in striking contrast from the quality of Leopold Senghor, marrying Senegalese independence with a deep facility in French literature and poetry.

29　Customs officers, police, lawyers, know this situation only too well, and teachers too, who sense their will to friendliness being "cultivated" by ingratiating students.

30　"Unprofitable" is in the text of Matthew 25:30 and Luke 17:10. The Greek *achreios negates cheira* – "uselessness".

31　This was exactly the distinction on which the Muslim League came to insist and which, by a belated conversion to it, Muhammad Ali Jinnah seized on like a gift-horse. Fearing, by aligning with All-India nationalism, to be a permanent minority, he and the League opted for "nationhood"; the demand for Pakistan, firmly ruling out their being merely "a community". By contrast, the deeply Islamic thinker, Maulana Abu-l-Kalam Azad, believed that a "true Islam" could properly share the sub-continent in the form of an All-India nationhood. He suffered much obloquy for his reading of Islam in those eirenic terms. They were terms which, by the logic of Pakistan's necessity to a viable Islam, exposed Islam in India to a "withering away". It did not happen so.

32　It has often been conjectured that *satyagraha* would never have availed to terminate a Hitler Raj in a negotiated political withdrawal. For it needed an imperialism susceptible to its soul-force, something in the Gandhian logic that owed itself to the Sermon on the Mount and the likes of John Ruskin rooted in the English heritage.

33 The worst features of the caste system have been curbed in ways susceptible of legal prescript, such as the suffrage and citizenship but *daljits* still suffer heavy privations in respect of popular attitudes especially in village and rural areas. The Indian Government in 2001 was resisting efforts to include the caste factor in international discussion – and legislation – concerning "racism". Its line was that "caste" was within India's domestic aegis and was not a "race" issue rightly to be covered by the concept of "human rights". Yet it remains a still powerful sanction of "apartheid".

34 Chief among them the wane of British imperial power after the exhaustion of two world wars and the pattern of negotiated withdrawals of which the Indian was the salient example.

35 Depending on the criteria one brings, verdicts about "disinterest", the absence of "ulterior motive", can be highly debatable. Gandhi's *ahimsa* could be sharply at odds with "tolerance" when "indianism" was involved. He resisted Christian evangelism sharply out of fear, for example, of losing numbers from Hindu electorates. See the illuminating study in Susan Billington Harper, *In the Shadow of the Mahatma: Bishop V. S. Azariah and the Travails of Christianity in British India*, Grand Rapids, 2000.

CHAPTER THREE   "So Help Me – Who?"

1 It was the characteristically Hebraic – and, indeed, Islamic – understanding of a divinely purposive creation entrusted, riskily, to humankind, a creation for which God was "responsible". Out of the "responsibility" came guidance, law and prophethood for its discipline and direction. Uniquely, then, in the Hebraic tradition, that divine stake in human history kindled an extension of "responsibility" towards what eventuated when human history went so darkly wrong (whereas Islam stayed with legislation only as sufficing to "order" such perversity). Such was the Hebraic matrix of "hope" – sharpened, to be sure, by a Jewish conviction of special "election" – a hope enshrined in the Messianic concept, burdened with so many shapes and anticipations, all of them positing the "answer" God would have for the question of human history gone awry. The "Jesus-story" was for Christianity the measure and the realization of that hope.

2 In the sense that no one could state Christian faith without the "us" of one redemption, the "ours" of one "Lord and Christ", the "me" that cried: "The Son of God loved me . . .". See CHAPTER EIGHT below.

3 On two counts. In spite of what Muslim devotion has done with Muhammad's parenthood and "immaculate conception" and nativity wonders, Islam is strict as to his solely verbal mission and his status as a human prophet. Secondly, as noted in note 1, "Messiahship" in its Biblical sense (in both Testaments) pre-supposes a divine task more than "message" to us humans, whereas Islam holds that the *Shari'ah*, the *Din* and *Dawlah* of its structured revelation suffice.

4 Surahs 3.19 and 5.3.

5 The distinction is necessary in that "Judaism" in the strict sense only comes after the Fall of Jerusalem and the coming of the "sages" to Yavneh and so, at length, the Talmudic era.

6 The descriptive "Muhammadan" is only allowable in this context of what pertains to him personally (cf. "Augustan" or "Dantean"). Those who belong to Islam are only properly called "Muslims".

7 To use the modern term, in contrast to the Judaic dictum that YAHWEH, while "universal" is not "international", because of a singular relation to the "nation" of Israel.

8 "Credences" in no derogatory sense. For that is what they are. It is this duty that has been tardy in contemporary Islam (due to be noted elsewhere). It is not, for any living faith, a subversive activity but rather one of purging and refining, seeing that what "came about faith-wise" has abiding quality within such due academic sifting.

9 This conviction about enclosing and perfecting all previous "scriptuarizing" by Allah of the world's peoples confirms – by its very shape – the point being made. It is a piece of faith, self-enclosed inside the assurance of Muhammad's destiny. It was not, there and then, a product of studied investigation or explicit research into the kind of "proved evidences", these being neither feasible nor sought.

10 Surah 33.56.

11 John Milton, *Samson Agonistes*, line 1729.

12 The Chapter (1) in Isaiah is a quite vehement indictment of society, politics and religion in the prophet's day. He reaches for what one might think outrageous comparisons reducing "chosen-people" status to the worst pagan levels of guilt and crime. Yet it is precisely his moral reading of that status which undergirds his bitter disavowal of it. That paradox has always attended on the Jewish mind – and its Zions – at their truest.

13 "Derive" in a dual sense, i.e. stemming from their religious reflection on "hopes proper to their situation", but also essentially from the nature of God as told – for them – in creation and covenant.

14 With the hyphen, "man-age" has a curious propriety here in the sense of a *magisterium* entrusted to human hands. The word has undergone a certain diminution.

15 The term "Christlikeness" must initially seem dubious to Muslims as somehow bringing "Allah" into conformity to Christ – and this as "limitation". Properly understood, all is authentic if we understand the conformity as willed, indeed demonstrated, from the divine side – which is exactly what Christian faith holds and says.

16 "Kenotic" from the Greek *kenosis* (see Paul in Philippians 2:5–11). Divine self-expending is evident not only there in "the Word made flesh" but also in creation itself and then further in the activity of the Holy Spirit inside all that is "grievable" to Him in our human attitudes and hardness of heart.

17 It needs to be remembered that the actual command to repeat and so perpetuate the Eucharist of "bread and wine" comes only in Paul's account in 1 Corinthians 11:23–26 and not explicitly in the Gospels. But the reference in

Matthew 26:29, Mark 14:25 and Luke 22:19 to "drinking it anew in the kingdom . . ." can only refer to the ongoing sacrament. See further CHAPTER EIGHT.

18 Such is the clear meaning of the Greek *eures gar charin para to theo*. The "grace" Mary has "found" is wholly hers in the vocation to Christ-mother-hood. Christian devotion may have "developed" the further meaning of a "grace" inherently hers to bestow on suppliants. However, such concepts of "developmental" liberties in the Church to identify and warrant hidden, latent meanings are surely subject to the authority of the first and original sense and should not arrogate worth against the grain of the "master-narrative".

19 Muhammad Iqbal, *Zabur-i-ʿAjam* (Persian Psalms), trans. A. J. Arberry, Lahore, 1948, p. 22.

20 Dag Hammarskjöld, *Markings*, trans. L. Sjöberg and W. H. Auden, London, 1964, p. xvi.

CHAPTER FOUR   Pronounal Jewry – God's Own People

1 Esau was very much "the other party" in the Genesis 32 story, the "disad-vantaged" by Jacob's "advantage" and its meaning for his conscience. Dow Marmur thinks that the "angel" at Jabbok was "the guardian angel of Esau", meant to symbolize Jacob "extracting blessing" from surrounding non-Jewry. *The Star of the Return: Judaism after the Holocaust*, New York, 1991, p. 118. See CHAPTER FIVE below. However, with Moses all was corporate and collective, out of a retrospect of liberation and into a communal prospect of a "promised land".

2 1 Corinthians 10:1–2. His Jewish–Christian aside about "that Rock was Christ", belongs with his thoroughly Jewish emphasis that Sinai had incor-porated all generations. Nor need we be concerned here over the technical point, raised by scholars as to whether there were "Hebrew tribes" entering the land from the east who had never "come out of Egypt".

3 Not that the triads correspond directly, though "the ethnic" bears on "creation faith", "the land dimension" on tangling history and memory, and so embracing "communal story". It is significant that the Israeli flag has its two equilateral triangles, pointing downward and upward – land, people and story; power, hope and righteousness.

4 Making plural a cherished form of words in the singular, to suggest that at least the option of reading vocation in the same three denominators might be open to all – though emulation of Jewry can be highly dangerous.

5 The true omnipotence is not incapable of such magnanimity, but has the grace of "delegation" of authority without forsaking Lordship. Is it not such a *kenosis*, a Self-limiting in divine creation, in which there is a creaturehood like ours as humans?

6 In the one case misdirected, in the other not from right auspices.

7 There is the mysterious narrative of a "fighting, king-like Abraham" in Genesis 14, but for the most part he is a kindly nomad supremely anxious

about a son and heir. It is a different kind of land tenure and "territoriality" we reach with Joshua and the Judges.

8　John Milton, *Samson Agonistes*, lines 1712–15.

9　Sanhedrin 4:5. See also, Maimonides, Mishnah Torah, Laws of Sanhedrin 12:3. The same words come in the Qur'an, Surah 5.32.

10　Pirke Aboth 5:21. It is a wonderful saying in that it might silence all that is raucous and unseemly where religious faiths engage in controversy. But it may also admit the "championing-of-truth" role that can so far mislead.

11　Rabbi Abraham I. Kook. See his *Lights of Penitence etc.*, trans. B. Z. Bokser, New York, 1978, p. 11.

12　See, for example, James Barr, *Old and New In Interpretation*, London, 1960.

13　It could hardly be otherwise, in that sensitive souls could scarcely avoid a painful self-query about sustaining, even placarding their exceptionality. What, for example, of Malachi (1:11) about YAHWEH's "Name being great among the Gentiles", with incense purely offered in every place? The sense of "seeking peoples" was alive for the Isaiah of Chapter 40 onwards, while Haggai (2:7) could write of "the desire of all nations". Was this invariably in the oddly menacing terms of Psalm 2?

14　There are many examples of nations aspiring to read their identity as a God-given vocation to put all other peoples into debt. Russia, in a classic writer like Dostoevsky, is a notable example, articulating with passion what his countrymen understood. America, with its "independence" and "virgin" soil, cherished the same theme, which runs like a thread through all American literature and was notable in, for example, Herman Melville.

15　The emphasis found repeatedly in the writing of Elie Wiesel.

16　It would seem that, somehow, divine "election" spells human "rejection". It cannot be said that the two facts are not related – not, certainly, as due "cause and effect", but evidently as conviction and comment.

17　See Robert McAfee Brown, *Elie Wiesel, Messenger to all Humanity*, St. Louis, 1983, p. 167, stressing how the Shoah under the Nazis transcended all comparison with other and earlier acts of genocide.

18　It is clear that, but for passionate zealotry in Jewish part, the Fall of Jerusalem need not have occurred. The Romans were loathe to be provoked and were not averse to non-political Jewish liberties. Titus may have had little love for Jewry but he was not heartless. When he returned to Antioch after the capture of Jerusalem, the Greeks there asked him to expel the Jews from their city. He refused to do so, on the ground that the Jews no longer had their homeland in Judea and should not be further harassed.

19　This very abidingness of Jewry under diaspora conditions clearly interrogated the territorial idea. "Next year in Jerusalem" might be liturgical yearning but it was the very spirit that breathed it which ensured that it need not be fulfilled. It is this deep irony of the diaspora that the Zionist initiative had to overcome, only to carry forward yet another irony – that of denouncing what was also its reliance. See W. D. Davies: *The Territorial Dimension of Judaism*, Berkeley, 1982, for a careful study of the land/diaspora issue in Torah and Talmud.

20　The Greek aura of the Johannine *Logos* theme should not have been misread as unfit to carry, in its own terms, the essential Semitic theme of "divine agency" from which the Messianic form derived. Prophets and other "word-bearers" were "agents" on divine errand, enshrining in their mission the "divine wisdom". It was entirely fitting that *logos* should – in "Gentile" context – avail for this common meaning.

21 Even so, the perennially Hebraic features remained – the Jewish authorships behind so much of the Greek New Testament, the concerns of the Letter to the Hebrews, the Church's devotion to psalmody and the Hebrew Canon, and – supremely – the Messianic theme itself.

22 The words "Give me your tired, your poor . . ." inscribed on a plaque inside the pedestal of The Statue of Liberty, were written by Emma Lazarus (1849–87) in her sonnet: "The New Colossus". She was an ardent promoter of Jewish nationalism, translated Hebrew poems in *Songs of a Semite*, and wrote a play around mediavel persecution of Jews as allegedly "poisoners of wells".

23 It is not hard to imagine what might have happened to the "hope of Israel" had Hitler's forces broken through to Egypt and Palestine in 1940, or if the Palestine Police had not painfully held the ring for a UN Resolution to emerge in 1947, warranting partition and state creation. See Elie Wiesel, *One Generation After*, New York, 1971, pp. 129–36. "Truth for a Jew," he wrote "is to dwell among his brothers,' *ibid.*, p. 189 – but how far does "brother" reach?

24 "Ripe for brooding dispute" because the recovered terrain lay in the bosom of long non-Jewish tradition, stretching from ancient Palestinians into an extensive Arabism simultaneously anticipating their "sovereign indepen-dence". When Golda Meir used to remind Americans that they had "colonized" a territory to which they had no historical right whereas Israelis were re-possessing "a motherland" she overlooked, in the equation, the fact that the Arab world was in no way analogous to the hapless Iroquois and the other tribes of "Indians" unable effectively to react to invasion.

25 Echoing the suspicion – according to Josephus – that troubled the mind of Eliezar, leader of the warriors on Masada when he saw that their "game was up" and that they ought "to have conjectured the will of God much sooner". That is always the agony when dire events shatter tenacious hopes.

26 It needs to be remembered that the Balfour Declaration from which all else followed in 1917 had no legal standing. It was merely a piece of correspon-dence between Balfour and Lord Rothschild expressing an "attitude" towards an idea. The Mandate was set to implement its dubiety and that League of Nations remit was made to pass into that of the United Nations which voted the partition on which all else rested.

27 For one interesting example extending Israeli interests into US policy towards Iran see: Hossein Alikhani: "The Power of the Lobby", in *Global Dialogue*, Nicosia, Vol. 2, No. 3, Summer, 2000, pp. 45–54. There are many others.

28 A descriptive cited by Chief Rabbi, Jonathan Sachs, *Radical Then, Radical Now*, London, 2001. "You get it from your parents, pass it on to your chil-dren and not a small number of people have died from it." Yet he also avers

that Judaism is "pluralist". See also *The Times*, London, no. 2, March 28, 2001, p. 4.

29 "The contribution to Jewry's psychological health by the State of Israel and the Zionist presence in the diaspora cannot be over-estimated." Jacob Neusner, *Stranger at Home*, Chicago, 1981, p. 200.

30 *Ibid.*, p. 200.

31 *Ibid.*, p. 9.

32 Herman Cohen (1842–1918) in Alfred Jospe (ed.), *Reason and Hope*, New York, 1971, pp. 166–70.

CHAPTER FIVE   The Self-Encounter in Judaism

1 Genesis 32:22–32. Perhaps, strictly, the usage "Judaism" should be reserved for developments after 70 CE but it is fair to use it with that reservation to denote all things Hebraic throughout the long history.

2 Elie Wiesel, *And the Sea is Never Full: Memoirs, 1969–1998*, London, 1999, p. 169.

3 We are now so familiar with Israel being Israel that it is an effort of mind to realize that the State was never so named before it was achieved. The final choice had dire implications for Palestinian hopes. It clearly ruled out "bi-federalism", and gave solidity to the initial objective of "a national home for the Jewish in Palestine". Yet to call the partitioned entity in 1948 "the Jewish State" would have been ambiguous concerning the ever-Jewish diaspora in the wider world. It would seem that the name "Israel" must be linked with the choice of "the Rock of Israel" in the Constitution's Preamble. This was a compromise between the "religious" mind that wanted divine "mention" and the secular mind that – as did Ben-Gurion – vetoed formulae like "the God of Abraham" or "the Lord YAHWEH".

4 Gerhard Von Rad, *Genesis: A Commentary*, rev. edn, trans. J. H. Marks, London, 1972, p. 322.

5 It was not that Peniel should be read as inconclusive, rather that Jacob "came through" only as a different "Jacob" and this was how the numinous "wrestler" also "prevailed" over him in the form of a "defeat" that made Jacob have "mastery".

6 Quoting G. M. Hopkins on humankind in general but borrowing the descriptive aptly for how Jewry perceives its Jewishness. *The Poems*, 4th edn, ed. W. H. Gardner and H. H. MacKenzie, Oxford, 1970, p. 68, "The Sea and the Skylark".

7 We do not know what matters re eponymous ancestors, or place names, lie behind the story, nor what "strands" it may have passed through. Does Penuel represent an important city? (cf. 1 Kings 12:25). Did Jacob think that in "staggering" his gifts he was establishing an "obligation" on Esau, a sort of "bribery" (the servants were to say: "He is behind us"). Why the fivefold times the word "face"?

8 Cf. the old tradition that "spirits" must "vanish" when dawn is near, as in *Hamlet*: "It faded with the crowing of the cock."

9　The ancient Semitic idea that to know a name was to possess power over its owner, whether by evocation or by curse. Even in Paul's day Greek religion too felt a need to be prudent in not neglecting some deity of still unknown name. Hence "the altar to a god unknown" (Acts 17:23)

10　Psalm 114:1–2. The "dominion" over which He "ruled": the "dominion" ruling on His behalf or in His Name.

11　For there is the same triad everywhere – territory denominating inhabitants, inhabitants occupying territories, either mutually historical in and by the other. Thus "Mogai, the Divider of the Universe . . . made a big mountain which he called Kere-Nyaga as his resting place when on an inspection tour . . . And he took the man Gikuyu to the top of the mountain of mystery and showed him the beauty of the country that Mogai had given to him." So Jomo Kenyatta tells of the "right" of the Gikuyu people to their lands in "Kenya". In *Facing Mount Kenya, The Tribal Life of the Gikuyu*, New York, n.d. p. 5.

12　R. S. Thomas, *Autobiographies*, trans. J. W. Davies, London, 1997, p. 92.

13　Or unless it can somehow be "internalized" so that inwardly it remains what it ever was but externally need not insist that YAHWEH cannot have "chosen peoples plural". See below.

14　The theme of Americans being "new world" people of divine destiny runs steadily through all American literature from the first pilgrims. The tallies were obvious – a migrant race, a virgin territory, pagans to displace or subdue, and God-given destiny to attain, not to say a "Pharaoh" and a tyranny left behind (to which, however, like exiting Israel they owed much.)

15　As, for example, in Judges 11:24 where the Amorites are told to "possess what Chemosh their god has assigned them" while Israelites will take what YAHWEH conquers for them.

16　For what "the coat" represented was what most galled them and taunted their pride, born of "lesser mothers", Leah's sons apart. There was a venom in their strategy. Reread the scene in Thomas Mann's *Joseph and His Brothers*.

17　As, for example, the notion in Zechariah how "seekers" could take hold of the skirt of a jew" (why not the hand?) (8:23) after hearing how "God was with them". Or the gratuitous inclusion in "the hereafter" of "the godly Gentiles".

18　John Milton, *Samson Agonistes*, lines 1206–7, in the mouth Samson, challenging Harapha, the Philistine warrior.

19　It is noteworthy how far early Zionist case-making drew on "Gentile" depiction of Jewry as "effete, cowed, or self-despising" in their ghetto condition, in order to galvanize them into the vibrant activism of "auto-salvation" of which Zionism dreamed when it represented a tiny minority element in world Jewry.

20　Cited in Momme Brodersen, *Walter Benjamin: A Biography*, trans. M. R. Green and I. Ligers, London, 1996, p. 12.

21　Zvi Kolitz, *Yosi Rakover Talks to God*, London, 1998. The text, found in 1992, was not the work of a ghetto fighter. It was written in 1944 in Buenos Aires, by a twenty-six year old agent of the Irgun Zvi Leumi, of Lithuanian birth. It was a propaganda story meant to enlist recruits for the Irgun and was first printed in Yiddish. But it made a passionate statement of Jews as "the choosing people" having YAHWEH in their debt for the fidelity with which – even in the direst seeming absence of His relevance – they still confessed His Name and their inalienable status with Him.

22 The play is so often seen as an exercise in "anti-Jewish sentiment", has been played in those terms and enjoyed in them by Graziani-style "groundlings". Yet it is equally, if not more aptly, possible to read and act it in the contrary sense. If Shylock is pilloried as vindictive and callous, fit to be caught out on a legal technicality, he is also plainly a figure of deep pathos in the end, a victim doomed by a conspiracy, no-less callous if more urbane. The picture of "Gentile" levity and the incongruous lyricism of the play emerge as unseemly in the context of such passion. Nor should the anti-anti-Semitism be missed in the "Hath not a Jew eyes . . . ?" speech with its appeal to undifferentiated humanity.

23 Echoing Elie Wiesel, *And the Sea is Never Full*, London, 2000, p. 48.

24 As, for example, in Nikiprowetsky's "Ethical Monotheism" in *Daedalus*, Vol. 104, No. 2, 1975, p. 80. "Yahwism's claim to exclusivity did not tolerate peaceful co-existence with other cults". Cf. the view that "YAHWEH is not an international God".

25 No intelligent reading of the New Testament could ever doubt that "Jesus was a Jew". The abiding issue is "what sort of Jew?". There has been welcome commitment in the twentieth century of Jewish scholarship to "Jesus the Jew" – the title of a notable examplar of it in Geza Vermes.

26 "Fraudulently" in that so much tracing of the Holocaust (and age-long anti-Semitism) directly to the crucifixion has been prolific in the twentieth century but only by ignoring the insistent New Testament witness to the inclusively human character of the compromises of state justice and religious integrity that occurred in the crucifixion of Jesus. "Behold the sin of the world" – rather than "Look what Romans and Jews commit" was the cry of the faith. The will to implicate could only be universal. See note 27

27 George Herbert, *The English Poems*, ed. C. A. Patrides, London, 1974, "Self-Condemnation", p. 176.

28 See G. K. Anderson, *The Legend of the Wandering Jew*, Boston, 1965, and M. D. Conway, *The Wandering Jew*, London, 1881.

29 Albert Memmi, *Portrait of a Jew*, trans. from French by Elizabeth Abbott, London, 1963, pp. 2–45.

30 *Ibid.*, pp. 172f.

31 *Ibid.*, p. 325. See further this chapter.

32 Jacob Neusner, *Stranger at Home*, Chicago, 1981, pp. 4f.

33 *Ibid.*, pp. 28f.

34 *Ibid.*, p. 80.

35 *Ibid.*, p. 122 and pp. 90f. He makes a distinction between *golah* (exile *qua* place) and *galut* (exile in being). There is an existential *galut* in being "at home" in America. Yet dwelling in Israel will not fully end *galut* since Zionism is a therapy for Jewish self-hatred. If there is "the Jewish problem solved by Zionism", there is "the Zionist problem addressed to Judaism", p. xxx.

36 *Ibid.*, p. 164.

37 Vladimir Jabotinsky, genius of what grew into the Likud dimension of the Israeli mind and an uncompromising "displacer" of non-Jewish population, saw from the outset that there would be no accommodation. He knew that "every nation . . . sees its land as its national home and fights the settlers (sic) as long as there is a glimmer of hope of getting rid of them". From the Russian of his *On the Iron Wall*. see my *Palestine: The Prize and Price of Zion*, London, 1997, pp. 55–6. Max Nordau was, likewise, a no-compatibility realist in the Zionist vision of Jewish self-redemption.

38 Moshe Shamir, *My Life with Ishmael*, trans. from the Hebrew by Rose Kirson, London, 1970, pp. 12f. He cites the Muslim *Bismillah* oddly, in a note on Arab funerals, as *La Allah il-Allah wa Madkhamad* etc., p. 11.

39 Moshe Shamir, *Beneath the Sun (Tahat Hashemesh*, 1950), cited in *Modern Hebrew Literature*, Vol. 3, No. 3, p. 15.

40 See the discussion in Abraham Avi-Hai: *Ben-Gurion: State-Builder: Principles and Pragmatism 1948–1963*, Jerusalem, 1974, in a chapter headed "the Jews who left Zionism behind" (pp. 219–46). Other Jews still had a "Zionism" with the role it had *before* the achievement of the State of Israel. It was a measure of the degree to which Ben-Gurion sought to disavow diaspora, despite its continuing to be vital to the very existence of the State. As Herzl had it: "Zionism is the Jewish nation on the way" (note 42, p. 491).

41 Ben-Gurion, *Recollections*, p. 120, and pp. 116f.

42 Ben-Gurion, *Rebirth and Destiny of Israel*, trans. from the Hebrew by M. Nurock, New York, 1954, p. 409, and "This demands from each of us a new accounting of self", p. 403.

43 Elie Wiesel, *All Rivers Run to the Sea, Memoirs, 1928–1969*, New York, 1996, and *And the Sea is Never Full*, London, 2000.

44 *All Rivers Run*, p. 19. *Sea Never Full*, p. 68. *The Jews of Silence*, New York, 1968. *Sea Never Full*, p. 67.

45 *Sea Never Full*, p. 171, also *All Rivers Run*, p. 19.

46 *All Rivers Run*, p. 84 and p. 104. He cites the Rabbi of Kotyk, who said to God: "I shall continue to call You Father until You become our Father", accepting the pain of faith in God in order not to lose it.

47 *Sea Never Full*, pp. 125f. He tells Germans: "I do not believe in collective guilt", p. 153.

48 *Ibid.*, p. 172 and *All Rivers Run*, p. 388.

49 Ben-Gurion, *Recollections*, p. 131 and *In Vigilant Brotherhood* (The American Jewish Committee's Relationship to Palestine and Israel), New York, 1966, p. 57.

50 Simone Weil (1909–43). She found it "resolved" in a small Chapel in Assisi, kneeling – for the first time in her life – when the Passion Liturgy came home to her soul, strengthened by the impact of George Herbert's poem: "Love". The divine love at the centre of all human pain confirmed the self-expending love discernible in the creation and humankind being "let be" within it.

51 The sort of guilt-complex that prompts some Christians to find "a direct line from Good Friday to Auschwitz", or had there been no "imaging" of Judas and Caiaphas, Jewry would have been spared the need for their Yad Vashem Memorial.

52 "Dubious" because it completely abandons the New Testament openness to all and sundry in Christ, and because it has the hidden implication of the Christian Church as "somewhere" where Jews are unwanted, not expected, and in short, excluded in an oddly ironical form of anti-Semitism. Yet the theory becomes subtly attractive as, nevertheless, facilitating relationships and fostering a "Gentiles only" Church.

53 Franz Rosenzweig, *The Star of Redemption*, trans. W. W. Hallo (1930), New York, 1970, p. 403.

54 *Ibid.*, p. 341.

55 See critique of Rosenzweig in Jacob B. Agus, *Jewish Identity in an Age of Ideologies*, New York, 1976, pp. 280ff and 313.

56 Rosenzweig, *The Star of Redemption*, p. 396.

57 Martin Buber: *Two Types of Faith*, trans. N. P. Goldhawk, London, 1951, p. 43, which has – unlike Christianity – "the hereditary actuality of faith", p. 98.

58 Martin Buber, *I and Thou*, 2nd edn, trans. R. Gregor Smith, New York, 1958, p. 11. The point was crucial in Chapter 1.

59 Robert Browning, *Poetical Works*, Oxford, 1940, "An Epistle of Karshish, the Arab Physician", p. 426.

60 For Paul had said much the same in "not setting affection on things", and echoing the words of Jesus about "where moth and rust corrupt".

61 Notably that of birth-determined faith-status which means that non-Jewish birth *ipso facto* excludes and, for all such, "conversion" into Judaism makes a very high hurdle. See David Daube: *Appeasement or Resistance*, Berkeley, 1987, "The Burdened Convert", pp. 59–73.

62 Abraham Heschel, *Man Is Not Alone*, New York, 1951. The literature on Heschel is large. See, e.g., John C. Merkle, *The Genesis of Faith: The Depth Theology of Abraham Heschel*, New York, 1985; D. J. Moore, *The Human and the Holy*, New York, 1989; and Lawrence Perlman, *Abraham Heschel's Idea of Revelation*, Atlanta, 1989.

63 See my *Troubled by Truth*, Edinburgh, 1992, pp. 108–26. Eliezer Berkowits, for example, found "divine pathos" as "unJewish". God, being perfect, had no "need" of man, and was "indifferent" to the creature. Leon Roth saw the "divine pathos" theme as "a revolt" against the Judaic truth of divine "immunity". Such critics, however, ignored the evidence Heschel had drawn from the Hebrew prophetic tradition in his masterpiece, *The Prophets*, New York, 1962.

CHAPTER SIX   The Muslim Personal Pronoun Singular

1 These are the two passages which tell of the "burning bush". Others, with them, in Surah 79.15 refer to Tuwa and 27.7 tell of the "firebrand" Moses might bring, 27.8–9 adding: "As he came near to it there was a voice saying to him: 'Blessed is He who dwells in the fire and encircles it. Praise be to God, the Lord of all realms of being'." All the passages move on to the throwing down of the staff which the Bible places in the presence of Pharaoh.

2   That act, too, has its own point to make, namely that the meaning of the *Salat*, its prostration most of all, is to be taken out into the business of daily Muslim living. The person made prostrate behaves accordingly in erectness.

3   The grammar requires that emphasis. "An apostle" would be differently phrased. See below. Moreover, Muslim cognizance of other "apostles" – and indeed of other religions – is always subject to the theme of their "confirming" what the Qur'an makes final, as the condition of their being heeded as authentic.

4   As happens when the cry is used as a rallying of Islamic "causes" – as the criers see them, or as a clarion call to confrontation. Truly understood, *Allahu akbar* is what all humankind should confess, proclaiming a universal Lordship.

5   As in the aberrations (by New Testament criteria) of a Christendom that made "the name of Christ" its exclusive pride, or a type of Hinduism which confines itself to the pursuit of an extreme Indianism.

6   Surah 4.125 "God took Abraham for a friend". Even Hakluyt in his *Voyages, Travels and Discoveries of the Early English Nation*, Vol. ii, 1, 209, remembered how "the Merciful God commanded his secretarie Abraham to build Him an house in Mecca". On the significance of the nomad for later "election" by "seed", see CHAPTER FIVE. Can we think that Allah was "grateful for Abraham's faith in Him"? as suggested by Sholem Asch in *My Personal Faith*, trans. Maurice Samuel, London, 1942. pp. 33–7.

7   The feature, so central in the Hebraic tradition, is displaced (for the most part) in the Qur'an by Abraham's repudiation of idolatry. As a *hanif* he is a "father of theists", a people of universal progeny.

8   Surah 21.87–88 – from the context about "going away in anger" usually identified with Yunis, i.e. Jonah "crying out in the darkness" (of the fish) and being "rescued from his anguish".

9   Grammar creates a big problem here for theology, in that God is thus "joined" to as the "possessor" (not the "acquirer") of the *mudaf*. The word "Allah" can never be in the construction the other way round. Thus, for example, when Surah 114 speaks of "the God of men" it uses *Ilah al-nas*, the "common noun".

10 The term *ummi* has been variously translated, often as "illiterate" (when it has sustained the view that the Prophet could "neither read nor write"). On many counts it is more likely that it carries the sense of "native" provided that we understand what "native" here signifies – not to disparage but to underline that Arabs were a "people without a native scripture", i.e. "not lettered" in that sense. Hence the plural *ummiyyun* used of non-Jews (Jews were "people of the Book"). Muhammad was *ummi* as sharing that condition. Indeed, doing so was a main part of his credentials. He would be making them, via the Qur'an, "a scriptured people".

11 In contrast to the nineteenth-century "renewal movement" in India, the Ahmadiyyah who – in a disputed or ambivalent way – impugned, or were alleged to impugn the status of Muhammad as "sealing" divine revelation. Hence their being proscribed in Pakistan as "non-Islamic" in 1974. Thanks to their doctrine of the "Hidden Imam" and other characteristics, Shi'ah

Muslims take a different approach to Quranic commentary and the readings of Tradition.

12 Surahs 39.44 "To God alone *shafaʿah* belongs": 21.28 and 53.28, "those whom God permits": that of idols avails nothing (30.13 and 43.86) and "none in hell" (74.48).

13 Islam makes this familiar distinction between humans who hold a "trust" by which to order and direct their world, whereas stones and beasts are subject to laws or ways from which rational volition is excluded. Yet there is – appropriate to all – an *islam*, or "submission".

14 *Istiʿmar*, now a hated word, i.e. "imperialism". But Surah 11.61 notes that God has "made us imperialists in the earth . . ." (*istaʿ marakum fi-li-ard*) – agriculturally, that is, not politically in other people's lands.

15 The theme of "original sin" has been badly misconstrued on many hands. "All sinned in Adam", not as personal guilt pre-contracted like a virus before we had ever lived or acted, but because birth ushered us into a world enmeshed in social tangles and historical legacies. The vital comprehension of meaning is missed, for example, by Mohammed Lahbabi when, commenting on the Surahs quoted here, he says: "Le musulman, par contre, ne repond que des conséquences de ses propers actes à l'exclusion de toute responsabilité diffuse ou de pèche herité de quelque ancêtre que ce soit". *Le Personnalisme Musulman*, Paris, 1964, p. 109.

16 Perhaps not until years 2 or 3 of the Hijrah. See CHAPTER SEVEN.

17 Those credentials had much to do with issues close to any hearer's mind. He was "one of them", an *ummi* in their *ummiyyun* quality. He was – he claimed – scripturizing them in their own language. He was restoring the ancient Abrahamic associations of their city. The directness of the message was "democratic" in its range.

18 *Ijtihad*, or initiative in application and interpretation of *Shariʿah*, led to "consensus" or *Ijmaʿ*, which Sunnis needed for their validity. But who could participate in the vital *Ijtihad*? If only the experts in its niceties, then these would have a stranglehold on change. The issue loomed large in twentieth-century "modernism" and remains contentious still, as the battleground between the will for, and resistance to, innovation and reform.

19 Perplexities stem sharply from "the western factor", from the irresistible penetrations of technology, and – notably – from Muslim minority status, deprived of the age-long security of the Islamic state – so long indispensable to authentic Islamic faith and life.

20 *Tahannuth* denotes the practice of withdrawal for meditation which, according to Tradition, took Muhammad to the "cave" on neighbouring Mount Hira'. It should not be confused with *tahannuf*, denoting the Abrahamic "monotheism" of the *hunafa'* (sing. *hanif*) who were a possible impulse to Muhammad's prophethood.

21 Type-name of a "holy sage" in Najib Mahfuz' short story about a man's search to find this saint to cure him of an un-named disease. Reports of the saint's whereabouts all end in futility.

22 See, for example: "In a Naqshabandi Circle", R. Simac, *The Hibbert Journal*, Vol. 65, No. 258, Spring, 1967, pp. 104–5, concerning the celebrated

Nasruddin. The stories made acute psychological point and were a popular teaching means. Many can be found in the sundry publications of Idris Shah.

23 The translation of A. J. Arberry, *The Ruba'iyyat of Jalal al-Din Rumi: Select Translations into English Verse*, London, 1949, p. 29.

24 Matthew 10:39 (cf. 16:25), Mark 8:35 and Luke 9:24 and 17:33.

25 Editions of Al-Dirini were well-nigh legion, often undated and without page numbers. On Prayer Manuals and the Muslim devotion they exemplified through the centuries see: Constance E. Padwick, *Muslim Devotions: A Study of Prayer Manuals in Common Use*, London, 1961, 2nd edn, Oxford, 1997.

26 Where the theme of praise suggests the ground of the plea as in: "O God, whose nature and property is ever to have mercy . . . Let Thy great mercy loose us (from the chain of our sins) . . ." In Islamic usage "the Name" is both a "theology in worship" and "a plea in prayer".

27 *Al-Fuyudat al-Rabbaniyyah* assembled by one who describes himself as "the poor servant depending on the kindness of his Master the glorious, named Al-Jilani of Baghdad", n.d., p. 108.

28 The sense is elusive. Was it the voice of God speaking within him? Or his own witness to that which God said of Himself? Or a claim on the part of Al-Hallaj to mystical union? In the third case, it was a "mystery" Al-Hallaj was unable, or unwilling, to explain to his judges, with their incapacity to think anything but their own fixed, Sunni prejudice on behalf of a dogmatic "that Allah is One" in the bare statement sense. It may be that Al-Hallaj almost courted martyrdom as the "keeper" of a "mystery" beyond all vulgar explication. "In the ear of the infidel," sang Rumi, "mystery is no mystery."

29 From the root "to communicate a message". There were sundry times when Muhammad in Mecca was warned that he had no other obligation than the verbal mission (3.20, 5.92 and 99, 13.40, 16.35 and 82, 24.53, 29.18, 36.17, 42.48, 64.12).

30 On the slow recruitment of disciples in the Meccan years, see W. Montgomery Watt, *Muhammad at Mecca*, Oxford, 1953.

31 Around the middle of the thirteen Meccan years of *balagh* there were crossings of the Red Sea into sanctuary in Christian Ethiopia – a measure of the local adversities but in no way an ultimate solution which only the logic of the Yathrib "exile" could afford, as – still hazardous – occasion to establish an independent quasi-political base.

32 CHAPTER ELEVEN needs to study contemporary aspects – intellectual and religious – of Muslim personalism.

CHAPTER SEVEN   The Muslim Personal Pronoun Plural

1 E. H. Whinfield, *The Masnavi*, London, 1898, p. 277.

2 In the Qur'an itself, apart from the use of the term *khalifah*, "caliph" for David, its use in singular and plural invariably relates to "humans" entrusted with the physical order – to be its peasants, managers, engineers, and grateful developers. However, the whole logic of Muhammad Medinan leadership

demanded a perpetuation of *hukm*, rule and authority – the more so when prophethood was decisively concluded.

3   The distinction in the *Fatihah* (1.6–7) is applied to Muslims ("on whom Allah's favour rests") "those on whom, straying, anger rests" as Jews and Christians. On more denunciatory passages see Surahs 5.18 and 72–75, 9.31–35 (but cf., for example, 2.62)

4   Abraham as the builder of the Ka'bah and Ishmael are central to the Meccan tradition. Abraham is the true iconoclast forsaking the idols of his people and even demolishing them, rather than – as for Jewry – the great progenitor of the "right" line through Isaac and Jacob.

5   Using "ecumene" in the sense it might carry as exclusive to Islam. The world round the Ka'bah when at prayer has been – if crudely yet vividly – likened to a wheel of innumerable concentric circles all directed by geometrical *qiblah* to their "hub" in Mecca like the spokes of a wheel. That figure in the praying mind makes for deep solidarity.

6   The five are not Quranic though there are references to "dawn, sunset and night" in 50.39–40 ("hymn and prostration") and to "fixed hours" (4.103). See also 30.17 ("night and morning"), 17.78 ("sunset, dark and dawn") while 20.130 has "sun-rising, its going down and the two ends of the day". It is clear from these verses that there was *Salat* in Mecca towards Jerusalem before there was the *Qiblah* towards Mecca.

7   It is true that Arabs and Arabism enjoyed a primacy in the origins of Islam: the Qur'an as "matchless Arabic" and Muhammad's being – significantly – "Arab-born". But his being "a mercy to the worlds" surmounted the instincts of some early Muslims to give Arabs special status or demur about others entering into recipience of *Zakat* or exemption from the *Jizyah* tribute, that followed on conversion to Islam.

8   The loved phrase as to "manifest victory" – achieved and seen to be achieved – varied by *al-fawz al-'azim*, "the great victory".

9   The current concept of "human rights" requires that no state can plead that only its own writ runs in its own land, or resist "human rights" by claiming: "None of your business here". It is this that makes it uncongenial to some insistently self-sufficient polities.

10 For the reason that the Quraishi regime saw it to be inimical to their tribal hegemony, based on pagan *haram* status.

11 The civil indignities they suffered varied greatly, often in relation to the attitudes of local officials or the temper of Muslim communities. Even high positions might be accessible to them, but common citizenship was excluded in any recognizably "modern" terms. The system bound religion to the *millah*, or birth-community where one would perforce remain, unless acceding into Islam. It was a "tolerance" on its own Islam-contrived terms.

12 Seeing that the Hijrah meant that the faith which was first religious response in Mecca became an "institutional cause" for which "fighting was made legitimate" (2.244; 8.15, 39, 65–66; 61.4 and sundry other verses concerning booty, captives and ransoms.

13 See medieval examples in James Muldoon *Popes, Lawyers and Infidels*, Liverpool, 1979. There could also be other *"dars"* like *Dar al-Bida'h* ("abode

of heresy"), *Dar al-Baghi,* ("... of usurpation") and *Dar al-Maslubah* ("... of despoilation").

14 The Khawarij "seceders, disputed Umayyad Caliphs as being unworthy to be recognized as "Muslim" and against whom therefore the duty to deny them obedience must be put into effect. Much turned on precisely what was minimally vital in denoting a Muslim, or perhaps maximally. The problem is perennial – creed-recital or worthy works?

15 The issue around the meaning of Jihad runs far and wide. It can readily be internalized as a discipline of deeply personal Islam and it can be the distorted head-line word of "Islamophobia". More soberly, the basic theory of a *Dar al-Islam* means that in a non-Muslim regime the sincere Muslim must be inwardly "subversive" of it and, therefore, duty-bound to a Jihad to change what, meanwhile, is only tolerated. Most Muslims, at least in diaspora, would repudiate that reading. See below.

16 Speaking historically of the Hijrah as "the event of the *Sirah*" not impugning the Muslim belief that Allah gave it.

17 The familiar distinction in the initial "I" in small case is crucial. (There is the same point with Muslim and *muslim* as the "name of the doer".) As 49.14 and other passages show, one might "submit" while withholding faith. Patriarchs were *muslim* long prior to the Qur'an in Arabic and to Ramadan and *Shari'ah* as known to Islam, tall "I".

18 Zakaria Bashier, *The Hijrah: Story and Significance,* Leicester, 1983, p. 71. He notes there was no word *munafiqun* "hypocrites" in pre-Islamic Arabic.

19 *Ibid.,* p. 101.

20 *Ibid.,* p. 103.

21 All religions face this danger – that of role on behalf of transcendence so readily turning into supreme arbiter. "The royal banners forward go" as a crusaders' hymn has it, or *"Islamu akbar"* for *"Allahu akbar"*.

22 It was on the basis of that defensive undertaking that Muhammad was able to entrust his cause to its Yathribite shelter. The Pledge did not anticipate that it would be his springboard for campaign. Hence the chagrin of those influential people in Yathrib who had not been party to the Pledge. The first Pledge had only concerned an interest in the teaching.

23 Bashier, *The Hijrah: Story and Significance,* p. 81.

24 Though the two Surahs are listed as Medinan, some scholars think they may be "Meccan-composite". The Prophet may have been looking back over his Meccan experience of how obdurate his hearers had been. Or the words may reflect how Yathribites, too, were ill-disposed, despite the *Ansar* among them.

25 With those "locks" in the two verses, are we close to something like a "Behold, I stand at the door and knock" situation? Perhaps not, but is there not a point in the saying that "truths only become true when our faith has made them so"? – "made", that is, not that our credence "constitutes" them as truths, but that it "verifies" them such to be.

26 Though the bitterness of partition and its tragic cost did mean extreme vulnerability for Muslims staying in divided India. They could be suspected as "delaying spies", "potential – and so subversive – emigrants", while their great educational institutions were downgraded by Indian nationalism.

Could Nehru ensure the long tenure of the "secular" principle on which, apprehensive of its breakdown, remaining Muslims had to rely?

27 "Revolutionary" might be modified by the fact that the long British Raj (and especially after the failure of uprising in 1857) had meant a long deprivation of Islamic statehood, the more bitter given the former Mughal splendours. But the British Raj was destined to depart so that what Pakistan created might at length eventuate. That is not a scenario to be envisaged by today's dispersed Muslims.

28 The once-for-all Hijrah is not historically undone and remains – as ever – the monitor of the Islamic mind as to what ought to obtain. It is, however, the virtual Islam of pre-Hijrah Mecca that now fits Islam's diaspora away from where its various Medinas (Riyadh, Islamabad, Baghdad, Teheran, Kuala Lumpur and the rest) still fulfil their versions of its role and power.

CHAPTER EIGHT   The "We" and the "I" in the New Testament

1 William Shakespeare, *Macbeth*, Act 1, Sc. 4, lines 28–9, 31–2.

2 Romans 16:1–24. The chapter may well be a kind of "appendix" and many have wondered how Paul could have had so many friends in Rome, person- ally known, when – as he said – he had never yet visited the city. But that, in itself, could be witness to how far given to travel church-folk were and how far people who had not actually met could be fully party to friendship.

3 Verse 6, or ". . . help them on their journey in a way that God would approve". Was it the traditional "three days' right" to board and lodging? Pilgrim-folk should be sure of acceptance but should not overstay their welcome, being *bona fide* travellers. Paul himself owed much to this pattern of things.

4 As, with so strange an analogy, in Zechariah 8:23: "Out of all languages of the nations ten men shall take hold of the skirt of a Jew: saying: 'We will go with you for we have heard that God is with you'." Elsewhere in psalm and prophet the Hebrew sense of non-Jewry is that of suppliants and enquirers. In high paradox Psalm 2 warns all powerful ones to "be wise" and be on the right side of the small "elected" nation, lest its "Son be angry".

5 "Common" is Tyndale's translation where "salvation" also becomes "health". Perhaps he felt that Jude had in mind some "national" well-being, or "commonweal" society could find in true citizenship. But the sense of *koines* has better to do with "sharing the shared", i.e. the grace of God in Christ.

6 The Book of Genesis, opening in the majesty of creation, ends with Joseph "embalmed . . . in a coffin in Egypt", whence Hebrews 11:22 has him "giving instructions" as to the final transfer of his "bones" to "the land of promise".

7 Luke 16:1–9. The agent knew well enough how his master, a would-be "lender", regularly "sold" X quantity of goods to a "buyer" (no goods changing hands) for a "bond" to buy them back at a higher price. Thus he had his "interest" and the other party his "loan". There is a striking range and acuity to Jesus' parables.

8   *Who is Man?*, Stanford, 1965. Just as "one can never remain aloof from one's own self" (p. 14) so one can never well remain aloof from one's neighbour. It could be said that this profoundly Jewish meditation is a truly "Gentile" thing.

9   "Different" in two senses: (1) in the greeting Jesus had for the renegade (as the basis for his ceasing to be one) and (2) that very transformation in "the Jew" Zaccheus.

10 The range and diversity of scholarship, conjecture, surmise and verdict on the theme of "the real Jesus" are dauntingly wide and bewildering, expertly tackled and non-expertly claimed. For my part some attempt was made – not needed here – to formulate the "learning Christ" in *The Education of Christian Faith*, Brighton and Portland, 2000.

11 The imagery in John 12:32–33 (cf. 3:14–15) about "all being drawn" to him through the significance of his death could never be a coercive thing. The "all" has to do with unlimited range and universally significant appeal, not of guaranteed success – of which, witness the Cross itself, there is none in the realm of grace.

12 See note 10. For "Sonship" was not "honorary" bestowal of a dignity but the steady fulfilment of a vocation. It could only be made real in action as the sphere of its reality in fact.

13 A potential difficulty for all New Testament readers is that we are presented from the outset with what only became evident by the process. The wise reader needs to appreciate doctrine about Christ as the confession reached only via the story in which it had its ground – a ground always there but only cumulatively evidently so.

14 Those of Romans 11–13 and Galatians 4. See below.

15 Robert Frost's actual lines are in *Complete Poems*, New York, 1964, p. 47.

16 That fact itself carries a deep significance, given the sanctity of Hebrew, and also eloquent of the "exportability" of the faith in Christ. To be sure, Jesus and some disciples may well have used Greek as a second language but the Scripture's Greek character marks a remarkable transition, given – again – how diverse, from *koine* to elegant, the Greek quality is.

17 These numerous folk were "enquirers", "asking to learn" (as the Greek is). It is odd that the English equivalent now takes "proselytism" as a wanton urge to propagate. What most deterred "proselytes" from Judaising was the tall hurdle of "circumcision", a faith demanding "the mark in the flesh".

18 The point is made, according to Acts 15:11, by none other than Peter: "We (Jews) believe that through the grace of our Lord Jesus Christ) we (Jews) shall be saved even as they ("Gentiles") We would expect him to say: ". . . they even as we . . ."

19 It is clear how keenly they sensed some sort of inclusion of the "nations" in YAHWEH's providence and grace but, always, the honour of the mission serving it remained unilaterally in Jewish hands. Even the "universalism" of the Book of Jonah needs the context – and saga – of a Hebrew messenger.

20 Exceptional in that, unlike any other, it names a "people" as such, not citizens of this or that place or region, not an individual and not, like 1 Peter, "the dispersion", though such the readers of Hebrews may well have been.

21 He uses angelic and Mosaic comparisons, struggles in what would later be Talmudic style with Melchizedek and draws on things Levitical to tell of "Christ the Mediator". But his most powerful case-making is how he draws as one the ministry and the Passion of Jesus as "the learning Christ". That theme occupies chapters 1 to 4 of my *The Education of Christian Faith*, Brighton and Portland, 2000.

22 "Erstwhile" depending on how we date the Letter, pre- or post the Fall of Jerusalem in 70 CE

23 Galatians 3:24. Paul's imagery is of the slave who ensured that the school-boy did not play truant but duly arrived at school. Discernment of, and obedience to, "the Law of Christ" replaced (but also compatibly included) the Law of Moses in the new Christian tradition and being "in Christ" was a habitual rendezvou-ing at the "Temple".

24 It was this steady esteeming of the body which contrasted in the Biblical world with the *soma/sema* ("the body a prison") theme of Greek thought, and also underlay the deep pathos of the fate of "the disembodied" souls in Sheol, before Hebrew thought came to hold a "resurrection" of the body. This deeply religious perception of the body was in further contrast with the wondering, but finally only wistful, aestheticism of Greek statuary and art.

25 Philippians 4:5: *epieikes* "largeness of mind", and 2 Timothy 1:7: *sophrosune*, "a mind whose thoughts are sound", in the derivative *sophronismos*, enshrining the Greek theme of "moderation" and/or "modesty", i.e. "unpretentiousness".

26 2 Corinthians 5:14: *sunechei*, as of one pressed in a crowd who has to go along with it, or on a road that admits of no deviating – provided we know the "constraint" as wholly within us, while yet deriving from love to Christ.

27 Given the self-understanding of Jewry as "the people of YAHWEH", it is not surprising that Messianic hope should sometimes take a collective shape. To be sure, the "idea" of a "Son of David" and the principle of monarchy and Temple readily inspired expectation in personal form – a view agreeing with the sense that it was precisely the "nation" that needed rescue and could never – in effect – be its own "saviour". However, perhaps a right sort of "nation", keeping a perfect "Sabbath", might avail. Or might the concept of "the remnant" suggest that a part of the whole might be its "Messianic secret"? In any event, the Church was heir to the principle that the Messianic thing, once inaugurated decisively, would need to grow into a sub-Messiahship of "all of us".

28 "Impossible" seeing that – at least in mortal terms – the self has to be there in order to forego itself. Can abnegation ever happen without requiring the abnegator? There was always the perplexity as to what "it" was that "entered" Buddhist Nirvana.

29 This would still be the case even if we regard the First Letter of Peter as written by some other carrying his name. This "other" understands his "mentor" that way.

30 See 1 Cor. 16:1 and Acts 24:17 and the whole of 2 Cor. 9. When Paul decided to take the proceeds personally to Jerusalem, to bring home to the Jewish citizens its sacramental meaning, he forfeited his very freedom to evangelize.

CHAPTER NINE Two Great Sexes Antimate the World

1 John Milton, *Paradise Lost*, Book viii, line 151. John Donne, *The Poems*, ed. H. J. C. Grierson, Oxford, 1933, p. 47. In point of fact, Milton's "two sexes" are "sun and moon", the luminaries of the earth. For present purposes we ignore whatever Milton may have had in mind in thinking them "sexual", and what he meant by implication of an inferiorizing of any "feminine" moon as lesser luminary.

2 Not to ignore the puzzle of "sex-change" more frequently contrived of late through techniques earlier unknown. It seems strange that people who feel themselves "in the wrong body" have usually – at an earlier point – contrived a part in parenthood.

3 Milan Kundera, *Laughable Loves*, 1973, London, p. 94.

4 Adapting to terms of the human body how Raphael describes to Adam the acts of angelic love. *Paradise Lost*, Book viii, lines 627–9. ". . . union of pure with pure desire, nor restrain'd conveyance need."

5 The root from *purus* is clear enough but "purity" has always been at risk to those who felt an implied stigma in its presence. The suffix -itan comes from the sixteenth/seventeenth century naming of those who wanted a deeper "purifying" of the English Church. As "puritanical" the term descended into reproach of the morally fastidious.

6 Long study of the matrix of the two narratives and of the complexity of early Genesis ventures the view that Chapter 1 belongs to the sixth-century BC while Chapter 2 to the tenth century. The canonical order does well to reverse the chronology.

7 The English compound "helpmeet" or "helpmate" comes from two Hebrew words "help answering to". The noun *'azer* is frequently applied to God as in Psalms 33:29, 70:5 and 121:2; also in Hosea 13:9. There is a deep "theology of sexuality" in that "answering to . . ." though it is also capable of less positive interpretation, depending – as all exegesis does – on the predilections of the reader.

8 Ibn Qutayba (838?–899), the ninth-century sage of Baghdad, was both grammarian and theologian, trans. R. A. Nicolson, *A Literary History of the Arabs*, London, 1930, p. 77, from *Kitab al-Shi'r wa-al-Shu'ara'*.

9 Jonathan Swift's *Gulliver's Travels* demonstrated his capacity for nausea about humankind sharpened by a caustic wit. Even his tombstone in his Cathedral in Dublin recorded his "savage indignation" ever "lacerating his spirit". On ending *Gulliver*, ironically he wrote: "I have finished my *Travels* . . . they will wonderfully mend the world."

10 Albert Camus, *The Outsider*, trans. S. Gilbert, London, 1946.

11 It is intriguing to note how electrification and the advent of new amenities can significantly reduce the birth rate in communities thereby finding new interests and pursuits.

12 They happen when not willed, fail to happen when they are willed and what of "wet dreams"? These were odd arguments to plead irrationality in *eros* when so evidently susceptible to the disciplines of *agape*. But Augustine was obsessed with the idea that "sinful lust" had ensued from the Fall.

13 Jerome, *Epistles*, 22:20.

14 In that event, however, a second, or even a third, marriage did not have the blessing of the Church; though its civil validity was recognized and Church auspices laid stress on due penitence. Ideally, Orthodox theology saw marriage as belonging beyond mortal demise.

15 Official Roman Catholic pronouncements (at odds with some of its theologians and scholars) still confine marital intercourse to the possibility of procreation, thus casting doubt on the sacramental quality (or potential) of sexual exchange within marriage as transacting "bodily delight" in the context of a total mutuality.

16 John Donne, *The Poems*, ed. H. J. C. Grierson, Oxford, 1933, opening line of "The Canonization", p. 14.

17 Though when, in "Universal Unions", he used sexual metaphors for the sundry "kissings" of "fountains and rivers", "mountains and skies", and "sunlight clasping the earth", he ignored their dispassionate quality and so the "soul of sex" which, as Donne knew so well, alone could say:

> Nothing in the world is single.
> All things by a law divine,
> In another's being mingle.
> Why not I with thine?

For only humans are pronounal. P. B. Shelley, *Complete Poetical Works*, ed. T. Hutchinson, Oxford, 1934; "Love's Philosophy", p. 583.

18 F. Engels, *Origin of the Family, Private Property and the State*, London, 1884, p. 126.

19 Jeremy Taylor, in his *The Mysteriousness of Marriage*.

20 Thomas Hardy, *Collected Poems*, 1932, p. 213.

21 See: F. E. Hardy, *The Later Years of Thomas Hardy, 1892–1928*, London, 1930, p. 272, and ed. M. M. Millgate and R. L. Purdy, *Thomas Hardy: Collected Letters*, Vol. 2, Oxford, 1939–58, p. 99. Hardy's *Jude the Obscure* was published in 1896. One central question in Jude is why their partnering should be deemed "illicit". More deeply still, Hardy was asking "What of women like Sue who may never have been meant for the mandatory sex that marriage pre-supposes?". Did she then, rejecting Jude maritally, wed Phillotson out of self-hatred? Hardy himself seems to have been confused as to what he intended and about what can feasibly be addressed in terms of the novel. Hence, no doubt, his intense pain over its reception.

22 D. H. Lawrence, *Women in Love*, Gudrun speaking, Chap. XXI.

23 D. H. Lawrence, *Selected Literary Criticism*, Chap. XXI, ed. Anthony Beal, London, 1956, p. 356, writing on "Nathaniel Hawthorn and The Scarlet Letter".

24 Gerard Manley Hopkins, *The Poems*, rev. edn, W. H. Gardner and N. H. MacKenzie, Oxford, 1967, p. 86, "At the Wedding March".

25 "Coitus," he wrote, "weighs down reason because of carnal pleasure it makes men inept for spiritual things." *Summa Theologica*, Suppl. 64.5. He failed to appreciate how far culture, not "nature", decided what was abnormal. In the

mid-sixteenth century, the Council of Trent adopted Aquinas as official doctrine, despite *Summa Theologica*, 1.92.1., ad 1, finding woman "a misbegotten foetus".

26   George Eliot, *Middlemarch*, London, 1872, Chap. 3.

27   E. B. Browning, *Aurora Leigh*, London, 1857, Book 1, lines 458–9.

28   This was to turn the "nature" argument on its head, reversing the merely physical case about "the female" into the loving one. See Gordon Haight, *George Eliot: A Life*, Oxford, 1978, p. 402. (viii).

29   The theme of "signs" is central to the Qur'an with their appeal, as here, to intelligent cognizance. Perhaps one could then say, with Geoffrey Chaucer in *The Merchant's Tale*, "Marriage is a full greet sacrement . . . a wyffe is Goddes gifte verily". Surah 7.189 speaks of "finding rest in her", while 4.21 seems to imply that martial experience should not be subject to irreverent rupture. 2.228 says that men have a status over women and 2.223 uses the analogy of fertility in the ploughed field (*tilth*) and via intercourse in marriage.

30   See, for example, Surah 24.2, how adulterers repudiate God's sovereignty, corrupting each other, and committing the sin of *shirk*. *Zina* is frequently reprehended.

31   For a recent example of how the Quranic view of sexuality might be best presented and how the presentation might dismay a feminist see: Muhammad Abdel-Haleem, *Understanding the Qur'an: Themes and Styles*, London, 1999. In my *Islam among the Spires*, London, 2000, ch. 6, are other aspects of the theme.

32   As in note 31 where ardent feminists might feel that the apologia fails its own case. See pp. 42–58.

33   Fatima Mernissi, *The Harem Within: Tales of a Moroccan Girlhood*, London, 1994, p. 254. "A cosmic frontier splits the planet in two halves". See also the same writer's *Beyond the Veil: Male/Female Dynamics in Modern Society*, Bloomington, 1987, and Margo Badran (trans.), *Harem Years: The Memoirs of an Egyptian Feminist* (author Huda Sha'rouri), London, 1988.

34   Echoing the Qur'an's words about the unbelieving: "They did not think worthily of God" – *ma qadaru Allaha haqqa qadrihi*. Or, more loosely, "their idea of God was all awry" (Surahs 6.91, 22.74 and 39.67). See my: *Returning to Mount Hira': Islam in Contemporary Terms*, London, 1994, pp. 61–82.

35   In his Preface to *Jude the Obscure*, London, 1896.

36   John Milton: *Paradise Lost*, Book viii, line 269.

37   *Ibid.* Book v, line 844, adapting how Milton has his angels available to God – "Freely we serve because we freely love."

38   *Essays of Montaigne*, Book III. 8.

39   So marriage is defined in the English *Book of Common Prayer*. Its note about "a remedy against sin" could never mean that marriage was some "second best", for those unable to be celibate but that it bars all wanton-ness rather as a Highway Code does the impetuosity of drivers. The first step newly-weds take in the Service is towards "the Holy Table".

40   *Book of Common Prayer*.

41   Charles Williams, *He Came Down from Heaven*, London, 1950, "Only

Christianity has affirmed the spiritual significance of matter and the flesh", p. 106.

42 Percy Bysshe Shelley: *Complete Poetical Works*, ed. N. Rogers, Vol. 1, Oxford, 1972: the phrase later borrowed by E. M. Forster for his novel *The Longest Journey*. The journey poor Harriet Westbrook took with Shelley was all too short. "Conjugal minds will seek their kindred soul", p. 71.

43 "Discard" as "discarding", though it would also be true of the rejected party. See below of "divorce".

44 Cecil Day Lewis: *The Burial Day*, London, 1960, p. 505.

45 Cesare Pavese: *The Burning Brand*, Diaries, p. 71.

46 Garry O'Connor: *William Shakespeare: A Life*, London, 1991, pp. 81 and 254. See also *Julius Caesar*, Act 2, Scene 1, lines 271–3 and 282–6.

47 How else might we disown the mind-set in the statue – erected in the heart of Amsterdam – as symbol of the massive industry known as "Interclimax", namely the penis?

CHAPTER TEN   Our Dividual Being – The Irony of Mystical Union

1 "Self-absentness" is still unsatisfactory but it is closer than "self-transcendence". The problem in making the point (which will come below) is that one can aim to be "free of self" in the moral way of being "unselfish" – which still requires the self: or in the total way of being "unselfed". It is the latter that mystic ways seek. The same ambiguity attaches to being – or not being – ego-centric. Does the term mean an (ethical) egoism or our being by nature in a self?

2 The issue has to be taken up in the sequel. There is no intention to imply that religions may not contain paradox – they all do – but that they must be willing to admit that situation.

3 Fyodor Dostoevsky, *Notes from the Underground*, trans. Constance Garnett, London, 1912, p. 115.

4 William Wordsworth, *Poetical Works*, ed. T. Hutchinson, Oxford, 1905, p. 492, line 37.

5 "Spoil" is a telling word here, since it can mean what is stripped off a dead foe in battle, so that we "gain at cost". It also means "decay" or "go bad", while a "spoiler" is one who frustrates.

6 Psalm 86:11. What the Buddhist seeks, and e.g. Muslim mystics, for the most part, is a state of "union" where there is no conscious "heart" asking to be unified.

7 C. S. Lewis, *Collected Poems*, ed. Walter Hooper, London, 1964, p. 133.

8 George Herbert, *The English Poems*, ed. C. Partridges, London, 1974, "The Church-porch", line 424, p. 45, "Christ purg'd his temple" and "Giddiness", p. 138.

9 The point is clear from many familiar language usages – "the hour is come", "at the end of the day", "there is a tide . . ." – where bare "measure" is taken over by "meaning". The Greeks made the distinction between *chronos* and *kairos*, i.e. time as a "when" merely and time as a "what".

10 The temptation was always present to make mystical experience a badge of distinction, a charisma others lacked and thus a warrant for exemption. Such cherished withdrawal was the more likely when esoteric lore, Kabbalistic subtlety and spiritual élitism sharpened indulgence in it as a hidden form of self-esteem.

11 As in Psalm 63:1 and Surah 21.87. Several of the basic terms of rigorous doctrine could be brought to carry esoteric meaning.

12 There is a certain quandary here, in line with the irony we are studying. If the fire itself is "desire" can the fuel be also? If the fuel is this and that "desire" the fire must be the self per se, unless we suppose that "kindling" is inherent – in which case what need of fuel? The analogy can work well but leaves open the possibility of a self able to discriminate between fuels "right for its fire".

13 Though that word may also confuse, not escaping the subtlety between "not a thing any more" and "ending the illusion about a supposedly real".

14 As in note 13 – it is clearer if we distinguish between "nothing" and "no-thing". Alice (in her Wonderland) asked where she would be if she were "blown out" like a candle. It would be as if she had never been there at all. That "as if" fits the rigorous Buddhist view of the human self.

15 In the long history of Christian faith there has been much diversity in respect of the human body. However, it is clear that there is no "spiritual grace" that does not know and tell itself in some physical act – "take a hand", "say it with flowers", "lift a finger", "share a look". Faith in the Incarnation makes it the most materialistic of religions, with its "bread and wine". Hence the deep sacramental principle of all things as candidates for holiness.

16 See *Simone Weil as We Knew Her*, ed. J. M. Perrin and G. Thibon, London, 1958, p. 114.

17 In the sense that, if there is a destiny to futility belonging to human existence such compassion in response to it should be included in the futility. As with Albert Camus in his quite different context, absurdity can be defied as well as deplored. We need not act our pessimism. We can live a courageous irony.

18 Thomas Traherne, *Centuries, Poems and Thanksgivings*, ed. H. M. Margoliouth, Oxford, 1958, Vol. ii, Stanza 1, p. 177.

19 Chapter 6, note 23.

20 The one is simply the ego-centric situation, the other the ego-centric perversity.

21 On the Sufi Orders, see: J. Spencer Trimingham, *The Sufi Orders in Islam*, Oxford, 1970, and M. Gilsenan, *Saint and Sufi in Modern Egypt*, Oxford, 1973.

22 Ahmad al-Tijani: *Prayers*, repeatedly printed in many scattered and undated pocket texts. Al-Tijani founded the widespread Tijaniyyah Order in the eighteenth century. He belonged to the great University at Fez and his Order spread throughout the Maghreb and far into the Sahara, Nigeria and the Sudan. That we "send forward" our deeds into eternal reckoning is a central emphasis of the Qur'an.

23 Surah 2.10, 5.52, 9.125, 22.53, 24.50, 33.32, 47.20, 74.31. It would seem a

more hopeful analysis than bare condemnation inasmuch as, presumably, "sickness" can be treated. 74.31 makes a distinction between "those in whose hearts there is a sickness" and "disbelievers". Is it a less than lethal inability to recognize truth?

24 The question characteristically runs through the entire sequence of Muslim spirituality and echoes Biblical faith in "the most moved Mover", the "desiredness" of the world and of the human scene on the part of the great Originator. Hence the hope of human sanity and responding "Desire".

25 Mahmud Ibn 'Abd al-Karim Shabastari, *Gulshani Raz* ("The Mystic Rose Garden", written in 717 AH), trans. E. H. Whinfield, London, 1880, pp. 14–15.

26 *The Faith and Practice of Al-Ghazali*, trans. W. Montgomery Watt, London, 1953, pp. 56–7.

27 *Shaikh Abu-l-'Abbas 'Alawi*, Martin Lings, London, 1961, p. 102.

28 R. A. Nicholson, *Diwan Shamsi Tabrizi (Manaqib al-'Arifin)*, Cambridge, ed. 1952, p. xxii.

29 A. J. Arberry, *The Ruba'iyyat of Jalal al-Din Rumi*, London, 1959, p. 187.

30 *Op. cit*, note 28, p. 210.

31 Abu Said ibn Abu-l-Khair, cited in E. G. Browne: *A Literary History of Persia*, Cambridge, 1902, Vol. 2, pp. 261–7.

32 Husain Ibn Mansur al-Hallaj, *Seven Poems*, trans. Mustafa Badawi, *Journal of Arabic Literature*, Vol. 14, 1983, pp. 46–7.

33 The steady emphasis of, e.g., Fazlur Rahman, that the Qur'an – and so Quranic Islam – are not about the divine nature but "imperatives" concerning human conduct and action. See: *Major Themes of the Qur'an*, Minneapolis, 1980, pp. 1–5. "The aim of the Qur'an is man and his behaviour, not God", p. 3.

34 *Sharh al-sadr*, the "opening of the bosom" to insight and truth, as affirmed of Muhammad in his "Ascension". It is used in Surah 39.22 about the individual Muslim "expanding" his heart to receive Islam.

35 This plea for unification is the central theme of Sufi poetry. Cf. also E. J. W. Gibb, *A History of Ottoman Poetry*, Vol. 3, p. 114. Also R. A. Nicholson, *The Idea of Personality in Sufism*, Cambridge, 1923.

36 A. J. Arberry, *Sufism*, London, 1950, p. 59.

37 Certainly any neglect, by us, of nature, history and experience in their immediacy and long-range memory out of a past, would hardly allow of search for "comprehension" in any sense of that inclusive word – knowing and the known.

38 A. J. Arberry, *Fifty Poems of Hafiz*, Cambridge, 1947, p. 97.

39 Cited in R. A. Nicholson, *Literary History of the Arabs, 1941*, p. 234.

40 'Abdallah Ansari, *The Invocations*, trans. Jogendra Singh, London, 1939, p. 31.

41 Cited in Philip Callow, *Vincent Van Gogh: A Life*, London, 1990, p. 48.

42 It seems to have taken its rise in Meister Eckhart to be given new currency by Don Cupitt in a book of that title, London, 1980.

43 For *shirk* – the worship of what is not "God" must include, not only idolatries of every kind, but worship accorded in line with misreading theologies.

44 "Evident" may be disputed by the sombre Thomas Hardys of this world but – though "beneificence" on their view may be overridden or outweighed by "malice" – any such evaluation means that it is present and claims to be reckoned with in patient realism. It makes no sense to say that "the only excuse for God is that He does not exist."

45 John V. Taylor, *The Go-Between God: The Holy Spirit and the Christian Mission*, London, 1972, p. 93.

CHAPTER ELEVEN   Faiths' Pronoun-Users Now

1 Citing William Shakespeare, *King Lear* Scene 11, lines 97 and 29–30.

2 "A deciding thing rather than what we decide", yet – nevertheless our "decision" in the recognition of its worth to warrant our attesting of it. Cf. Paul in 2 Corinthians 5:14: *sunechi* – "makes up our mind", "leaves us no option but . . ."

3 I.e. "springs of judgement" and "conviction" if these are sincerely sought, open, generous and determinative of action, then – these being all "religious" attitudes – they are significantly "religious" even in aloofness from any explicit faith-confession. Cf. note 25 below.

4 For the grim origins cf. Gerhard Von Rad, *Holy War in Ancient Israel*, trans. M. J. Dawn, Grand Rapids, 1991.

5 The term in its elusive or poetical meaning served to satisfy both piety and "secular" prowess, avoiding the tension between these, involved in a use of "the God of Israel".

6 Before and after partition in 1947 and the separation of the (then) two Pakistans – western and eastern, there were many Pakistani Muslims who averred that Islam in India "would wither away". That opinion was only logical if statehood was a *sine qua non* of survival. Despite its deep tribulations, Indian Islam has demonstrated a strong survival nerve and mind.

7 An outstanding personal example was independent India's first Minister of Education, the Meccan-born Maulana Abu-l-Kalam Azad, author of a notable Urdu study of the Qur'an, who suffered sharply at the hand of those eager to disavow his vision of an Islam fully compatible with Indian nationalism. See Ian H. Douglas, *Abu-l-Kalam Azad: An Intellectual and Religious Biography*, New Delhi, 1982 and I. H. Azad Faruqi, *The Tarjuman al-Qur'an, A Critical Analysis*, New Delhi, 1982.

8 That adjacence, initially sharply and always tacitly, tended to suspicion. Why had staying Muslims not gone there? Was their staying sinister? How much "spying" might be latent?

9 It surely does in the clear priority of Mecca. See below. Nor was the diaspora situation or that of "statelessness" unprecedented. The "modern" pioneer, in founding what became the University of Aligarh, Sir Sayyid Ahmad Khan, had argued after the collapse of rebellion (seeking power) in 1857 that Muslims under the British Raj were still in *Dar al-Islam* and should cast off despair and gloom in the enjoyment and fulfilment of their religious amenities and "Pillars" – all of them intact.

10 The point has often been made by legists in Islam, especially in the West. The established principle is that "occasions" have to be the clue to "texts". Can this be true only for the calendar ones of the Qur'an's *Tanzil* during the years of Muhammad's *Sirah* and not also of the century ones that consider what it might mean that the Qur'an was given *then* but was meant for every later time, including the present? "Finality" is meaningless unless it belongs developmentally agelong.

11 Surahs 56.60 and 70.41. God is not 'taken by surprise' in somehow not being alert to all that eventuates whether in time or beyond time, so that nothing is 'overlooked', whether in what awaits us eternally or here and now.

12 The familiar term, "tied back to itself", so often used in twentieth-century Muslim pleaders for renewal and "abreastness" of intellectual tasks, such as Ahmad Amin, Taha Husain, Fazlur Rahman, 'Ali 'Abd al-Raziq and numerous others. They sought to break out of traditional mind-sets living in ancient margins of *Tafsir*.

13 In that no text, however revered, can contradict what readers choose to find it meaning. This does not make for chaos but has to sober rash or opinionated claims that "we have got what it means". In the twentieth century so-called "post-modernist" theories of "readership" have had unnecessarily dire affect on religious "texuality".

14 History being irreversible, it may be assumed that a given religion has been preponderately part of it in cultural and other terms. Providing that the "dominant" one does not domineer, stability of identity – and several other factors – indicate that it should continue, if only as the major guard against the pressures of sheer secularity (assuming it has what being such will take).

15 Echoing the familiar – and ludicrous – comment: "I do not believe in belief."

16 It seems also to be the logic in Surah 2.256 in that the "no compulsion" rubric rides with the statement: "The right has been clearly distinguished from the false" and "the believer has laid hold of the most sure hand-hold that will never break."

17 The Roman "deputy" or "official" who dismissed contemptuously the violent case made against Paul in Achaia, as Luke has it in Acts 18:12–17.

18 "Prehension" – "the act of grasping or holding" – more familiar in the prefixed forms of "apprehension", and "comprehension". All have place in religious awe as what "seizes" us with wonder, fear, guilt and joy – in all "the numinous".

19 To speak of "entering Nirvana" implies that a "something" does so, since the verb is "active", yet, by definition, what "takes place" is an end to all "taking place". It has, then, to be understood as an end to "pronounality" itself, a conscious (?) cessation of "me-ness". The common western error in describing Nirvana as "extinction" consists in not realizing that, truly, there was nothing to extinguish.

20 "Come ye unto prayer: come ye to the good" – the call of the *Adhan* from the minaret.

21 George Herbert, *The English Poems*, ed. C. A. Patrides, London, 1974, p. 66, "Sinne". The opening line: "Lord, with what care Thou hast begirt us around!" has a very Islamic ring.

22 Using "divine" as a noun. The "resource" is surely there in the concept of *Al-Qadir ala kulli shay* "over all things competent".

23 William Wordsworth, *Collected Works*, ed. T. Hutchinson, Oxford, 1905, "The Excursion", Book 1, line 216, p. 759.

24 D. H. Lawrence, *Collected Letters*, ed. H. T. Moore, Cambridge, 1984, Vol. 1, p. 273. He made a "religion" of the body's sexual passion and, doing so, came – if only clumsily – towards the sacramental quality of "what we do after the flesh". For him religious faith was far from being merely "at best a legitimate myth to which one pays lip-service but does not engage one's mind with", as, for example, thought the historian H. Trevor Roper. See Naim Atallah, *Of a Certain Age*, London, 1992, pp. 74–6.

25 Dylan Thomas, *Collected Poems*, 1934–52, London, 1871, author's note, p. vii.

26 Echoing Philip Larkin's poem "Churchgoing", in *Collected Poems*, ed. Anthony Thwaites, London, 1988, p. 89.

27 T. S. Eliot's phrase in *Collected Poems and Plays*, London, 1969, p. 194, from "Four Quartets", "Little Gidding", lines 101–2.

Index of Names and Terms

Index of Themes

Biblical Passages

Quranic Passages

Surah 2
v.143	121
v.149–50	115
v.163	97
v.183–85	116
v.191	117
v.213	121
v.217	117
v.223	99, 150
v.256	24, 190, 228
v.272	105
v.286	99

Surah 3
v.19	121, 197

Surah 4
v.25	213
v.82	124
v.84	99
v.108	176

Surah 5
v.3	197
v.18	197
v.48	119
v.105	100

Surah 6
v.125	197
v.153	99
v.164	99, 197

Surah 7
v.159	121
v.172	197

Surah 9
v.107–8	123
v.118	104

Surah 10
v.20	121

Surah 11
v.47	104
v.118	119

Surah 13
v.22	105

Surah 16
v.93	119
v.120	121

Surah 17
v.10–11	200
v.15	99, 197

Surah 19
v.18	104

Surah 20
v.11–14	94, 97

Surah 22
v.34	119
v.67	119
v.78	115

Surah 23
v.97–8	104

Surah 28
v.39	94

Surah 29
v.69	115

Surah 30
v.21	159, 160

Surah 38
v.82–83	100

Surah 39
v.7	99, 197
v.22	197
v.44	214

Surah 40
v.5	121

Surah 41
v.44	102

Surah 42
v.8	119

Surah 47
v.24	124

Surah 49
v.13–14	118, 119

Surah 53
v.38	99, 197

Surah 57
v.2	105